The Cold War Past and Present

The Cold War Past and Present

Edited by

RICHARD CROCKATT and STEVE SMITH
University of East Anglia

London
ALLEN & UNWIN
Boston   Sydney   Wellington

Allen & Unwin, the academic imprint of
Unwin Hyman Ltd
PO Box 18, Park Lane, Hemel Hempstead, Herts HP2 4TE, UK
40 Museum Street, London WC1A 1LU, UK
37/39 Queen Elizabeth Street, London SE1 2QB

Allen & Unwin Inc.,
8 Winchester Place, Winchester, Mass. 01890, USA

Allen & Unwin (Australia) Ltd,
8 Napier Street, North Sydney, NSW 2060, Australia

Allen & Unwin (New Zealand) Ltd in association with the
Port Nicholson Press Ltd,
60 Cambridge Terrace, Wellington, New Zealand

First published in 1987

British Library Cataloguing in Publication Data

The Cold war past and present.
1. World politics – 1933–1945   2. World politics – 1945–   3. Soviet
Union – Foreign relations – 1917–1945   4. Soviet Union – Foreign
relations – 1945–
I. Crockatt, Richard II. Smith, Steven M.
327'.09171'3   DK267
ISBN 0–04–327101–4
ISBN 0–04–327102–2

Library of Congress Cataloging-in-Publication Data

The Cold War past and present.
"This book is based on a colloquium held in April 1986 at the University of
East Anglia, Norwich . . . " – P. xiv.
Bibliography: p.
Includes index.
1. World politics – 1945–   – Congresses.
I. Crockatt, Richard.   II. Smith, Steve, 1952–
III. University of East Anglia.
D840.C64 1987   327'.0904   86–32149
ISBN 0–04–327101–4 (alk. paper)

Typeset in 10 on 12 point Bembo by Computape (Pickering) Limited
and printed in Great Britain by Billing and Sons Ltd,
London and Worcester

Contents

List of Tables

Contributors

Mike Bowker is a Research Associate at the Royal Institute of International Affairs, Chatham House, London. He is in the process of completing a book with Phil Williams on the subject of Superpower Détente.

Richard Crockatt is Lecturer in American History at the University of East Anglia. His main interests are American foreign relations and political thought, on which he has published a number of articles.

Wayland Kennet (Lord Kennet) is currently SDP spokesman on foreign affairs and defence in the House of Lords. After a period in the Foreign Office, 1946–47, he held a number of political offices, including Delegate to the Council of Europe, 1962–65 and Member of the European Parliament, 1978–79. Among his many books are *The Italian Left* (1949), *Strategy for Survival* (1959), and *The Futures of Europe* (1976).

Bruce Kuniholm is an Associate Professor of Public Policy and History at Duke University, North Carolina. He has served on the Policy Planning Staff of the US State Department and has written numerous articles and books, one of which, *The Origins of the Cold War in the Near East* (1980), was awarded the Stuart L. Bernath prize by the Society for Historians of American foreign relations.

Sir Frank Roberts, GCMG, entered the Foreign Office in 1930. Among the posts he has held are British Minister in Moscow, 1945–47, and Ambassadorships to Yugoslavia, 1954–57, to the USSR, 1960–62, and to the Federal Republic of Germany, 1963–68. He is on the boards of several international companies and is a frequent participant in conferences on international affairs.

David Robertson is Dean and Fellow of St Hugh's College, Oxford. He previously taught at the University of Essex. He has written a number of books on electoral behaviour and has recently begun to research in British defence policy. He is editor of the *Penguin Dictionary of Politics* (1986) and will shortly publish (with Robbin Laird) *Strains Within NATO* (Wheatsheaf, 1987).

Victor Rothwell is Lecturer in Modern British History at the University of Edinburgh. His books include *British War Aims and Peace Diplomacy 1914–1918* (1971) and *Britain and the Cold War* (1982).

Jacques Rupnik is Senior Fellow and Lecturer at the Center for International Affairs (CERI) of the Fondation Nationale des Sciences Politiques in Paris. He studied at the Universities of Paris and Harvard, and has worked as a research associate at Harvard. He has written extensively on East European affairs, most recently co-authoring *Totalitarismes* (Paris 1984) and *L'Amérique dans les têtes* (Paris 1986). He contributes regularly to BBC External Service broadcasts.

David N. Schwartz is currently at the London office of Goldman, Sachs and Company, working as an investment banker. He was educated at Stanford and MIT. Before starting his present job in 1986, he spent five years at the US State Department, most recently serving as Director of Strategic Nuclear Policy. He has also been on the staff of the Brookings Institution in Washington, where he published, among other things, two books – *NATO's Nuclear Dilemmas* (1983) and, co-edited with Ashton Carter, *Ballistic Missile Defense* (1984).

Steve Smith is Senior Lecturer in International Relations at the University of East Anglia. He has also taught at the State University of New York (Albany). He has published widely in the areas of foreign policy theory and strategic weapons/arms control. His books include *Foreign Policy Adaptation* (1981), *Foreign Policy Implementation* (edited with Michael Clarke, 1985), and *International Relations: British and American Approaches* (edited, 1985).

Brian White is Senior Lecturer in International Relations at North Staffordshire Polytechnic. He has published widely in the field of foreign policy analysis and British defence policy, and is currently completing a major study of the British role in the origins of Détente, to be published by Allen and Unwin in 1988.

Phil Williams is Lecturer in International Relations at the University of Southampton. He previously taught at the University of Aberdeen and from 1984–86 was Research Fellow at the Royal Institute of International Affairs, Chatham House. He has published widely in the field of US defence policy, and among his books are *Crisis Management* (1976), (as co-author) *The Carter Years* (1983), and *The Senate and US Troops in Europe* (1985).

Lord Zuckerman OM, KCB, FRS, trained as an anatomist and was engaged in research until the Second World War, when he was appointed Scientific Adviser to the Supreme Allied Command. He has since held many senior scientific and defence-related posts, notably as Chief Scientific Adviser to the Minister of Defence, 1960–64, and subsequently to HM Government, 1964–71. He is currently Professor at large at the University of East Anglia. Among his many books are *Nuclear Illusion and Reality* (1982) and *Star Wars in a Nuclear World* (1986).

Acknowledgements

This book is based on a Colloquium held in April 1986 at the University of East Anglia, Norwich, as one of an annual series organized by the UEA Seminar in Atlantic Studies. This Colloquium, like the previous ones, was made possible by a fund established by the late Sir Geoffrey De Freitas and we are most grateful to Lady De Freitas for her continuing support of the Seminar. Thanks are due to Professor Howard Temperley, Chairman of the Seminar in Atlantic Studies, and to Dr John Charmley for their help in organizing the Colloquium. Thanks also to Clara Crockatt for valuable editorial assistance on Chapter One. Gordon Smith of Allen and Unwin has been an unfailingly patient and supportive editor.

Foreword

SIR FRANK K. ROBERTS

In this foreword I shall draw upon my experience of Western relations with the Soviet Union since 1938 to suggest that the thread of continuity in what appears a frequently changing scene is more significant than the alternation of periods of 'Cold War' and 'Détente'. The use of these terms conceals fundamental East–West differences and they convey what could be a dangerous impression that periods of tension (Cold War) are even more serious and periods of dialogue (Détente) more hopeful than they have hitherto proved to be.

My first connection with Soviet affairs was in the prewar period of mutual suspicion marked by the Munich agreement of 1938, followed by the brief but unsuccessful negotiation in 1939, rudely terminated by the Molotov–Ribbentrop Agreement, this in its turn terminated by Hitler's invasion of Russia in 1941, resulting in the Anglo-Soviet Alliance against Hitler. In the Foreign Office between 1941 and 1945 I found that this ('Détente') period with the Soviet Union barely disguised serious controversies, especially over the future of Poland and of Germany. It was, however, the intention of the Western allies to base the postwar order on continued co-operation with the Soviet Union, above all in the United Nations and in the Occupation Regime in Germany. This ('Détente') policy was continued throughout 1945 and 1946, although from Moscow, where I then was, hopes of Stalin's continued co-operation in peace after victory seemed, and indeed proved to be, illusory. The stages in the transition from Détente back to Cold War were: (1) Stalin's rejection of the Western invitation to join the European Recovery Programme of 1947; (2) the Soviet-engineered *coup d'état* in Prague in 1948; (3) later in 1948, the Berlin Blockade.

Stalin's death in 1953 broke some of the ice of this Cold War, and in 1955 a new period of Détente was ushered in by Khrushchev, who met Western leaders and went to Belgrade to restore relations with Tito's Yugoslavia. Above all, Khrushchev realized that war, hitherto regarded in Moscow as an inevitable stage in the final defeat of capitalism, was in the nuclear age no longer an acceptable part of Marxist-Leninist ideology. He re-emphasized instead Lenin's concept of peaceful coexistence, which contributed to his breach with Mao's China, but was misunderstood in the West as implying a degree of genuine world-wide co-operation with the Western 'capitalist' world, which was never in Khrushchev's mind. 'Peaceful coexistence' included commercial and cultural exchanges as well as high-level discussions and personal meetings. But in political and strategic terms it was limited to the control of nuclear weapons and to crisis management in Europe and the Atlantic. In the outside world there were no such restraints upon Soviet actions; competition was the order of the day under the slogans of support for 'national liberation movements' and of the pursuit of the ideological struggle. And, nearer home, increased personal, commercial and cultural exchanges were overshadowed by the second major Berlin crisis, leading to the building of the Berlin wall in 1961, and by the even more dangerous Cuban missile crisis of 1962, which brought the two superpowers close to the brink of war.

These major crises did not, however, herald the return to another Cold War. Khrushchev's more cautious successor, Brezhnev, picked up the Détente element in Soviet policies and, on the Western side, NATO added Détente to deterrence and defence. Nixon and Kissinger pursued Détente with the Russians with their hands enormously strengthened by their successful Détente with China.

This renewal of Détente in the 1960s and 1970s had its successes, above all in several major agreements on nuclear arms control and in the German Ostpolitik and the Four-Power Agreement on Berlin. But all this was within the framework of crisis management and nuclear arms control in the major area of East–West and superpower confrontation. In the outside world, apart from mutual superpower caution in the Middle East, there were no corresponding achievements. On the contrary, in the 1970s the Soviet Union took the opportunities afforded by the post-Vietnam and post-Watergate climate of introspection in the USA openly to support 'national liberation movements' in the Horn of Africa and in Southern Africa and eventually with its own armed forces in Afghanistan, while also changing the balance of military forces with the USA very much in its favour.

To the USA, which had marked time with its armaments throughout the 1970s, Détente therefore seemed to be a one-way street for Soviet advance. With Reagan's election, the USA regarded the Soviet Union primarily as an adversary rather than a potential, if difficult, partner; the emphasis in Washington moved towards restoring the military balance. The stationing of Pershing II and Cruise missiles in Europe was the pretext for the Russians to break off all East–West talks on arms control. But negotiations under the Helsinki agreement of 1975 for Security and Co-operation in Europe (CSCE) were not interrupted then or later, and the Soviet Union soon returned to the negotiating tables on arms control in Geneva and Vienna. Despite Soviet attacks on Mr Reagan's brain-child of the SDI, or even perhaps because of the potential strains this might place upon the Soviet Union's inferior high technology, top-level superpower meetings were resumed in 1985 after a gap of six years, bringing East–West relations back on a (Détente) course of negotiation.

The conclusion I draw from this unduly compressed review is that, although it is convenient to discuss the history of East–West relations since 1947 under such headings as the First Cold War, Détente, the New Cold War, and now perhaps the renewal of Détente, such arbitrary divisions may also lead to misunderstandings: first, in underestimating the continuity of Soviet policies and ambitions thoughout the periods of tension and of discussion alike; secondly, over the depth of the ideological divide between Soviet Marxism–Leninism and our Western market economy social systems; thirdly, over the limited significance of changes in Soviet leadership from Stalin to Gorbachev; fourthly, over the extreme difficulty of trying to reach increasingly complicated arms control agreements, especially in the nuclear field, before rather than after a high degree of political understanding and mutual tolerance has been reached between the two contending camps. To avoid creating any misunderstanding myself, however, let me emphasize in conclusion the importance, precisely because of this adversarial relationship and also because of the nuclear challenges facing us, of maintaining and developing a realistic dialogue with the Soviet rulers and, so far as is allowed, with the Soviet people. But this will bring better results if we resist the temptation to expect too much from the periods of Détente and from more outgoing leaders such as Khrushchev and Gorbachev, and if we also avoid the other extreme of assuming the worst in the alternating periods of disappointment and disillusion that recall Stalin's original Cold War.

PART I

Introductions

1 The Cold War Past and Present

RICHARD CROCKATT

Cold Wars New and Old

In the 1830s Alexis de Tocqueville wrote that two nations would before long 'sway the destinies of half the globe'. He was referring to the United States and Russia (de Tocqueville, [1835] 1945, p. 452). Were he alive today, de Tocqueville might congratulate himself on his foresight, but we can assume that he would wish that the Russo-American sway over mankind had taken a different form. He based his prediction on the enormous potential for growth in both countries provided by the existence of vast areas of land and natural resources. Although he recognized that these two nations even then represented competing principles of political organization, he can hardly have foreseen the form that this competition would take or the extent to which it would dictate the conditions of international affairs. Nor could he have predicted the existence of the nuclear nexus, which binds these two nations even as their social systems separate them. It was left to a twentieth-century political theorist, Hannah Arendt, to take the full measure of the conditions under which de Tocqueville's prediction would be fulfilled. Writing in 1962 as an exile from a Europe now dwarfed by the superpowers, Arendt observed that 'wars and revolutions have thus far determined the physiognomy of the twentieth century' (Arendt, 1973, p. 11). A quarter of a century later, there is no reason to revise this statement. The armed truce of the postwar years, which we call the Cold War, represents, not so much the triumph of peace over war between the superpowers, as acceptance that a military and ideological stand-off is the best substitute for peace available.

From one point of view the Cold War of the last forty years is of a piece: the comings and goings of governments and the oscillations between antagonism and accommodation are so many eddies in one continuous stream. On closer inspection, however, substantial shifts in East–West relations are discernible. One such shift occurred in the late 1970s with the advent of what has come to be called the 'new' or 'second' Cold War (Halliday, 1983). The succession of crises from Angola, in 1975, to Iran, Afghanistan, Poland, the Horn of Africa, Nicaragua and El Salvador, coupled with the deployment of new intermediate-range nuclear weapons by both sides in Europe and the halt in the SALT process, ushered in a period of hostility in East–West relations comparable in scope and intensity with the early postwar years. Détente, already moribund in the later years of the Carter administration, was effectively buried by the time of the election of President Reagan.

These developments raise a number of questions, which this book seeks to address. What were the conditions which made Détente possible in the late 1960s and early 1970s? Why did Détente prove to be so fragile? What are the connections between the 'first' and 'second' Cold Wars? What are the prospects for East–West relations in the late 1980s and beyond? In drawing together contributions from historians, international relations specialists, and participants in the events of the last forty years, this book examines postwar East–West relations in the light of three major phases: the first Cold War, covering the decade following the end of the Second World War; the period of Détente in the late 1960s and early 1970s; the new Cold War of the 1980s. Discussions of Britain and continental Europe are included as integral elements of the larger picture of superpower relations. No scheme can hope to capture all the complexities of historical change and, in any case, as will be clear, the contributors' perspectives vary. Taken together, however, the chapters of this book aim to provide a comprehensive assessment of the conditions affecting East–West relations in the last forty years.

To a striking degree the policies of the United States and the Soviet Union since the late 1970s reflect their respective interpretations of the failure of Détente. From the standpoint of the Reagan administration, the complex structure of Nixon–Kissinger Détente had in effect been a form of appeasement. 'Linkage', which had been intended to operate as a check on Soviet behaviour by making arms agreement and trade concessions conditional upon Soviet restraint in the Third World, had not worked. The Soviets had cynically exploited America's move towards accommodation to build up their arms far beyond parity with the USA and had engaged continuously and aggressively in adventurism in the Third World. Détente, in the oft-repeated phrase, had been a one-way street. The Carter policies too had failed. The attempt by President Carter to pursue linkage by other means in his human rights policy had borne little fruit, and in any case conflicted with his aim of playing down the ideological conflict with the Soviet Union and reorienting American policies on a North–South basis. By 1979 Carter himself was forced to concede that gestures of co-operation had made little impact on Soviet actions. For the incoming Reagan administration the only possible route lay in a reassertion of American political resolve to oppose Soviet advances, coupled with a build-up of American military power. Negotiation, particularly on nuclear arms, must remain on the agenda, but the USA must 'negotiate from strength'.

Viewed from the Kremlin, the new Cold War represented a renewed challenge to two principles long considered vital to the Soviet Union's standing as a great power – security and legitimacy. With the experience of the Second World (or 'Great Patriotic') War still a powerful memory more than forty years on, the Soviet Union could not afford to compromise on the means of self-preservation. The United States, the Soviets pointed out, had been the first nuclear power and had thus initiated the arms race. Soviet advances in weaponry since then had been aimed at redressing the balance, which had been consistently in the United States's favour. Soviet vulnerability to encirclement by the Western powers – to say nothing of China – meant that the USSR needed to maintain a substantial conventional military capability in addition to its nuclear arsenal. Détente seemed initially to promise recognition by the USA of Soviet security needs and also to confer legitimacy upon the Soviet Union's aspirations to be treated as an equal by the United States. In so far, however, as the Americans interpreted Détente as a means of restricting the Soviets' legitimate interests in the Third World, then it represented an unacceptable interference in Soviet affairs. The Americans, it was observed, placed few comparable restrictions on their own activities. Like the Americans, the Soviets by the late 1970s had come to view Détente as a one-way street, though in the contrary direction. The Reagan administration's return to strident Cold War rhetoric and policies undermined whatever had been achieved under Détente, provoking a dangerous destabilization in international affairs, above all in the field where superpower relations mattered most – control of nuclear arms.

These contrasting readings of recent history reflect, as both David Schwartz and Mike Bowker make clear in their contributions to this book, different Soviet and American expectations of Détente. Both sides, writes Bowker, viewed Détente competitively, which meant that gains by one side would be interpreted as losses by the other. The American principle of linkage clashed with the Soviet preference for compartmentalization of the main areas under discussion, with the consequence that only limited progress was possible in the most compelling area of mutual interest – arms control. Détente, concludes Schwartz, did not alter the fundamentals of the US–Soviet relationship.

Among the features of the new Cold War frequently cited by observers is the intensity of ideological conflict between the superpowers, which has served to reinforce bipolarity in the international system. This development is clearer on the American side for two reasons. In the first place, the Reagan administration's stance on foreign affairs has been fuelled by a powerful swing to the right in domestic politics. A strain of moral and religious fundamentalism has issued in a repudiation of permissive social values at home and a corresponding distaste for compromise abroad. Secondly, the Soviet Union continues to insist on its adherence to Détente and on the paramount need to detach negotiations on arms from conflicts in other areas. Such compartmentalization is uncongenial to the Americans, and in this sense 'linkage' is no less a priority for the Reagan administration than was the case for Nixon and Kissinger. There is a difference, however. As a matter of policy Nixon and Kissinger resisted invoking absolute principles in dealings with the Soviet Union, on the grounds that it risked exacerbating tensions without materially affecting Soviet behaviour. President Reagan, however, who is evidently more at home with moral principles than with the minutiae of policy, far less with the kind of geopolitical scheme that informed Kissingerian *Realpolitik*, believes that the current challenge to US policy-makers lies above all in the sphere of fundamental values. Since his election, Reagan asserted in 1983, there has been a 'reawakening' within the United States, 'a new sense of confidence in America and the universal principles and ideals on which our free system is based' (Reagan, 1984, p. 3). The tone of public statements by the Reagan administration thus seems closer to that of, say, John Foster Dulles in the early 1950s than to the period of Détente in the later 1960s and early 1970s. Going further back, we can assume that President Reagan would experience little difficulty in endorsing the words with which Truman announced his Doctrine in March 1947, perhaps the classic utterance of American Cold War ideology:

> At the present moment in world history nearly every nation must choose between alternative ways of life. The choice is too often not a free one.
>
> One way of life is based upon the will of the majority, and is distinguished by free institutions, representative government, free elections, guarantees of individual liberty, freedom of speech and religion, and freedom from political oppression.
>
> The second way of life is based upon the will of a minority forcibly imposed upon the majority. It relies upon terror and oppression, a controlled press and radio, fixed elections and the suppression of personal freedoms.
>
> I believe that it must be the policy of the United States to support free peoples who are resisting attempted subjugation by armed minorities or by outside pressures (Truman, 1963, pp. 178–9).

Truman had Greece and Turkey in mind; Reagan's concern is El Salvador and Afghanistan, among other Cold War flash-points. Both Presidents, however, were also thinking in global terms and, indeed, as Fred Halliday has pointed out, the salient feature of periods of Cold War is not so much the existence of superpower conflict or the absence of negotiation, but the subordination of all world conflicts to the overriding one of East–West antagonism (Halliday, 1983, p. 9)

It is reasonable to ask, however, how far we can push the contrast outlined here between periods of Cold War and of Détente. Has not ideological conflict been a consistent element in East–West relations since the war, including during the high tide of Détente in the early 1970s? Have not negotiations continued through periods of high tension in US–Soviet relations, as they are doing now in a range of fields? There is the problem too of periodization. In his foreword to this book Sir Frank Roberts, drawing on a possibly matchless depth of personal experience in British–Soviet affairs, considers continuities over the past forty years to be far more significant than the periodic alternation of Cold War and Détente. From this point of view, the 'Détente proper' of the early 1970s was merely one among a number of comparable episodes and, in any case, was conditional upon the continuous and overriding fact of US–Soviet conflict. Lord Zuckerman, who shares Sir Frank Roberts's depth of experience in public affairs, recognizes only one Cold War, with the added complication that he dates its inception from 1918, the year of British intervention in support of Tsarist forces opposing the Bolshevik Revolution. And, even if we accept that Détente proper did represent a new departure in US–Soviet relations, we must reckon with Phil Williams's observation that Détente was a short-lived exception to the rule of Cold War relations between the superpowers. Is not Détente in any event only definable in relation to the Cold War?

There is much more at stake in these questions than the meanings of words. The issue involves the kind of interpretive framework we bring to bear on the postwar era as a whole. This book establishes broad divisions of the period into the origins of the first Cold War, the antecedents and the consequences of Détente, and the new Cold War of the 1980s. As the references to the contributions by Roberts and Zuckerman suggest, the periodization adopted is not to be taken as a rigid mould but rather as a convenient framework within which a range of perspectives can be accommodated. Much depends upon the type of question asked and the point of view adopted. It may be that generational differences produce markedly different perspectives on the course of events. A lifetime of continuous involvement in public affairs stretching back before the Second World War may encourage perception of continuities in postwar international affairs by its very contrast with prewar circumstances. Those with shorter memories may be more impressed by local shifts in the tenor of East–West relations and be predisposed to grant that significant movement has taken place and could take place in the future. But, even if there is such a thing as a generational divide on these issues – and it would surely be rash to overstate the case – the question of relative weight to be assigned to continuities and discontinuities arises in any case in the attempt to relate short-term changes to longer-term structural features of the international system. In the remainder of this introduction, as a basis for the detailed papers that follow, I shall explore various ways in which this relationship might be established.

Ideological Conflict

The most obvious element of continuity in postwar East–West relations is the ideological face-off between communism and democratic capitalism. The passage from Truman's 1947 speech quoted above testifies to the depth and intensity of the divide, and many sources from the Soviet side can be cited that express the same conviction of the mutual incompatibility of the two systems. The point scarcely needs to be laboured. More significant is the degree to which the United States and the Soviet Union have become national embodiments of these ideologies, to the extent that it is only with difficulty that we can conceive of these nations in the way that we view, for example, France and Britain in the eighteenth century – as great powers with manifestly conflicting interests but inhabiting a more or less common conceptual universe. James Reston's comment, made in 1947, that 'negotiating with the Russians is like playing tennis on a court without lines or umpire' (Reston, 1976, p. 19), expresses the frustration often felt by Western Kremlin-watchers and diplomats when confronted by their Soviet counterparts who do not appear to 'play by the rules'. The cloak of secrecy that surrounds decision-making in the Kremlin, the difficulty of constructing a rationale for Soviet policy in terms of traditional diplomacy, has fed the suspicion that the Soviets operate on the basis of a master-plan for Soviet world-domination, and there are enough statements on the record to lend plausibility to this theory for those predisposed to seek it. For their part, the Soviets have expressed distaste for the deep strain of moralism in American diplomacy, the reliance on what Bruce Kuniholm in this volume calls the 'diplomacy of principle'. To the Soviets, such documents as the Atlantic charter and the Declaration on Liberated Europe were suspect not only because they got in the way of the pragmatics of great power diplomacy but because they seemed ideologically loaded against the Soviet Union. As Kuniholm makes clear, the moralistic strain in American diplomacy has deep cultural and historical roots and has been geared as much to satisfying the domestic appetite for principled justification of foreign policy as to the specific requirements of relations with other countries.

From the European point of view, the crusading element in the foreign policies of the two superpowers puts them both at a remove from 'traditional diplomacy'. To that extent, as a number of the

contributors to this book observe, there has always been a disjunction between European and US/Soviet perceptions of international relations. As for the superpowers themselves, if mutual
trust is the main ingredient of successful diplomacy, then its absence
accounts for much that is characteristic of US–Soviet relations, and
the lack of a common framework of understanding must in turn be
put down to the radical divergence in ideology between the two
powers.

Admittedly, ideological difference does not explain everything.
One historian found it possible (at least in the opening pages of his
book) to describe the early postwar years without reference to
communism or capitalism. He cited traditional power rivalry and,
above all, geopolitical factors as the chief sources of the breakdown
in the wartime alliance between the United States and the Soviet
Union (Halle, 1967, Chapter 1). It can also be said that both the
USA and the Soviet Union have acted in ways that their ideological
positions would not lead one to expect. The Soviet Union has
frequently pursued an opportunistic or pragmatic line in the Third
World, supporting heterodox nationalist movements in preference
to orthodox communists when trade advantages and political stability seemed most likely to result from such moves. Often too, as in
the case of Allende's Chile, the Soviet Union has offered little aid to
potential allies when the price would involve open confrontation
with the United States in its own sphere of interest. By the same
token, the United States has recognized political limits to its
capacity to dictate the course of events in line with pure ideology,
above all in Eastern Europe. For all the aggressive noises that have
issued from Washington in response to Soviet enforcement of its
power, the United States has accepted that the costs of an open
challenge to the Soviet Union in this area are too high. Finally, as is
routinely pointed out by Russian specialists, there has been substantial continuity between Tsarist and Soviet goals and in the
general character of Russia's relations with the West since the time
of Peter the Great. From this standpoint, the Soviet Union represents a twentieth-century version of the 'Eastern question'. But
when these (and many other comparable) points have been made,
there remains the fact, which has psychological as well as political
dimensions, of sustained ideological competition between the
United States and the Soviet Union. Explaining the Cold War
without reference to ideology is like explaining black–white rela-

tions in the United States without reference to race. It can be done, but only at the cost of radical distortion of reality.

The Division of Europe and the Alliance System

A second element of continuity lies in the division of Europe, a peculiarly literal translation of ideological conflict into geopolitical fact. Two related factors, both consequences of Allied victory in the Second World War, determined the split: the disposition of troops and subsequently of political power, in May 1945, and the failure to reach a settlement on Germany. With some minor adjustments, the line of the Iron Curtain corresponds to the military positions reached respectively by the Soviet Union and the Western Allies in 1945, and the current border between East and West Germany matches the zones of occupation devised by Churchill, Roosevelt, and Stalin. The subsequent reinforcement of the divide in the form of parallel military, political and economic organizations on each side of the line has become such a familiar feature of the postwar scene that it takes an effort of imagination to conceive of any other possible arrangement. However, for a number of reasons, the line through Europe has proved to be more blurred than the miles of barbed wire and concrete would suggest.

In the first place, Finland and Austria stand as examples of compromise between the superpowers. Both these countries have been effectively detached, though for different reasons, from the central arena of Cold War conflict. Secondly, trade between the Eastern and Western blocs, particularly since the signing of the Helsinki Accords in 1975, has forged substantial links across the European divide. More dramatic signs of cracks in the ideological wall have come in the series of uprisings in Eastern Europe against Soviet-style communist rule: from East Germany in 1953, to Hungary in 1956, Czechoslovakia in 1968, and Poland in 1980. Less explosive but none the less significant has been Yugoslavia's successful pursuit of the role of independent communist state since 1948 and Rumania's defiance of the Kremlin on defence policy. Albania has pursued a consistently hostile line towards the Soviet Union. More generally, the Soviet Union is confronted by an asymmetry in its economic relations with the nations of Eastern Europe, most of which have a considerably higher standard of living than the Soviet

Union. Not only does this loosen these nations' dependence upon the Soviet Union, it carries the threat of dissatisfaction among the Soviet people, should they be able to make comparisons with their better-favoured comrades within the Warsaw Pact. It is no accident that, among the nations of Eastern Europe, the Soviet Union places the tightest restrictions on foreign travel. Soviet fears about the economic imbalance within the Eastern bloc are compounded by the threat posed by trade with the West to ideological purity and political reliability, a point well brought out by Mike Bowker in this book. The Soviet Union can afford neither to give free rein to the nations of the Eastern bloc nor to ignore the pressures for diversity within its sphere of interest. In short, influence over Eastern Europe is something that the Soviets have had to work at; it has involved Soviet concessions as well as Soviet impositions.

America's relationship with the nations of Western Europe has been less tense because, in principle, the basis of the NATO alliance and of America's economic and political relations with Western Europe is consent. Nevertheless, alliance politics have been subject to strain in Europe on a number of counts. Britain's role, discussed in three contributions to this book, illustrates both the opportunities and constraints set by the terms of the American relationship. As Victor Rothwell observes in his chapter on Britain and the early Cold War, in the immediate aftermath of the Second World War British and American perspectives on the Soviet threat showed a marked divergence, with Britain initially pressing for a firmer line in the face of the Soviet Union's tightening grasp on Eastern Europe. The United States soon assumed its role as senior partner in the relationship, based on overwhelming economic and military predominance, while Britain adjusted to a trimmed down post-imperial role as a minor great power. But Brian White offers substantial evidence in his discussion of Britain and Détente that Britain made a decisive contribution in the late 1950s and early 1960s to the easing of tension between East and West, most notably in the nuclear test ban negotiations between 1959 and 1963, in which British diplomacy played a 'catalytic role'.

Other aspects of the British relationship with the United States, however, demonstrate the strains caused by differing interests and diplomatic perspectives. The 'special relationship' has never closed all the gaps between Britain and the United States. The McMahon Bill of 1946, which excluded Britain from co-operation in atomic research after close wartime collaboration in the Manhattan project, provoked sharp resentment in Britain and led to the development of the British independent nuclear deterrent. The USA's support for the UN resolution condemning the action of Britain and France in the Suez crisis produced perhaps the most damaging split in the special relationship, either before that date or since. Through these and other incidents NATO has remained firm. But, although there are sufficient examples of co-operation in moments of high risk beyond the NATO theatre – Britain's tacit endorsement of America's role in Vietnam, support for the US bombing of Libya, and the United States' backing for Britain in the Falklands War – co-operation in these instances has been contingent upon Britain's acknowledgement of US superiority. The first two instances, furthermore, aroused powerful opposition within influential sectors of British public opinion, and led many in Britain to question the American relationship. Recently, NATO itself has come under close scrutiny. In David Robertson's reading of Britain's defence options in the 1980s and 1990s, the financial demands of the NATO alliance weigh heavily on defence costs and, he observes, 'it is no longer obvious that they are fully consonant with home defence'. Even the Conservative government concedes that rising costs of nuclear and conventional arms may dictate cuts in the number of separate functions that Britain's forces currently undertake. The Labour Party's policy of moving towards non-nuclear defence, if implemented, would represent not only a radical restructuring of British defence policy but, as Robertson points out, an abandonment of the consensus that has governed Britain's commitment to NATO for close to forty years. The effects on the American relationship with Britain are incalculable, but we must assume that the 'special relationship' would become a piece of history.

Looking beyond Britain, European and American interests have clashed frequently in the economic and military fields: witness US suspicion of the threat posed by the European Economic Community to the American economy, the attempt during Reagan's first administration to halt European co-operation with the Soviet Union on its gas pipeline project, the reluctance of a number of European nations to accept the deployment of Cruise and Pershing II missiles (originally, it must be noted, requested by Europe) and, more recently, European doubts about America's Strategic Defense Initiative (SDI). The list could be extended, but the message is clear:

there has been considerable divergence in American and European perceptions of the Soviet threat and in the means of dealing with it, in addition to 'in-house' friction caused by the inherent imbalances in the US–European relationship. The signs are that in the past year (this is being written in July 1986) relations have never been worse since the Suez crisis. 'Who needs allies?' asked a columnist for the 'liberal' *New Republic* in December 1985 in exasperation at Europe's mealy-mouthed response to American action in Grenada, the Achille Lauro hijacking, and against international terrorism generally (Krauthammer, 1985, pp. 17–20). In Europe there has probably never been a time when the NATO alliance was more openly or more widely questioned.

Once again, however, we must ask whether these signs of strain within both blocs have materially affected the basic lines of division in Europe and whether they are likely to. A categorical answer is hardly possible, though the record thus far suggests that the threat of decoupling has tended to reinforce the division of Europe and the alliance systems, because of the two factors in the East–West relationship that were mentioned at the beginning of this section as the original grounds of Cold War antagonism – the position of Germany and the issue of military security.

During the 1950s it was still possible to find advocates of a reunified neutral German state. This had originally been the goal of the Soviet Union, as one possible means of containing the threat of German resurgence. However, with West Germany's incorporation into NATO in 1955 and the formation of the East German state in the same year the likelihood of reunification was sharply reduced. The Austrian Treaty (also 1955), under which the occupation forces were removed and Austria was re-established on a neutral basis, removed the danger of a 'Greater Germany' on the Hitler model, but also provided an unwelcome precedent of Western-oriented neutrality. In these circumstances a divided Germany seemed the safest bet for the Soviet Union. The building of the Berlin wall in 1961 effectively signalled the end of Soviet aspirations for a reunified Germany within the foreseeable future, and the settlement of Germany's borders in 1972 as the culmination of Willy Brandt's Ostpolitik set an official seal on the *de facto* division of Germany. On the American side, we need only recall the furore aroused by George Kennan's suggestion, made in his Reith Lectures of 1957, that Germany be reunified as a neutral state, to be aware that the

American leadership had already accepted that keeping Germany divided was of critical importance in holding the line in Europe.

Neither side professes to be happy with a divided Germany and a divided Europe. When, in 1975, Henry Kissinger's chief adviser on communist issues, Helmut Sonnefeld, made a statement in which he effectively conceded that the Soviet Union had a 'sphere of interest' in Eastern Europe, others within the administration rushed to deny that America could ever grant legitimacy to Soviet domination in that region. Recently, the record of the Yalta conference of February 1945 has become yet again the subject of scrutiny by American conservatives, according to whom American weakness at that crucial meeting sealed the fate of Eastern Europe. Things could have been otherwise, and might yet be, the implication seems to be. Hopes are one thing, however, reality another, and the reality is that both sides have much to lose from a radical change in the status quo. Better the evil you know than the evil you don't is the principle that has generally guided the policies on both sides.

The overriding factor, however, promoting the continuance of the status quo in Europe is the issue of security. The Soviet Union has never permitted liberalization in Eastern Europe to progress beyond the point of threatening the solidity of the Warsaw Pact. Military security and the preservation of socialism are inextricably intertwined. On the Western side, but for some parties on the left in Europe and the extreme right in the United States, both pillars of the NATO alliance have generally accepted that the American nuclear umbrella, coupled with the presence of American conventional forces in Europe, is a necessary, if unfortunate concomitant of Cold War politics. Above all, nuclear deterrence has served to reinforce the division of Europe during the past forty years and is thus among the central points of continuity in the East–West relationship.

The Arms Race

The term, deterrence, suggests a defensive posture; it carries the implication that aggressive intentions lie exclusively with the other side and that therefore 'our' weapons are deployed as a necessary counterweight to the threat of offensive action by the other side. But given the explosive power, speed of delivery and increasing accuracy of nuclear missiles, the theory of deterrence readily shifts towards the claim that defence can only take the form of an offensive power that matches that of the enemy (Prins *et al.*, 1983, p. 156). We can imagine a perfect model of deterrence in which each side would possess exactly the same equipment. If we assumed, furthermore, that certain other conditions for stability were satisfied – rough comparability in economic performance and technological capability, wholly compliant allies and minimum political disturbance from outside the blocs – then we can envisage room for a gradual scaling-down of this balance of terror to the point where only token forces are necessary to maintain stability. In these circumstances disarmament would be not only possible but logical.

We have only to posit such a situation, however, to comprehend why such stability as has been produced by the East–West arms race is of a different order. Only one element in the actual postwar situation fully corresponds to the situation described in the model – fear of the consequences of a nuclear exchange. This is certainly a powerful force for restraint on both sides. But, in all other respects, despite certain rough correspondences, there are significant imbalances in the East–West military relationship that, if allowed to grow, could disturb the overall balance and even ultimately override the restraint imposed by the fear of nuclear war. A glance at some of the main aspects of the nuclear arms race will show how fragile this balance has been.

The Cold War began with an asymmetry that had great ramifications for the future – a United States atomic monopoly coupled with Soviet superiority in conventional forces in Europe. Following the failure of proposals for the internationalization of atomic research, the first produced the inevitable Soviet response in the form of its own atomic programme. As Lord Zuckerman points out in this volume, the Soviets had been engaged on it for some years, in any case. The second created a strategic dilemma for the United States that has persisted until the present day – the possibility of a Soviet invasion of Western Europe, in which the United States and its allies would be confronted with substantially superior numbers of Warsaw Pact conventional forces, and with the need therefore to reserve the option of a nuclear response in such a case. No matter that the Soviets disclaim any intention of invading Western Europe or that American leaders similarly protest their peaceful intentions: this disjunction has fuelled mistrust on both sides. Why, ask the Soviets, will the Americans not join them in a public declaration of 'no first use' of nuclear weapons? Why, ask the Americans, does the Soviet Union maintain such large conventional forces in Europe? Such questions are symbolic of further areas of suspicion regarding motives on each side. Soviet civil defence plans for evacuation of its major cities seem to imply the belief that a nuclear war is winnable, Soviet leaders' protestations to the contrary notwithstanding. And there were enough public statements from the American Defense Department and the military in the late 1970s and early 1980s to arouse Soviet (and Western European) fears that America too envisaged the theoretical possibility of nuclear victory (Halliday, 1983, pp. 52–5). Behind it all lies the 'logic' of the arms race itself, which has technological, political and economic dimensions.

From the outset, the arms race has been dictated to a degree by technological imperatives, and in this sense weapons technology reflects the pace of modernization generally in the post-industrial society. Each new solution to a technical problem creates its own set of new problems, as military planners and scientists anticipate responses to the initial solution. The result has been, writes Lord Zuckerman in this volume, that 'politicians have been dragged along by their technological advisers'. One example among many is the development of MIRVs in the late 1960s (the placing of multiple independently targeted warheads on a single rocket) in response to the threat posed by the anti-ballistic missile systems (ABMs) developed by both the United States and the Soviet Union in the 1960s (Prins *et al.*, 1983, pp. 128–30). By the time MIRVs were in place, however, both sides had concluded that existing ABM systems presented insuperable technical problems and they were thus prepared to contemplate a qualified ban on ABM systems in the form of the ABM treaty of 1972. Meanwhile, MIRV development continued, with the Americans in a decisive lead in this field, while the Soviets favoured larger heavier rockets with single warheads. Research on ABM systems, which was not prohibited by the ABM treaty, also continued on both sides, the outcome of which has been the American 'Star Wars' programme or Strategic Defense Initiative (SDI). Less is known about Soviet developments in this area, but we must assume that they exist, although at a less advanced stage. The result, if deployment of SDI takes place, will presumably be a reprise of the late 1960s situation, only at a higher level of technological sophistication and fire power, necessitating a search for means of incapacitating or circumventing SDI by novel developments in missile technology. Indeed they already exist in the form of Cruise missiles and 'stealth' bombers.

If there is a logic in the record of nuclear weapons development then it surely indicates that each technological innovation will be matched by another. There is no guarantee, however, that the action–reaction cycle will work out in a balanced way if, as seems clear, the Americans maintain a technological lead and if, as also seems to be the case, the Americans count on their lead to give them political advantage. The effort to out-modernize the Soviets with SDI is only one more case of a technological innovation that has great potential implications.

In his chapter on SDI Steve Smith provides a detailed analysis of the technical conundrums involved in the programme, to which he adds the observation that SDI is a search 'for a technical fix to a political problem', based on the 'fallacy of the last move'. In Reagan's theory – and we must assume that he is sincere in this belief – SDI represents the ultimate form of defence, which will render offensive weapons redundant and usher in a period of genuine reductions in nuclear armaments. From the Soviet Union's point of view, however, SDI threatens a radical destabilization in the strategic relationship in that the United States appears to be after unilateral advantage. There is the paramount problem, as Steve Smith notes, of how to manage the transition from a world dominated by 'offensive' weapons to a world dominated by 'defensive' weapons. Should SDI prove technically feasible and should the US retain a decisive lead in this field, could the Soviet Union be expected to negotiate reductions in its own offensive weapons without evidence of good faith on the American side? This could only mean (following the logic of the SDI philosophy) either sharing knowledge of SDI technology or an American offer of substantial reductions in its own arsenal, or both. The situation is comparable in certain respects to the period of American atomic monopoly between 1945 and 1949. Such good faith was not forthcoming then, nor is there reason to think it might be now, and for the same reasons. The conditions do not exist which would permit a technical solution to a problem that is so patently subject to political calculations.

The record of the arms race demonstrates the profound influence of political pressures, domestic and foreign, on perceptions of innovations in arms technology. The purported 'missile gap' of the late 1950s is now known to have been non-existent, but proved useful to President Kennedy during the 1960 election in his effort to picture the Eisenhower administration as weak on defence. The result was a marked stepping-up of America's Intercontinental Ballistic Missile programme. The evidence suggests that the massive Soviet military build-up of the 1960s was a direct consequence of Soviet awareness of its politico-strategic inferiority demonstrated in the Cuban missile crisis of 1962. The search for parity in nuclear weapons was thus also a search for political equality on the part of the Soviet Union. As the subsequent history of arms negotiations shows, the difficulty of establishing what parity means, given the differences in technical character of the nuclear arsenals and in the strategic purposes they are designed to serve, has proved to be one more focus of political discord between the superpowers. More generally, as many historians have observed, successive American presidents have found it expedient to play up the Soviet threat in order to extract appropriations from a cost-conscious Congress. On the Soviet side, the American threat has served as a useful means of maintaining ideological conformity within the Warsaw Pact nations.

The economic systems of the powers also reflect Cold War priorities. The devotion of large proportions of national budgets to armaments exact huge costs on national wealth, most notably in the Soviet Union, which fears, not without justification, that its faltering economy may place it at a decisive political and military disadvantage. Thus far both sides have been willing to pay the costs of what amounts to a partial war economy, but the costs are more than merely economic. A ceiling may well be set as much by political as by economic factors, as the militarization of the domestic political economies threatens to undermine fundamental political principles. President Eisenhower warned in his farewell address of the dangers of the 'military–industrial complex', posing the question of whether liberty and democracy could survive the potentially 'disastrous rise of misplaced power' (Eisenhower, 1961, p. 1038). Eisenhower's cautious optimism that eternal vigilance should prove a sufficient protection against this danger is not shared by those in the anti-nuclear movement, for whom the rationale of the arms race is inherently irrational and destructive of those values of consent and governmental accountability on which democracy is based, to say nothing of the danger of nuclear war itself.

In all these respects the arms race has become part of the fabric of the Cold War within and between the contending social systems. It is no surprise that, in the light of the combination of fear and mistrust, coupled with the existence of large arsenals, arms negotiations should have produced so little in the way of real achievement. Neither the Test Ban Treaty of 1963 nor the ABM Treaty of 1972 materially affected research and development in nuclear weapons. The SALT I and II Treaties (the latter not ratified by the United States but observed by successive American administrations, at least until late 1986) may have slowed the rate of growth in certain categories of nuclear weaponry but has not prevented modernization or development of new systems, even when, as is the case with SDI, they come close to violating existing agreements (in this instance the ABM Treaty). The ultimate 'logic' of the arms race is revealed in the argument that one or another weapons system must be developed or retained, not because it objectively increases security, but because it is required as a bargaining chip in the negotiating process.

There has thus been continuity in the arms race based on mutual recognition of the threat of nuclear war. There is a structure to East–West strategic relations provided by the doctrine of deterrence and a degree of comparability in the size of the arsenals on both sides. But the stability of the system, given the imbalances described above, is heavily contingent upon the assurance that neither side will seek or manage to gain unilateral advantage. In such circumstances, we must hope that Steve Smith will be proved wrong in his observation that SDI may be the most divisive issue between the United States and the Soviet Union during the next ten years.

The Question of Stability in Postwar East–West Relations

Two possible models of postwar international relations can be extrapolated from the foregoing discussion: one that emphasizes stability and one that focuses on the elements of change and instability in East–West relations. Each model can in turn provoke contradictory responses, according to whether we interpret stability and change positively or negatively. A positive or optimistic interpretation of the stability model would point to the caution that is induced in East–West diplomacy by ideological conflict, the division of Europe, the alliance systems, and the arms race. In a recent article John Lewis Gaddis adopts just such a stance. He observes that 'the Cold War, with all its rivalries, anxieties, and unquestionable dangers, has produced the longest period of stability in relations among the great powers that the world has known in this century; it now compares favorably as well with some of the longest periods of great power stability in all of modern history'. Furthermore, he sees a growing 'maturity' in the Soviet–American relationship, which contrasts favourably with the almost total lack of communication between 1947 and 1955 and the extreme swings between hostility and amiability in the following two decades. That maturity, he suggests, 'would appear to reflect an increasing commitment on the part of both great nations to a "game" played "by the rules"' (Gaddis, 1986, p. 142, 140). Gaddis is fully aware of the dangers of assuming too much about the permanence of the 'game', but on balance he is sanguine about the prospects. It is possible, however, to accept certain elements of Gaddis's analysis without accepting his conclusion. On this view, because the stakes in the game are being progressively raised in the form of increases in armaments on either side, stability takes the form, not of a steady state, but of a spiralling rise towards a potentially critical mass of armaments and mutual suspicion. It is not necessary to be a technological determinist to fear that the arms race is inherently threatening to world peace, if only because the political context in which it takes place has the potential to unbalance the military equation.

This raises the question of change and instability proposed by the second model of East–West relations. Once again, contradictory responses are possible. The optimist can point to a range of developments that suggest the possibility of movement of a positive kind in superpower relations. There have been occasions in the past, such as the period of summitry in the 1950s following the death of Stalin, when liberalization within the Soviet Union produced an easing of Cold War tension. Some would argue that the advent of Secretary Gorbachev promises a comparable improvement in East–West relations. Recurrent dissent within the Soviet bloc holds out the hope to many in the West that the Soviet Union may at length be forced to grant legitimacy to opposition groups. Other developments suggest that the bipolar divide on which the Cold War feeds has always been cut across by other divisions such as the Sino–

Soviet split and the emergence of the Third World non-aligned movement, and that multipolarity promises to diffuse the tensions of the Cold War. The idea of Europe as an independent 'third force' operating as a mediator between the superpowers and a check on the scope of Cold War politics reappears regularly as a possible solvent of the entrenched Cold War ethos. In the concluding chapter to this volume, Wayland Kennet voices the resentment felt by many Europeans at the sway exerted by superpower priorities over European affairs. The Cold War, he says, is an ossified irrelevancy, whose rigidities can only be loosened by the promotion of diversity within the contending blocs. In all these ways we can point to potentialities within the existing international system that could mitigate if not entirely remove the oppressive burden of Cold War tensions.

Pessimists, however, although recognizing that these possibilities may exist, at best doubt that they are capable of fruition within the foreseeable future and, at worst, fear that in any event they would be productive of destabilization in East–West relations. Recent history suggests, for example, that manifestations of dissent within the Soviet Union and its satellites will be summarily suppressed and that such liberalization as is allowed will be carefully controlled. There may be unwelcome justification in the argument that it is not in the West's interest to see dissent flourishing in the Eastern bloc, in so far as it encourages the Soviet Union to reassert an uncompromisingly anti-Western stance. The Sino–Soviet split has not been an unequivocal gain for the West to the extent that it has fuelled Soviet fears of accommodation between China and the West at the Soviet Union's expense. The extension of the Cold War to the Third World from the Korean War onwards has produced multiple new flash-points between the superpowers, both where they have succeeded in superimposing the Cold War on local situations and where they have not. The Middle East presents perhaps the most dangerous of these flash-points, because the superpowers' economic and political interests in this area are not matched by an ability to dictate the course of events. Superpower relations are peculiarly vulnerable in those areas where the rules of the Cold War least apply. And, finally, we can speculate on the consequences that might ensue from the adoption by a British Labour government of its proposed non-nuclear defence policy, which could well, as David Robertson suggests, 'destroy the solidity of NATO'. On the basis of past performance it is reasonable to expect the superpowers to attempt to rein in their allies in the face of threats to the status quo. Viewed in this light, the superpowers are highly sensitive to changes that might affect their interests and correspondingly determined to resist their effects.

Whatever conclusions we draw from an examination of East–West relations in the postwar period, they must surely be able to take account of the elements of stability and the potential for change and, hence, instability. On the evidence of the contributions to this volume, a salient feature of Cold War politics is the existence of limits to the power that can be exercised by each side. To adapt a formulation used by Phil Williams in this book, opportunities are matched by constraints in every sphere of East–West relations. 'Stability' may not be the appropriate term to describe a situation in which the pressures for change and for preservation of the status quo exist in a dynamic relation with each other. At the very least we must hope that there is sufficient fluidity in East–West relations to allow opportunities to be taken when they arise, and sufficient solidity in the relationship to restrain either side from exploiting such opportunities to their own advantage.

2   *Technology for a Cold War**

LORD ZUCKERMAN

Although this book is based on the idea that there have been two
Cold Wars, with an intervening period of Détente, I have always
assumed that there has been only one. My preferred date for its start
is the intervention in 1918 of British forces to help the then Tsarist
government to suppress the Bolshevik Revolution. That historical
event sticks in my mind mainly because of a story that the British
troops which had then been sent to North-west Russia all but
mutinied because, so it was said, they had got fed up with 'all that
black butter'. When I was told that the black butter was caviar, I had
the feeling that the counter-revolutionary forces were less deserving
of sympathy than were the revolutionaries whom they had been sent
to suppress.

In truth, I do not in fact know when hostility between East and
West began. Does it predate 1917, or was it a consequence of the
Revolution of that year? Had it to do with the existence in the
interwar years of what were in effect small Tsarist organizations in
exile, about some of which books are now appearing? Was Western
Europe as hostile to communism, because it was seen as a threat to
the existing order, as was the United States? When I was at Yale in
the early 1930s, I discovered for the first time that people were really
scared of the idea of Bolsheviks.

I must, however, also confess that in those days I paid very little
attention to these matters, and that it was not until just before the
Second World War that I started to be aware of the existence of
anti-Soviet feelings. What I cannot recall now is whether, at the time
of the Hitler–Stalin pact, there was any general feeling that the
USSR was the real enemy of the West, or whether that came when
the Second World War ended. What I remember is that from the
mid-1930s there was fear, fear of Hitler and fascism.

As I recall it, public attitudes to the USSR were transformed

---

* This chapter was originally presented as an after-dinner lecture at the Colloquium
on which this book is based.

when Hitler turned on the Russians after the start of the war. Winston Churchill then spoke of 'our brave ally', and pro-Soviet feeling became widespread. A story used to be told about a certain Duchess who laid on a grand dinner for Mr Maisky, then the Russian Ambassador in London. 'It is so good', she said, 'that your brave people and ours are now allies. We can forget about the past. But what a pity, Mr Ambassador, that Stalin has killed all your generals' (she was referring to the purges of the 1930s). There was a pause before Mr Maisky replied: 'What else could he have done? We don't have a Cheltenham to which to retire useless generals.'

In the first two or three years of the war I was the convenor of a small dining-club, to which we used to invite eminent people, including cabinet ministers, ambassadors and military leaders. Maisky was our guest on one occasion, but he decided not to intervene in the after-dinner discussion until he had heard what everyone else had to say. When he did speak, he started by saying, 'I don't quite understand why you all seem to think that Russia is going to be defeated. We are not going to collapse, but I cannot tell you what price my country will have to pay for victory. Nor can I tell you what that victory is going to cost you.' I have never forgotten those words. I did not meet Maisky again – according to *Who's Who* he died in 1975 aged 91. The next Russians I saw were a small group of senior officers in Normandy, a few days after our landings in 1944. They were there as observers.

There is much argument nowadays about the consequences of the Yalta Conference in 1945 and about who was responsible for what. In a recent issue of the *New York Review of Books* I read that Roosevelt thought that he knew how to handle Stalin, whereas Winston Churchill thought that he did. Who really enjoyed that honour, I do not know. Maybe it was Stalin who knew how to handle both of them.

But what I do know is that towards the end of the war, when I was strategic air planner to Marshal of the Royal Air Force, Lord Tedder, Deputy Supreme Commander to Eisenhower, the Russians kept us in the dark about the plans of their final push against the Germans, and that it was with great difficulty that Stalin was persuaded, mainly by Roosevelt, to allow Eisenhower to send his Deputy to see whether the Russian plans could be co-ordinated with those of the Allied leaders in the West. In his *Fringes of Power*, John Colville (1985a) implies that Churchill disapproved of the choice –

to send 'Tedder to Moscow to talk about purely military affairs is', he said, 'like asking a man who has learned to ride a bicycle to paint a picture'. Tedder did not include me in his party, and I envied his personal staff officer, Wing-Commander Leslie Scarman, now Lord Scarman and until recently a Lord of Appeal, who went with him. When they finally reached Moscow, it was only to discover that the Russian armies were already well on the way towards Warsaw. The Russian leaders did not appear to have been concerned to co-ordinate their plans with those of Eisenhower.

Well before the war ended I was also made aware that some of our own senior military people were not feeling friendly towards the Russians. I had spent the better part of 1943 in the Mediterranean theatre, and at the end of the year I passed through Algiers to say goodbye to some friends in Eisenhower's rear headquarters. As I was leaving the building, an American general rushed after me. 'Zuck', he said, 'we won't have finished when we've cleaned up in Europe. We've then got to take on the Russians.' That was the attitude among some of our people. There may well have been complementary views on the Russian side, but I do not know when the Russian political leaders and their military high command started to be suspicious of Western intentions. What has now become quite plain is that relations began to worsen even before the uprisings in the Balkans in the immediate postwar years, even before the Sino–Soviet pact of 1950, and before the West started to have fears of world revolution. Forty years on, the Second World War has not yet been closed in Europe by a formal peace treaty.

In March of 1946 Winston Churchill delivered his famous speech at Fulton, Missouri, the one in which he coined the term 'Iron Curtain'. The capitulation of Hitler's Germany had left Russia a nation in arms, and one that was soon making aggressive moves against West Berlin. The West reacted. It is on record that in September 1945 the American Joint Chiefs of Staff committed to paper a draft plan for a strike against the USSR, at a time when I should think they knew nothing about the problem of making nuclear bombs, or how many were available. There was also a private deal in July 1946 between the two men with whom I had worked very closely during the war, Lord Tedder and General Spaatz, who was then head of the US Army Air Force, to adapt seven airfields in this country for the reception of B.47 bombers and for the storage and handling of nuclear weapons. It is remarkable that that arrangement was made apparently without reference to the Cabinet (Campbell, 1984).

That was part of the background to the Cold War that the military of both sides provided. The West had reason enough to be wary of the Russians, and if their spying machine was anything like what it was cracked up to be, the Russians also had good reason to be suspicious of the West.

The advent of nuclear weapons had, of course, made a critical difference to the military scene. The Russians knew that the West had nuclear bombs well before we knew how far ahead they were in their development of corresponding weaponry. Most Western 'experts' thought that it would take the Russians ten or more years to catch up. In fact it was only four years after Hiroshima before it was clear that the USSR had also become a nuclear-weapon power. Then, in the very early 1950s, the Americans started to deploy nuclear weapons – free-falling bombs – in Europe. Jupiter missiles were stationed in Turkey, and Thors in Britain and Italy. It was obvious, of course, that deploying these weapons, and thereby giving military substance to George Kennan's 'containment policy', was bound to generate a vigorous arms race, the first phase of which ended, from a military point of view, with the Russians being forced to abandon their plans to position ballistic missiles in Cuba, and with the removal of American missiles from European soil. But this did not stop the race. As we know all too well, both sides now deploy missiles on static as well as mobile platforms, at home and at sea. The build-up of nuclear arsenals on both sides has generated increasing suspicion, and without question has intensified the Cold War.

The theme that I have set myself for this contribution is Technology for a Cold War. It is worth noting that the first serious claim that nuclear physics could be exploited to make atom bombs was not made in this country, or in the United States. It was made in Russia, way back before the start of the Second World War. Equally, the first proposal that there should be international co-operation in the nuclear weapons field was not the Baruch Plan of 1946, as is usually thought, nor was it the private agreement for Anglo-American co-operation between Winston Churchill and Roosevelt in 1943. It has become clear (Kramish, 1960) that it was made in 1941, with the full authority of the Soviet Academy of Sciences and of Stalin, by Kapitza, the Russian physicist who, in the 1920s and early 1930s, had been so distinguished a member of the

Cavendish Laboratory in Cambridge. Needless to say, as the German armies started to drive eastwards in June 1941, the Russians had to direct all their efforts to the manufacture of the conventional armaments they needed in order to halt and then drive back the invaders. But before the war had ended, Kurchatov, the leader of the Russian nuclear weapons team, had resumed his work on the bomb. Had the Russians not been invaded, it is conceivable that they might have had the bomb first, but it is impossible to speculate now what that would have meant. As recent American research has revealed, the Russians were certainly first in the field of ballistic missile technology. We have to assume, therefore, that they were not waiting to find out what was happening in the West before they embarked on the development of nuclear weapons and of missiles. And however sincere Kapitza's appeal, it is conceivable, as some argue, that these technologies were fostered because the Russians had in mind that they might be needed to spread communism – although how communism could be spread by the use of nuclear weapons is far from obvious.

Paradoxically, when Kurchatov resumed his work on nuclear weapons, the United Kingdom, having co-operated with the Americans during the war years, found itself shut out of the American nuclear programme by the McMahon Act, which the United States Congress passed in 1946. The United Kingdom was left to find its own place in the nuclear world.

In the years that have followed, the Americans have been ahead in almost every new step in the technological arms race – for example, in navigational techniques, in MIRVing, in nuclear propulsion, and in solid fuels for missiles. This has obviously acted as a spur to the Russians. But most major advances have taken much longer to mature than is usually appreciated. The possibilities of and technology for anti-ballistic missile defences, of which the Strategic Defense Initiative (SDI) is the latest manifestation, were being discussed on both sides in the 1950s. The only significantly new technical developments in President Reagan's ABM or BMD (ballistic missile defence) concept relate to space stations, and to laser and particle-beam weapons. But otherwise SDI takes us back to the debates of the 1960s when, correctly in my view, it was concluded that the ABM concept was basically flawed for both political and strategic reasons. Essentially that is why both sides agreed in 1972 to conclude an ABM Treaty.

To those versed in Newtonian mechanics, there are, of course, no secrets about what is or is not possible in space. There are no secrets about rocket-propulsion techniques or about nuclear warheads. There are no secrets about the technology of inertial navigation. There are no secrets about computer techniques, or about radar, even if one or other side may be ahead for a time in the exploitation of any one of these technologies. I am citing here what is generally accepted in the USA. But, as I have already said, every new technological step that is taken by one side encourages the other to do likewise – what armchair theorists call the 'action–reaction cycle'.

This, however, is not what emerges from the propaganda battle of the two sides. When the American administration puts its case for funds to the Congress, the Russians are always ahead, and therefore American security is being threatened. Today, for example, the message is that the USA cannot stop testing new nuclear devices because it is claimed that the Russians have just finished a series of tests that have put them ahead. The USA must therefore carry on testing. The Russians, we are told, are flouting arms control agreements. They are testing above the agreed threshold. They are breaking the SALT agreements. What is happening today in the battle of words and propaganda is little different from what has always happened since the 1959–60 moratorium on tests was breached by the USSR. Nothing seems to change. But neither side has achieved greater security by forcing the pace of the arms race.

It is sobering to discover from the papers of the General Advisory Council of the American Atomic Energy Commission for the period 1960–1 that this highly eminent body advised caution in pushing forward in the nuclear weapons field. They believed that it would be a mistake to force the pace. But, as everybody now knows, and to our cost, that advice was rejected. Robert Oppenheimer was one of those who advocated caution. For example, he believed that the development of the superbomb would be a mistake. Today we can ask whether anyone has benefited from the development of the superbomb? All it has done is provide more bars to the nuclear cage in which West and East are now trapped. Superbombs will be used only when one or other side is bent on suicide.

Yet, whatever they themselves may have wished, neither Eisenhower nor Kennedy nor Johnson was able to accept advice to go slow in the development of nuclear weaponry. Because such advice was not tolerable politically, the presidency was denied the opportunity to behave rationally by the nuclear enthusiasts in the weapons laboratories, in the armed forces and in Congress. No one fought more ardently to curb the nuclear arms race than did Harold Macmillan, but most of his efforts were also frustrated because of the strength of feeling in America about the need to build up their nuclear strength.

The arms race is part of the Cold War, with the result that the international political environment becomes ever more fraught with danger. The politicians are dragged along by their technological advisers. It was inevitable that they would be. They are conditioned by the environment of East–West hostility, of suspicion, and of fear. The public, the media, congressional and military leaders, call for more nuclear weapons, for different kinds of nuclear weapons, for all manner of arms. The bulk of the general public automatically believes that what is technologically new in the world of armaments is *ipso facto* good. To take a current example, I doubt very much whether President Reagan understands anything about the X-ray laser; no one would expect him to be able to pass even a simple examination in physics about the principle of the laser. But he has been persuaded that the X-ray laser is something America must have. A large slice of the American people have also been encouraged to believe that the President's SDI will make them immune to Russian ballistic missiles. Because of the President's belief, the development of the X-ray laser goes on. Tests of X-ray lasers, which are essentially tests of nuclear weapons, continue. But I am prepared to bet that however many tests are carried out, and whether or not a deployable X-ray laser ever results, it will not make any difference whatever to the security of the United States – or for that matter to the security of the USSR if it too goes in for X-ray lasers or for any kind of space-based laser.

In the past few months I have been re-reading the records of some of the debates on the ABM system that raged in the late 1960s, and which ended in the SALT agreements and the 1972 ABM Treaty. It is staggering how ignorant we were in Britain of the arguments that were being reported daily in the media of the United States. We treated the subject as top secret – why, I don't know. Did we just imagine that all would be best in the best of all possible worlds? Or were our politicians just insensitive to, as well as ignorant about, an issue on which the future of human society still hinges? SDI, as I have said, has provoked an acute re-run of the ABM debate of the 1960s.

All these debates could, in fact, be regarded as debates about the lure of technology. Public opinion, in America in particular, almost always forces politicians to take a stand on presumed technological advances. Promises of a technological advance in the field of defence become bones of political contention. That, basically, is why Senator John Kennedy had to argue in his presidential campaign of 1960 that America was suffering from a missile gap. However unreal that gap, he was driven politically to declare that the Eisenhower administration had lowered America's defences. The moment he became privy to the information with which Eisenhower had been supplied, he knew that there was no missile gap. The first time I met him after he had become President he asked me what I thought of his missile gap. 'Mr President', I replied, 'what missile gap are you talking about?' He roared with laughter. Election propaganda had demanded a missile gap, and the would-be President could not defy the presumed promises of technology.

Politicians in this and other countries do not seem to appreciate, do not understand, that scientists and engineers are at one and the same time buyers and salesmen, particularly in the fields of technology that affect national security – and so national politics. I have long hoped that the day might come when a political leader with the power to change the direction of events will realize that more advanced technology does not necessarily mean more security, that it often means the reverse. I cannot, alas, see such a politician emerging as some 'messiah' either in the United States or in the USSR. Possibly there will be a Western European 'messiah' one day. But if this is to make any difference to the momentum of the arms race, he or she will have to enjoy all the power of a true messiah. As I have said, Harold Macmillan, who was passionately devoted to the goal of stopping the nuclear arms race, was frustrated by forces that he could not control. He was inevitably impelled along by the same forces that were driving President Kennedy to the conclusion that it would be political suicide for him to insist on a comprehensive test ban that did not include verification measures.

It is strange to think that, in 1958, when the technical talks for a total test ban started in Geneva, John Cockcroft and William Penney, the leaders of the British team, were charged by Macmillan to return, if at all possible, with an agreement on the technical issues that were involved. Jim Fisk, who led the American delegation, was encouraged to do the same by Eisenhower. The Russians also then wanted an agreement for a total ban. Indeed, Kurchatov had been pressing Khrushchev in the late 1950s to take the initiative in calling for a comprehensive test ban.

When the three delegations returned from that first phase of the Geneva technical talks, they each reported to their political masters that they had reached agreement on the main technical issues, and that political negotiations for a comprehensive test ban could now start. But then the rats started to nibble away at what had been agreed, with, for example, arguments that more testing was necessary to assure American security, that the Russians were bound to find ways of cheating, that if there were to be a treaty, the Russians would have to agree to strict verification procedures. Harold Macmillan (1972) noted, during the course of a visit to Washington in March 1960, that the real reason why these arguments were put forward was that the Americans wanted to go on testing without restraint. He had discussed the matter of verification in Moscow in 1959, and had come back from his meeting with Khrushchev with a measure of agreement. But the Americans did not agree. And we were back to square one. American demands for more inspection fanned Russian suspicions. Inevitably both sides became more intransigent.

It is ironical that, whereas the political reason why a comprehensive test ban aimed at stemming the nuclear arms race could not be concluded in 1960 and 1961 was the fear that the other side would cheat, today the declared reason why we must go on testing is, as Caspar Weinberger stated recently, that so long as we have a nuclear arsenal we will need to test. We are no longer worried that the other side could or might cheat. Today we know that significant suspicious underground disturbances could be verified by means that do not demand intrusive inspection. The issue of a test ban has, in short, been turned on its head. It would seem that we no longer regard a Comprehensive Test Ban (CTB) as a measure that will help to curb the nuclear arms race. What matters is that our nuclear arsenal must be kept up to date, and to that end testing must continue. Politicians are often told by the 'weaponeers' that stockpiled nuclear weapons also need to be tested. I myself do not believe that this is ever done as a matter of routine. Norris

Bradbury, who became the director of the US atomic energy laboratories at Los Alamos after the end of the war, when Robert Oppenheimer retired, and who remained director until 1970, has put his name publicly to a statement to that effect. Surely it is obvious that one would not test stockpiled warheads as matter of routine? Where would the process stop if one were found to be defective? And what political or strategic difference would it make if, out of the thousands that exist, ten were found to be faulty? There are other ways of assessing the integrity of nuclear warheads.

The point I am trying to make is that, regardless of what the politician might like to see happen in order to achieve a peaceful world, he is driven into a corner by the reaction of the public to the claims of the technologist. That, essentially, is the story of SDI. President Reagan was entranced by the promises of national immunity to missile attack made to him by a few scientists. He had neither the first-hand competence to challenge their technical claims, nor the experience to deduce the strategic implications of those claims.

No doubt I shall be regarded as over-cynical when I say that it makes no difference at all which side in the arms race makes the more extravagant statements about its own or its opponent's advances. It would not have mattered if the Russians rather than the United States had been ahead in every step of the race. Either way, the technological arms race would have been with us.

I know, too, just how difficult it has become to get technologists of the three sides to agree. The UK tried to bring the Russians back to the technical negotiating table for a CTB in 1966. They agreed to come, but at the same time they cynically commented that, although they thought it would be wise to resume technical talks, they were concerned that were the Americans informed of their willingness, then the Americans would refuse to agree to the talks. They added that were the British to agree with the Americans, then they (the Russians) would not agree with the British. That is essentially what happened.

As I have said, the issue of a CTB has been turned on its head. Verification was once all-important. Today it no longer is. Even more ironical is the American invitation to the Russians – 'Come and watch how well we test' – and more so still the Russian acceptance of the invitation. I am prepared to bet that ten years from now the SDI story will have fizzled out, after a colossal waste of resources, and with only some trivial spin-off to show for it.

To return to my theme – there will never be any shortage of technology to fuel the Cold War. And the armament technologists can be relied upon to keep the temperature of the refrigeration of the Cold War low for as long as the public is encouraged to believe it should be kept low. It is up to the politician to end the Cold War – not the technologist. No one can win a cold war, any more than they can a nuclear war. But how the wise politician is ever to impose his will on the weaponeer I do not know. Today we have to accept the fact that nuclear weapons exist. We also have to realize that while one side remains armed, the other cannot disarm.

Could there ever be some kind of simultaneous political decision which allows a Reagan and a Gorbachev to cry 'stop' to their high priests of nuclear weaponry and of ABMs? Could a politically coherent Europe act as an effective middleman? Maybe. But, let me repeat, while we wait, do not expect the weapons technologist to stop the Cold War. He likes it.

PART II

The First Cold War

3 The Origins of the First Cold War

BRUCE R. KUNIHOLM

History, E. H. Carr tells us, is a selective system of cognitive and causal orientations to reality. It attempts to explain the past in the context of the present with a view to understanding the world around us. Causation, Carr feels, may be impossible to prove, but interpretations of causation none the less remain the most convenient method of adapting ourselves to the world; they enable us to interpret and order both past and present, and occasionally better manage our environment. The study of history Carr sees as a study of causes. The historian asks the question: Why? The great historian askes the question: Why?, about new things or in new contexts, and historical argument revolves around the question of the priority of causes (Carr, 1961, pp. 113–43).[1] It may be useful to keep Carr's definition of history in mind while reflecting in general on recent trends in the history of international relations and, in particular, on the extent to which a better understanding of the origins of the Cold War can illuminate the evolution of East–West relations and their prospects for the future.

Recent Trends in the History of International Relations

At the beginning of this decade, Charles Maier wrote a seminal essay, 'Marking time: the historiography of international relations,' that precipitated a spirited response. In that essay, Maier did not see the history of international relations among the promising fields of the discipline. He recognized the value of traditional skills such as mastering broad masses of documentation, bringing in multiple points of view, and recreating the 'plausible context' in which policy debate took place, but he fretted over the fact that innovation consisted more 'in the systematic inclusion of fields of activity

impinging on foreign-policy decisions than in the application of
new techniques' (Maier, 1980, pp. 357–8). He also appeared to
lament the fact that there was no acknowledged master in the field.

Subsequent judgements by American diplomatic historians – and
particularly by those who have written on the origins of the Cold
War – have been more upbeat than Maier's belief that international
history was 'marking time.' Where Maier observed that 'research on
the international system as system must mandate investigation of
domestic and internal pressures as part of one structure' and foresaw
'an exciting resumption of international history' *if* historians and
analysts accepted 'the systemic intertwining of domestic and international influences', Joan Hoff-Wilson and Thomas McCormick
pointed to the practitioners of the neocorporatist schools whose
methodological and interpretive frameworks they saw as laying the
foundations for the sense of collective enterprise and synthesis for
which Maier hoped.[2]

McCormick, in arguing the case, characterized the so-called
'post-revisionist' synthesis on the origins of the Cold War, subsequently discussed by John Gaddis in his thoughtful article on the
subject, as a pseudo-synthesis (McCormick, 1982, pp. 318–330; for
Gaddis's article, see Gaddis, 1983). What McCormick appeared to
reject were the post-revisionists' multi-causal explanations, which
he saw as inarticulate, unsystematic, and lacking both an analytical
framework and analytical sophistication. Asserting that there was
an increasing tendency for hard decisions on foreign policy matters
to be made outside parliamentary channels by 'the administrative
apparatus and associated corporatists in business and labor,'
McCormick called for a systematic analysis that located its bureaucratic subjects within a particular social structure, examined the
dynamic interactions of large aggregate groups, and discussed
patterns of behaviour over relatively long periods of time. Maier,
too, had stressed the importance of investigating those groups –
whether allied by class, interest, culture or ethnicity. Such groups,
he argued, sought 'an architecture across the frontiers of national
authority to preserve their influence within them.'

While Maier's argument – at least theoretically – makes sense to
me, and Michael Hogan's recent comparative analysis of America's
twentieth-century search for a stable, international economy strikes
me as a particularly thoughtful model of analysis (Hogan, 1984),
McCormick's more dogmatic argument poses problems because he

rests his corporate edifice on the foundation of productionism – a productionism, he asserts, that attempted to adjourn class war at home and national conflict abroad by forging a collaborative consensus on the imperatives of growth. McCormick's analysis is reminiscent of what Cold War revisionists were saying a decade or more ago, and has led Gaddis, responding to McCormick's assertion that post-revisionists are doing patch-jobs on traditionalist retreads, to raise the question of who is patching whose retreads? (Gaddis, 1983, p. 186). Whatever the merit of their respective arguments, the metaphor that McCormick and Gaddis both use, since it is circular, suggests the value of focusing on the hub of the question: causation.

Maier, in his article on the historiography of international relations, asserted that historians seemed ready (1) to accept the systemic intertwining of domestic and international influences and (2) to avoid insisting that one set of causes or another be given primacy. What he was seeking may well have emerged in what Jon Jacobson has characterized as 'the new international history of the 1920s – one that abstains from tired debates over the primacy of domestic or foreign policy, avoids the isolation of military and political relations from financial and economic concerns, and examines the interpenetration of the private and public sectors of the international political economy' (Jacobson, 1983, p. 617). Our concerns here, however, are not the 1920s but the period following the Second World War where, as Ernest May has observed, the challenge for the historian is times over more difficult (May, 1984).

McCormick agrees with Maier's first assertion on the systemic intertwining of domestic and international influences, but appears to reject the second on the primacy of causes. Clearly, he sees multicausal interpretations as unacceptable and, although covering himself by asserting that the emerging corporatist 'synthesis' (or, as I would prefer to call it, 'framework') is only one among a number of possible systems of analysis, he appears to believe that most interpretations beg fundamental questions answered only by his, and that rigorous systemic analysis, particularly along corporatist lines and building on the foundation he has outlined, deserve priority over others. Walter Lafeber, whom I suspect is sympathetic to McCormick's point of view, in a commentary on Maier's article has asserted that: 'The search for cause and effect might require historians to insist that one set of causes be given primacy, for only

in the scholarly dialogue that follows can the proper relationships
become clearer' (Lafeber, 1981, pp. 362–4). This is what McCormick appears to be doing.

My fundamental difference with McCormick is that I am more
comfortable than he with multi-causal interpretations. I also believe
that they better reflect the manner in which human history unfolds.
Although recognizing the value of the corporatist perspective and its
critique of pluralism when it comes to explaining the origins of the
Cold War, I cannot help but resist the tendency to interpret history
in a manner that runs roughshod over something as complex as the
diversity of the capitalist enterprise. Many of us, I believe, would
agree with Ernest May that 'political behavior consists of an
aggregate of individual actions, influenced by diverse factors and
therefore seldom if ever comprehensive in terms of any pervasive or
underlying purpose' (May, 1967, p. 133). To impose a comprehensive order on political behaviour often does violence to those
individual actions of which it is comprised. That this is true of
economic determinism, of Marxist-statist interpretations typical of
the radical revisionists (which thoughtful corporatists such as Joan
Hoff-Wilson reject), and of other such monocausal interpretations
of human behaviour, is evidenced, Robert Berkhofer has pointed
out, when those monocausal interpretations are applied cross-
culturally (Berkhofer, 1969, p. 57). Cross-cultural applications have
a habit of exposing the seeming rigor of monocausal interpretations
and showing them for what they are: heuristic devices which, unless
the historian or political scientist is careful in applying them, allow
the rationalization of anything in their behalf.

This judgement informs an earlier criticism by Arnold Kaufman
of the Cold War revisionists' Open Door interpretation: 'The theory
. . . is so resourceful that it can be made to explain any apparent
counterexample. But, more importantly,' he tells us, 'it is so
amazingly fertile that it also could have been made to explain the
opposite of what happened' (Kaufman, 1968, pp. 76–7). In the past,
as both Kaufman and Maier have pointed out, Cold War revisionists, no less than the traditionalists they criticized, were involved in
tautologies and relied upon propositions that could not be dispro-
ven. As Maier has noted:

> when the United States withdrew foreign assistance it was
> seeking to bring nations to heel; when it was generous, it sought

to suborn. When the United States bowed to British desires to delay the Second Front it justified Soviet suspicions; when it opposed Churchill's imperial designs it did so in order to erect a new economic hegemony over what England (and likewise France or the Netherlands) controlled by direct dominion.... (Maier, 1970, pp. 346–7).

Kaufman's verdict is that 'a theory that explains every possibility explains nothing ... It lacks intellectual basis because it destroys all significant distinctions.'

In spite of Maier's recognition that heuristic frameworks, unless carefully applied, allow a great deal of rationalization in their behalf when it comes to some of the revisionists, he nevertheless ran into the problem himself in an article he published in 1981 (Maier, 1981). In that article, Maier attempted – with greater insight than his critics allowed, but with less persuasiveness, I believe, than his future research will exhibit – to describe the continuing roles played by overlapping circles of civil servants, politicians, businessmen and academics in exploiting postwar circumstances to restructure the hierarchies they dominated in the first half of this century. The judgement that appeared to inform critiques of the article was that, in spite of Maier's laudable desire for imaginative synthesis, modern society was not a Gothic cathedral and did not conform to his blueprint.[3] Corporatism as an interpretive framework, it seems, has the potential for the same tendencies as other systemic interpretations.

Applications of the corporatist framework, at least as articulated by McCormick, I believe, risk making the same mistake and for more than one reason. Rather than offering an ecumenical way out of the differences among us about interpretations of American diplomatic history and the origins of the Cold War, I see the corporatist framework continuing in a more sophisticated way the 'tired' – or, if I may use a corporate expression, 'steel-belted' – debate between traditionalists and revisionists, and between revisionists and post-revisionists. Aside from the substance of the debate, I also see McCormick's framework generating the same set of familiar emphases by revisionists and neocorporatists on economic interest as the fundamental causative dynamic and by a host of others – either independently or in response – on pluralistically causative factors.

All of which does not deny that systemic interpretations in general and corporatism in particular have important contributions to make in explaining the origins of the Cold War. Such interpretations, certainly, have the potential for systematizing not only economic assumptions, but ideological, political, cultural, social, strategic, perceptual and other often inextricably intertwined assumptions as well. At best they can sweep away familiar frames of reference which, because they are taken for granted, present us with believable though distorted images, whose deviance from the true picture would otherwise go unperceived. They address the fact that how things happen is not synonymous with why they happen, and in attempting to infer the *real* reasons behind the actions they seek to explain, they are doing what Berkhofer has said the historian must always do. The crux of the problem is to recognize that a more elaborate explanatory framework may not necessarily result in better explanations of the past, to rein in a desire to make exhorbitant claims about the explanatory power of systemic frameworks and new techniques, and to apply them carefully to the problems posed by international history in order not to diminish their none the less important contribution to the illumination of human behaviour.

The Origins of the First Cold War

The purpose of this essay is not to elaborate on or extend continuing debates about historical methodology. Such debates are important in clarifying the different assumptions that historians bring to their analyses, but they will have little immediate impact on contemporary perceptions of either the origins of the Cold War or East–West relations (for example, see Combs (1984)). For this reason, I would like to go beyond questions of methodology and explore those that relate to values or norms. Values are important because they inform not only the methodologies historians choose, but the judgements they make when they attempt to shed light on the past. They also inform the perceptions of public officials and can illuminate the ways in which problems of perception become involved when officials attempt to carry out their responsibilities. An examination of values, in short, can raise important issues for discussion that will serve as a basis for thinking about the origins of the controversy between the United States and the Soviet Union over Eastern Europe as well as later phases of East–West relations.

In spite of the impression that might have been gained from the first part of this paper, the most fundamental issues debated in the hundreds of books and articles that have been written about the origins of the Cold War are not methodological. Nor are they evidenciary, although, as John Gaddis has pointed out, disagreements on occasion have led, 'most shocking of all, [to] the checking of footnotes' (Gaddis, 1983, p. 171). I would argue that the most profound questions that arise after we have sorted through all the evidence that can be marshalled on behalf of one or another argument, and when we attempt to explain the origins of the Cold War, revolve around the norms that should apply to the difficult judgements that historians make: How do we define 'legitimate' security concerns and to what extent can dominant perceptions and policies (whether in the Soviet Union, Britain, or the United States) be seen as 'legitimate' in the context of the 1940s? Given 'legitimate' security concerns, the question then becomes the extent to which the policies pursued by particular leaders were appropriate to their countries' legitimate security concerns? How, in short, do we get beyond the chauvinistic assumptions implicit in various nationalistic perspectives and assess the methods used by various leaders to achieve their ends, given their different political systems and the strengths and weaknesses of their respective countries? Where, to ask the question in a different way, does justifiably defensive behaviour stop and unjustifiably aggressive behaviour begin? (see Kuniholm, 1984).

I have argued elsewhere that there is an insurmountable difficulty in differentiating between aggressive and defensive actions, just as there is in distinguishing between nationalistic and ideological elements of a nation's policies, or between ideals and self-interest in the foreign policy of one or another country. This is particularly true when perceptions of the world held, say, by American and Soviet policy-makers are undergirded by a fundamental belief that their interests are compatible with those of other nations, and an even more profound conviction that the system of government they represent can best serve mankind. The question of the relative merit of each system is essentially a moral one, which continues the debate between Wilsonianism and Leninism that began back in the First World War (Kuniholm, 1980, pp. 428–30).

The problem of assessing the relative merits of different systems of government raises an important question: which principles should we invoke as a basis for judging the arrangements that leaders believe will best serve national interests as well as international security? Given the profound differences that separate Soviets and Americans, and the fact that their leaders would prefer an international security system that is compatible with their political systems and ideologies, such a task begs the question of a common standard and risks dissolving into moral relativism. If we exclude the two main principals in this debate, judgements about the relative merits of international security arrangements are subject to a host of considerations, including a country's historical experience (about which more later) and, occasionally, the dictates of propinquity. The closer a country is to a great power, we might generalize, the more it is vulnerable to and tends to resent the great power's imperial sway; the further away a country is, the less vulnerable it is, the less it has to fear, and the more it can call on that power to assist it.

When it comes to the early years of the Cold War, for example, the vast majority of people in countries that bordered the Soviet Union, such as Poland, Turkey and Iran, resisted a close alignment with the Soviets and, needless to say, preferred the US emphasis on self-determination to the Soviet desire for a sphere of influence over them. A good Marxist could contest this assertion by raising the question of who represents the 'people' and how one goes about making such a judgement with or without 'false consciousness', but let us assume, for the moment, that my assertion is correct. If it is, it probably has something to do with the fact that of the thirteen non-communist states that bordered the Soviet Union before the war, only five were independent when it was over. Finland was neutralized; Afghanistan retained its traditional role of a buffer state. Of the remaining three, Norway, Turkey and Iran, the last two were in jeopardy of being drawn into the Soviet fold, and the United States was the only power capable of seriously confronting this turn of events. Clearly, in the eyes of those whose territorial integrity was in question, the United States was seen as a counter-weight to the Soviet Union, whose influence was resented and feared and whose territorial aspirations were seen as illegitimate. Only principles such as those espoused by the United States could provide for the future independence of small countries which otherwise feared absorption into a Soviet sphere of influence.

We must concede that American policies toward Latin America in the early years of the Cold War could have developed to the point where they, too, were seen as 'illegitimate.' Such a development would have required that the United States be as vulnerable on its southern borders as the Soviets were on their western borders. A Soviet capacity to heighten American anxieties by establishing close political–military ties with countries in Latin America could have precipitated the process. The Monroe Doctrine, however, was never put to the test in those years. In recent years, however, the fact that countries such as Cuba and Nicaragua have resisted US-supported encroachments on their territorial integrity and have looked to the Soviet Union for succour may have as much to do with their proximity to the United States and their distance from the Soviet Union as with the character of their political systems, whose orientations also have something to do with indigenous opposition to perceived American imperialism and what are widely regarded as 'illegitimate' American policies.

Although the dictates of propinquity can have a profound influence on the orientation of a country's national security policies, they do not indicate the profundity of the national commitment to those policies. Such a commitment is best gauged by other factors, not least by the price people have been willing to pay for their own defence. During the Second World War, for example, the United States suffered 291,551 battle deaths; the British, 373,372; the Soviets, something in the neighbourhood of 11 million, in addition to approximately 7 million civilian deaths. Although there are no generally accepted casualty figures for the Soviet Union, and there is no means of distinguishing those who died as a result of Soviet policies from those who died in battle, or from the 3.3 million who were liquidated in German prisoner-of-war camps, or from the tremendous number of civilian casualties, there are rough calculations that can be made. Warren Eason, for one, has estimated that the Soviet Union's population declined by 24.1 million from 1941 to 1945. Of the 373,372 deaths suffered in battle by the British, 264,443 were citizens of the United Kingdom, which also suffered 60,595 civilian deaths (see United States Bureau of the Census, 1960, p. 735; Mellor, 1972, pp. 836–8; Eason, 1973, p. 53; Kassof, 1968, p. 230).

The point of citing these statistics is that, however those of us in the West might question the primacy of security as a motive for

Soviet control of Eastern Europe in the early years of the Cold War,
such statistics provide a convincing argument for the saliency of that
motive. To make this point is not to endorse the Soviet political
system. We cannot deny Stalin's cynicism, excuse his ruthlessness,
or make the case that Stalin's motives were based solely on security
concerns. But it is necessary to recognize that the Soviets lost sixty
times as many people as the United States in the Second World War,
that they suffered more than 200 times as many deaths in battle
during the Second World War as did the United States during the
war in Vietnam, and that the lives that were lost had a profound
effect on Soviet priorities.

The necessity of a Soviet sphere of influence in Eastern Europe
followed logically from the Soviets' view of their own history. How
could any Russian ignore the historic role of Poland as a route for
invasion of the Soviet Union? The Soviet view of history was also
influenced by the ideological lenses of Marxist-Leninism, which led
the Soviets to look with incredulity at the American assumption that
the principles of the Atlantic Charter could be universally accepted,
and to regard with cynicism the alternatives to Soviet control over
Poland suggested by the United States. Where Americans saw
themselves and the principles for which they fought during the
Second World War as devoid of self-interest, the Soviets, from their
point of view, could see such principles as little more than reflections
of American interests. They could argue that efforts directed toward
the maintenance of world order, embodied in principles espoused
by the United States, merely advanced US prosperity and power.

The Atlantic Charter, for example, endorsed a number of principles, among which was the access of all states, on equal terms, to
the trade and raw materials of the world. Since the United States
was competitively superior economically, the Soviets saw the
principle of free trade as propounding through philosophical 'false
consciousness' an ideology that served the interests of an American
ruling class, all the while discriminating against Soviet interests.
Lacking resources and the technical know-how to compete successfully, the Soviets were prepared to use force to secure an area they
believed should come under Soviet jurisdiction – especially when
the Soviet system was threatened by capitalist inroads into those
spheres. This inclination was undoubtedly reinforced by the
rationalizations to which Marxist-Leninist ideology lends itself.

Differing perceptions of the desirability of either spheres of

influence or self-determination as a basis for organizing Eastern
Europe are particularly sharp when it comes to the Polish question
and the international security systems envisaged by the Soviet
Union and the United States at the end of the Second World War.
Poland was a country whose symbolic importance was crucial to the
West: England went to war for Poland. It was also crucial to the
Soviet Union. The Nazi–Soviet Pact in 1939, which the Soviets
could argue was ˙ necessitated by Neville Chamberlain's
appeasement of Hitler at Munich in 1938, resulted in the division of
Poland more or less along a line that Stalin saw as consistent with
ethnic boundaries – defined not by him but by Lord Curzon as an
armistice line after the First World War. The Soviets subsequently
accepted the Atlantic Charter (and its pledges to seek 'no aggran-
dizement, territorial or other . . . ' and 'no territorial changes that do
not accord with the freely expressed wishes of the people concerned
. . . ') only, as Churchill reminded Roosevelt in March 1942, on
condition it not deny them the frontiers they occupied in June 1941
when they were attacked. The reservation they appended to the
charter put it more delicately: 'the practical application of these
principles will necessarily adapt itself to the circumstances, needs,
and historic peculiarities of particular countries . . . ' (Churchill,
1950, p. 327; Herz, 1966, pp. vi–vii).

As a result, the Soviet Union sought British recognition of its
frontier with Poland, ignored Roosevelt's plea to omit territorial
matters from the prospective Anglo-Soviet treaty in 1942 until the
very last, and then dropped territorial provisions only in turn for
promises of a second front, whose delay, from a Soviet point of
view, gave a measure of legitimacy to Russia's *de facto* possession of
the land it claimed from eastern Poland at the end of the war. At
Tehran in late 1943, meanwhile, agreements in principle were made
regarding Poland's eastern frontier, subject to Roosevelt's qualifi-
cation that political matters precluded his participation in such
arrangements. Stalin chose, not unreasonably, to disregard these
qualifications, and to regard the agreements as definite. At the
Moscow Conference in October 1944, Stalin saw the agreement on
de facto control of Southeastern Europe between Churchill and
Stalin, worked out after three days of negotiations, as sealed, and
Roosevelt's equivocation regarding such an agreement as not to be
taken seriously. Later events and conversations among the leaders,
moreover, tend to corroborate the assertion that Stalin (as well as

Churchill and Roosevelt) acted within his understanding that the agreement spelled out *de facto* control of Southeastern Europe. Finally, by the war's end, the Soviets had achieved in fact what had been denied them in principle: a sphere of influence in Eastern Europe. They did this not as the result of any agreement, but by the force of the Red Army.

In conjunction with military control over Eastern Europe, the Soviets exercised increased ideological and political control as well. This was necessary, presumably, because of the growth of the Soviet Union's hostage non-Russian population. Constituting only 35 per cent of the population in the Soviet Union during the interwar years, non-Russians grew to 44 per cent of the population after Stalin's accord with Hitler, to 50 per cent of the population by the end of the Second World War, and to more than 60 per cent of Russia's *de facto* 'empire.' The demographic and ethnic problems of managing large numbers of alien peoples account for Stalin's liquidation of the Volga Germans in 1941 and of the four autonomous Muslim republics of Crimea, Ingush, Chechen and Balkar in 1943–44 (Wesson, 1974, pp. vii–xi, 104–9; Conquest, 1970, pp. 1–12, 64–5). They explain Soviet suspicions of their own soldiers who had been taken prisoner and repatriated after the war, only to be subject to detention in the Gulag Archipelago. And they help to account for the Soviets' heavy-handed policies that began in Eastern Europe after its 'liberation' by the Red Army.

Whether Soviet intentions in Poland were foreshadowed by the Katyn massacres, or by the Soviet response to the Warsaw uprising, is a moot point; the fact is that Stalin's aspirations were evident even before the Second World War and that Russia's experience in Poland in 1920 could have left Stalin with no illusions about the reception that awaited him a quarter of a century later when Soviet forces marched into Poland. The Soviets felt they knew what they had to do and clearly intended to do it. Their own history, moreover, suggested the cost of doing less. As Stalin wrote to President Truman in April 1945, Poland had the same meaning for the security of the Soviet Union that Belgium and Greece had for the security of Great Britain (US Department of State, 1967, pp. 263–4). As a result, the Soviets circumvented the Declaration on Liberated Europe (which was intended to counteract the notion of spheres of influence and which restated the principles of the Atlantic Charter) by making sure that its operative clause was harmless. All that the declaration provided for was consultation, and unanimity was required before even consultation could take place. The Soviets also extracted a compromise on the crucial issue of the Polish government's composition.

American leaders, meanwhile, had been concerned with the fact that, in spite of their attempts to stay out of two world wars, the United States had been drawn into both of them – all within a thirty-year period. This was something they wanted to avoid repeating. To provide the appropriate moral context for US involvement in the war and to guarantee the peace after the war was over, Roosevelt had felt it necessary to adopt the principles of the Atlantic Charter and, later, the United Nations Declaration. While his primary motive appears to have been to cut the ground out from under America's isolationist leaders, and to avoid the mistakes of the First World War, the President also recognized that such principles fulfilled a public need: a peculiarly American need to justify either force or its potential use in terms of principles with which one could identify.

Roosevelt, apparently, believed that frank recognition of some of the issues that separated Americans and Russians, because they required compromise, would have smacked of cynicism; a public compromise of US principles would have appeared to condone traditional European politics, in which neither he nor the American public believed. Politically, such a course was worrisome, and its international implications were devastating. Revelations of a division of Europe into spheres of influence such as those apparently desired by Stalin could have damaged the United Nations, as the secret agreements of the First World War were damaging to the League of Nations. Bipartisan support would have eroded what Roosevelt saw as necessary mechanisms for the enforcement of the peace, and might have led the United States to return to isolationism. The cycles that led to previous wars would then repeat themselves, and Americans once again would be sucked into the fray.

Although Roosevelt was unwilling to make public concessions to Stalin for fear of alienating the American public in general and millions of Polish–American voters in particular, he recognized that private concessions were necessary if he were to maintain allied unity, secure Soviet assistance in the war against Japan, and obtain Soviet participation in the United Nations Organization. With hindsight, it is clear that the most immediate of these goals, Soviet assistance in the war against Japan, was unnecessary, but it was seen as imperative in early 1945 – particularly since the role that the atomic bomb would play was uncertain at the time. Few responsible American leaders would have been willing to risk the thousands of American lives that they thought would be saved by Soviet assistance in the war against Japan for the sake of the principle of self-determination in Eastern Europe.

In any event, at Yalta in February 1945, expedience triumphed over principle both in the Far East and in Eastern Europe, where Stalin acquired considerable territorial and other rights as quid pro quo for a commitment to enter the war against Japan. Since Stalin's position in Poland was supported by the Red Army, his will would have prevailed there anyway. There was little that could have been done either by Roosevelt, who did not intend that American troops should enter Eastern Europe, or Churchill, who could not have deployed troops there even if he had wanted to. Finally, both leaders recognized that the agreement on Poland was the best that could be obtained. In the world emerging from the war, principles espoused by the United States and Britain were useless unless respected or enforced; since Russia clearly did not respect them and neither American nor British troops were prepared to enforce such respect anyway, the Soviet Union would dictate the conditions that would apply; Soviet troops, in turn, would ensure that these conditions were enforced.

President Roosevelt had good reason to justify the expediency of the agreement. This is not true, on the other hand, if he intended to hold on to principle as the cornerstone of his policies. The practice of viewing international politics in terms of moralistic principles, however, was rooted in American history, and seems to have been as much a necessary response to public opinion as it was a determining factor in shaping the public mood. This practice raises the question of why Roosevelt felt it necessary to characterize national policies in such principled terms. Was it a function of his personality? Was it, as some would allege, an economically rooted need that was rationalized by rhetoric? Although historians differ in their responses to these questions, the consensus, with which I concur, is that Roosevelt's policies cannot be explained by either of these variables. A more thoughtful line of questioning concerns the possibility that the phenomenon we are examining was a more generalized public need whose expression found voice in principle, which Roosevelt articulated. If this is so, the question remains as to what fundamental needs of the nation's collective psyche the expression of such principles met? Since this question concerns problems that are systemic in nature, answers to it are unavoidably speculative.

In exploring the collective psyche of the American people, several authors have suggested that we must begin with an understanding of the role played by the rejection of Europe in the formation of America's identity.[4] 'Since it was Europe that colonized the world,' John Spanier tells us, 'the rejection of Europe is essential to the formation of the new nation's identity' (Spanier, 1971, p. 3). Albert Hirschman (Hirschman, 1970) also has observed that in a nation where success was symbolized by social mobility – a social mechanism in which the nation had unquestioned faith – there was a strong compulsion to like that (i.e. the United States) for which one had sacrificed so much, and to dislike that (i.e. Europe) which had been rejected. As a consequence, rejection of Europe was embodied: (1) in a vision of Europe as exploitative and evil; (2) in a consequent affirmation of self as peaceful and moral; (3) in the Monroe Doctrine, the first explicit expression of the ideological differences between the Old World and the New.

But if early insistence on the avoidance of entanglements was realistic, the American public's subsequent understanding of international relations was not. In the nineteenth and early twentieth centuries, the Monroe Doctrine justified a policy that was grounded in realism. Given the nation's distance from Europe, and the protection of the Royal Navy, insistence on the avoidance of entangling alliances made perfect sense. What made less sense was the American tendency to attribute to democracy and to American virtue the responsibility for what was in fact the result of geography and British maritime pre-eminence. The consequent depreciation of the role of power in international affairs was an indulgence that grew out of an isolationist past in which, because of a fortuitous set of circumstances, domestic affairs occupied the nation's energies. This preoccupation with internal affairs delayed the public's education regarding the realities of power and served to reinforce a tendency to attribute the country's relatively peaceful course to the democratic system and the moral superiority of all Americans.

Yet another factor contributed to America's depreciation of

power politics, and to the public's belief in ideological distinctions between Europe and the United States. As a non-feudal society, Louis Hartz argues, the United States lacked both a genuine revolutionary tradition and a tradition of reaction (Hartz, 1971, p. 16). If Americans were revolutionaries, they were different from others in the sense that their revolution did not have to destroy any established feudal institution; their liberalism, in short, was what Santayana would call a 'natural' phenomenon. Democratic ideas, since they encountered no resistance, penetrated throughout society.

Another phenomenon helped to encourage a ready acceptance of these democratic ideas in the United States. American society had never experienced the 'inner struggle' of European society. Having their origins in physical flight (from Europe) rather than in social revolution, and provided with the opportunity to go West (however mythical that opportunity was), Americans had a ready-made paradigm for problem-solving – physical flight – which perhaps begins to explain the conformity of (and lack of tolerance in) American society noted by observers since de Tocqueville. Finally, in conjunction with a liberal norm, and a tendency to conform, the widespread ownership of property – or the apparent possibility of ownership – meant in effect that most citizens were of the same estate, and held the same capitalistic values.

Dominated by a capitalist middle class, and undivided by ideological conflicts (of the sort whose divisiveness could, as in France, separate one class from another), American society as a whole was committed to one set of values. And commitment to these values had important consequences. Many Americans attributed their country's prosperity to the economic laws of the market and gave little thought to their country's material resources and geographical isolation. They saw politics only as an impediment to economic laws. With the exception of blacks, most Americans could attribute the absence of domestic grievances, and the failure of a revolutionary ideology to develop, to the success of democracy and the capitalist system. By the same token, they saw class struggle and international conflict abroad as a reflection of a faulty and corrupt political system. Both perceptions tended to reinforce a misunderstanding of the nature and function of power. Believing in laissez-faire capitalism, and in the idea that free-trade and peace were one and the same, Americans sought economic (i.e. good) solutions to international problems. The unacceptable alternatives were political solutions, which smacked of power and were equated with European diplomacy, conflict, war and death. The logical extension of a national laissez-faire policy which benefited all individuals within the United States was an international laissez-faire policy which, it was thought, would benefit all countries. It was not recognized that liberal values were not national values in all corners of the globe, nor was it apparent that those values would not benefit all countries.

Given these attitudes, the American people entered the twentieth century and the First World War unaware of the power realities that made their participation necessary. Rather, with President Wilson's encouragement, they believed they were fighting a crusade for democracy. Once the crusade was over, they again withdrew into isolationism, seeing no connection between the realities of power and their own independence. By repudiating war as a political instrument, the United States came to see war solely as a means – a means to abolish power politics; hence, it was viewed moralistically and was not subject to compromise. Because of these moralistic restrictions, the United States up to the time of the Second World War rarely initiated policy – it merely reacted. Once provoked, it could justify the use of force only in terms of the universal moral principles with which it identified itself. This moralistic attitude, responsible for its 'all-or-nothing approach to war', also militated against what Spanier argues is the classic goal of diplomacy: 'to compromise interests, to conciliate differences, and to moderate and isolate conflicts' (Spanier, 1971, p. 16). Thus, by following a 'diplomacy of principle', and by regarding spheres of influence, alliances and the balance of power as the evil trappings of power politics, the American people, instead of seeing clashes of interest and power, viewed international politics in terms of abstract moral principles.

This view of international politics, whose roots are admittedly abstruse, but whose striking character has provoked a number of thoughtful explanations that I have attempted to synthesize here, constitutes one of the most elusive and yet one of the most basic domestic constraints on the conduct of Roosevelt's foreign policy. It is elusive because it was a phenomenon that did not lend itself easily to measurement. It is basic because the American people accepted its implicit assumptions, and the President operated in terms of those assumptions. Building on moralistic ideas that were deeply rooted

in American history, and on a philosophy inherited from Woodrow
Wilson, Roosevelt sought to correct errors of the past and to create a
peaceful post-war world. Sadly, he failed (perhaps unavoidably) to
educate the American public about the role of power in international
affairs. He also failed to recognize that in meeting the public's
psychic needs, the principles he embraced would only perpetuate
the public's misunderstanding of the nature of international relations and impede the classic goals of diplomacy as they applied to
US–Soviet relations.

Implications for the Future

If I were to debate the relative legitimacy of Soviet and American
security concerns in the early Cold War, I would argue that even if
the Soviets had legitimate security interests in Eurasia, their policies
toward the countries on their southern flank, the Northern Tier of
the Middle East, following as they did the USSR expansion into
Eastern Europe and the Far East, superseded the bounds of what a
majority of the international community was prepared to accept.
The resulting US commitment to maintain the balance of power in
the Near East and Europe made good sense, even if the rhetoric
associated with that commitment was misleading (Kuniholm, 1980,
pp. 231–49, 410–25). I would therefore agree with Vojtech Mastny,
who has convincingly argued that the primary source of conflict
between East and West was Russia's striving for power and influence far in excess of its reasonable security requirements (Mastny,
1979, pp. 35, 283, 292, 306).

My concern here, however, is not to debate this issue. Rather, it is
to recognize that clashes over the balance of power were virtually
inevitable after the Second World War, that differences were bound
to occur, and that those differences needed to be worked out. The
interesting question, it seems to me, is the extent to which a truly
workable basis of agreement could have been found – the extent to
which the security needs of the great powers and their coalitions
could have been accommodated in order to manage their differences
in a less acrimonious and mutually beneficial way. To that end, and
to the extent that the United States played a role in complicating the
process, the arguments of those who believe that the problem rests
in the transition between Roosevelt and Truman seem to me to be

misplaced. The problem is far more profound. It has to do with the USA's inability as a nation to deal with the realities of international politics, the resulting unrealistic rhetoric of US leaders, and the consequences of the public's sense of betrayal when administrations fail to match their rhetoric with concrete policies. This problem was as evident under Roosevelt as it was under Truman, and is as evident today as it was forty years ago.

In the years that followed the end of the Second World War, many would equate the Yalta agreement with *de facto* recognition of the division of Europe. Many of those who looked with favour on the outcome saw it as the only solution to the German problem. Others who were critical of the outcome but who came around to the same conclusion (i.e. that it was the only solution to the German problem) had to overcome years of unrealistic rhetoric by various administrations on the liberation of Europe. While such rhetoric created unfortunate expectations, particularly in Eastern Europe, those expectations were repeatedly dashed: by events in East Berlin and East Germany in 1953, in Hungary and Poland in 1956, and in Czechoslovakia in 1968. In 1975, under the Ford administration, the Helsinki accord would ratify Europe's postwar frontiers and, unofficially, the principle of permanent spheres of influence in Europe as well. According to John Stoessinger, Secretary of State Kissinger 'welcomed the Helsinki accord because it helped to institutionalize the principle of equilibrium in Europe and thus would stabilize detente in the geographic area that once had been the very center of the [C]old [W]ar' (Stoessinger, 1976, p. 110).

Others, particularly on the right wing of the Democratic Party and in the Republican Party in general, saw Yalta as a betrayal of the goals for which Americans fought in the Second World War, and as a symbol of appeasement. Most recently, responding to the psychic needs of an American public smarting from its humiliation in Iran, and in conjunction with a profound belief in the moral righteousness of American values that it believes should not be compromised, the Reagan administration has embraced this streak of unrealism. It has given voice to rhetoric that both fosters and perpetuates the public's misunderstanding of the nature of international relations. It has raised unrealistic expectations about the capacity of the United States to roll back Communism and achieve superiority over the Soviet Union – goals articulated in the Republican National Platform and shared by many of the principals in the Reagan administra-

tion. Articles and discussions in *Foreign Affairs*, *Commentary*, the
Washington Post, the *New York Review of Books*, and *Newsweek*,
meanwhile, with varying degrees of subtlety, have examined the
question of undoing Yalta, or repudiating its historic legacy; on the
fortieth anniversay of the Yalta Conference, President Reagan,
himself, has noted his desire to erase 'the dividing line between
freedom and repression in Europe.'[5]

More than forty years after the Yalta agreement, the arsenals of
the United States and the Soviet Union have increased massively.
Our capacities to destroy each other and the world are unquestioned
and incomparably greater than the relatively limited destructive
capabilities we had at the end of the Second World War. And yet, the
question before us remains the same: whether the domestic contexts
within which our national security policies are made can be suffi-
ciently receptive to the requirements of *international* peace and
security for our national leaders to find common ground, and the
extent to which our leaders can, and will, lead and educate public
opinion to this end. As a result, any examination of causes and their
priorities in explaining the origins and evolution of the Cold War,
particularly if it is to help us to better manage East–West relations,
must seek to better understand not only matters of substance but of
process as well, because such matters (and the values that affect
them) have impeded and continue to impede the process of
accommodation between East and West. Accommodation, it
should be noted, is not appeasement, nor is it an ideal espoused by
muddle-headed liberals. Under the circumstances that confront us
today, it is, very simply, a necessity.

Chapter 3: Notes

1 For the difficulty of dealing with the problem of historical causation, see
   Nash, 1969, pp. 228–99.
2 For the responses of Michael H. Hunt, Akira Iriye, Walter F. Lafeber,
   Melvyn P. Leffler, Robert D. Schulzinger, and Joan Hoff-Wilson, see
   Diplomatic History, 1981.
3 For critiques of Maier's article, see the comments by Stephen A. Schuker
   and Charles P. Kindelberger, as well as Maier's reply, in *American
   Historical Review*, 1981.
4 Especially useful are Hartz, 1955; Hirschman, 1970, pp. 106–19; Calleo,
   1970, pp. 100–22; Spanier, 1971, whose arguments I have attempted to
   synthesize and from whose first chapter I draw heavily for this discussion;
   Lipset and Bendix, 1959, pp. 76–113; Hyman, 1953, pp. 426–42.

5 See Brzezinski, 1984; Colville, 1985b, and subsequent discussions in later issues. See also articles in the *Washington Post*, 18 January, 12 February, and 15 February 1985 by Stephen Rosenfeld and Joseph Kraft, and discussions by Theodore Draper and adversaries in the *New York Review of Books*, 16 January and 29 May 1986, as well as Jonathan Alter's discussion in *Newsweek*, 28 April 1986. For Reagan on Yalta, see *Washington Post*, 6 February 1985.

4 Britain and the First Cold War

VICTOR ROTHWELL

In a public lecture delivered at the London School of Economics in 1955, at the end of the period under consideration in this paper, Sir Llewellyn Woodward, the Foreign Office official historian, complained that: 'In their search for security the Russians have in fact behaved like the hermit who went so far into a desert in search of solitude that he came out into a populous city on the other side' (Woodward, 1955, p. 285). Churchill had the same idea when, on New Year's Day 1953, he explained the outbreak of the Cold War with the argument that 'Russia feared our friendship more than our enmity' (Colville, 1985a, p. 658).[1] A sense of grievance based on the conviction that it was an unnecessary conflict, at least on the Western side, for which the entire blame lay with the Soviet Union, is a constant factor underlying British policy in the first Cold War, and one without which that policy cannot be understood.

An even more basic requirement for understanding Britain's role was met by the opening of the British archives in the 1970s, which has made it possible to place the much studied events in American policy beside what was happening in the country that was to revert to its wartime position as the USA's most important ally. Post-revisionist American work, which emphasizes the slowness and hesitation with which the United States took up what was seen as the challenge of a Soviet-led world communist movement, complements the work on Britain, which has shown that that country was far from being a minor actor. As Donald Watt has pointed out, between 1944 and 1946 American planners assumed that if the United States became involved in war with Russia it would be through being drawn into a Soviet–British war (Watt, 1984a, pp. 50–3).[2] This is not to suggest that the British themselves expected any such event. The experience of the war had given them cautious grounds for hope that the wartime Anglo-Soviet alliance could be preserved in some form on the basis of joint policies to prevent a revenge-seeking Germany from making another bid for European domination (Rothwell, 1982 and 1986, *passim*). To the British policy-making elite, this seemed a more realistic prospect than a postwar Anglo-American partnership, support for which in the United States of 1945 was negligible (Anderson, 1981, pp. 23–7). It was thought most probable that the United States would retreat into isolationism, apart from retaining an interest in weakening the British Commonwealth and Empire as an economic unit that imposed barriers against US exports (Gardner, 1956, *passim*). American treatment of Britain economically and financially during the war was not 'merciless', as a revisionist historian described it, but in some respects it had been ungenerous and, apart from specifically Anglo-American issues, there was immense and seemingly irresistible pressure in the United States well into 1946 for the return of servicemen to civilian life and for cuts in public expenditure including defence and overseas relief. The United States army was reduced to the world's sixth largest by 1947 (Kolko,, 1970, p. 287; Anderson, 1981, pp. 152, 154–6; Yergin, 1978, p. 178).

If the British needed any confirmation of these trends, President Truman's negative response to the stream of messages that Prime Minister Attlee sent him, appealing for Anglo-American control of the atomic bomb, appeared to provide it. Truman was to reject British appeals for nuclear partnership four times between 1945 and 1950 (Herken, 1980, pp. 29, 333). Under these circumstances, the advantages of friendship with Russia seemed self-evident to the Foreign Secretary in the new Labour Government, Ernest Bevin. His biographer, Lord Bullock, has summarized Bevin's attitude to America and Russia by the autumn of 1945 as being 'a plague on both your houses' (Bullock, 1983, pp. 116–18, 124, 195). This comprehensive curse indicated a weakening of the hope for co-operation with the Soviet Union, but what particularly irked Bevin was that US policy, under the guiding hand of Secretary of State Byrnes rather than of a President who was still finding his feet, was showing an impatient disregard for Britain. Byrnes, supported by fewer and fewer in Washington, regarded the problem of settling American–Soviet differences as limited and amenable to neat, legalistic solutions (Ward, 1979, pp. 22, 53–5, 100–2, 149–50, 175; Kennan, 1968, pp. 286–7). This phase in US policy ceased to have much relevance after Byrnes's resignation at the end of 1946, but it did foreshadow occasional West European fears that their interests might be overlooked by the United States during periods of Soviet–American détente in the late 1960s and 1970s.

Between the end of the war and 1955 there were three broad periods in the rise and subsequent development of the 'Cold War' – a term of mysterious origin that was in journalistic usage as early as the autumn of 1945 (Orwell and Angus, 1970, Vol. IV, p. 26). In the first period, from 1945 to late 1947, Britain still had hopes of salvaging something from the wartime Anglo-Soviet alliance, while being interested in forging security and economic links with its West European neighbours, especially France. This was the time when that pillar of British foreign policy, Con O'Neill, while temporarily absent from the Foreign Office, was writing *Times* leaders on the theme of one world in which the Soviet Union and the West co-operated (Charlton, 1983, pp. 39–40). In the second period, from late 1947 to the outbreak of the Korean War in 1950, there was a twofold change: not only did disillusionment with Russia become complete, but also Western Europe was almost totally eclipsed by the United States in British thinking about security. The third period, from 1950 to (for our purposes) 1955, might be described as mature Cold War. It was a time of almost complete immobility in Western–Soviet relations, in which notions of pushing back Soviet power by ending communist rule in at least some of the East European countries, and Churchill's hopes after he returned to 10 Downing Street of unlocking the East–West deadlock by a new summit, proved equally unproductive. For Britain, perhaps the most important feature of this period was increasing US impatience with the British notion of a three-cornered Western world. Under Eisenhower and Dulles, the United States ceased to be willing to conceal its preference for a two-cornered Western Alliance in which Britain's place would be in the West European corner (Manderson-Jones, 1972, *passim*).

At the start of the first period it was Soviet encroachment into the northern tier of the Middle East (Iran, Turkey and Greece, where the Greek Communists were assumed to be obeying orders from Moscow), plus the threat of expansion into the Arab areas farther south, that alarmed the British and almost monopolized Bevin's thoughts as 1945 gave way to 1946 (Bullock, 1983, pp. 214–17). In this respect Bevin mirrored the views of the British defence and foreign policy establishment, and Attlee was in a curiously isolated and maverick position in thinking that the Near and Middle East might be expendable for Britain – a heretical notion that the Prime Minister was compelled to abandon at the beginning of 1947 (Bullock, 1983, pp. 240–5; Barker, 1983, pp. 48–52; Ovendale, 1985, pp. 47–53, 98–101; Dalton, 1962, pp. 101, 105). The United States took a strong hand in this area from early in 1946, partly as a conscious act of atonement for its weakness towards the Soviet take-over in Eastern Europe; Truman, though not naturally an Anglo-phile, came to see a close identity of interests with Britain in most of this area, though obviously not in Palestine as the Arab–Zionist conflict neared its climax (Kuniholm, 1980, pp. 247–9, 301–2; Acheson, 1970, p. 197). Truman seems to have become convinced quite suddenly around the new year of 1946 that the worst interpre-tation of Soviet policy was the correct one, and the State Depart-ment had to fall into line with this view (Yergin, 1978, pp. 158–62; De Santis, 1980, pp. 206–8; Riste, 1985, pp. 60–9). Hence he issued the stern warning to Russia to quit north-west Iran in 1946, and the doctrine on aid to Greece and Turkey in 1947 in the wake of Britain stating that it could no longer continue financial aid to those coun-tries. To Britain this offered an instructive contrast to the failure to make much headway in relations with Western Europe, except for the Dunkirk treaty with France in 1947 with its already anachronis-tic commitment to co-operation against German threats. Dunkirk was negotiated with one eye on American and Russian likely reac-tions, and the other on helping the French socialist government of Léon Blum. The Blum government was seen as unusually deserving for a French government, because its views on policy in Germany were not totally at variance with British views, but Britain never-theless felt unable to help materially, for instance by increasing the amount of Ruhr coal that was sent to France. France was looking less and less valuable as an ally (S. Greenwood, 1983, *passim*; Young, 1984, pp. 47–51; Rothwell, 1982, pp. 335–6, 441, 445). At the same time, in Western Europe as well as in the Near East, the attractions of America loomed large. The one bright spot in Europe related to the USA: the co-operation in Germany that led to the economic fusion of the two zones under the agreement negotiated in late 1946. Meanwhile, the Soviet Union and the Western Powers finally ran out of subjects on which they could co-operate with the completion of the peace treaties with Germany's former allies in Europe in Paris

and New York during 1946. The 1947 conferences of foreign
ministers in Moscow and London reached deadlock on the problems
of Germany and Austria. British patience with Soviet actions was
wearing thin, and it snapped in a few cases such as that of the general
(later promoted to field-marshal) who, on a visit to Vienna in 1946,
told the young woman whom he had never met before and who had
the sensitive job of translating between the British and Soviet
military commanders in the city that Russia should be 'destroyed'
while it was still weak from the war (Williams, 1980, pp. 182–4; cf.
Winterton, 1948, *passim*). Bevin himself was highly conscious of a
break in his foreign policy in 1947, and the evidence now available
indicates that Stalin took a conscious decision in late 1947 to cease
the effort to restore any semblance of life to the former Grand
Alliance, while intending to keep the intensified confrontation with
the West from leading to armed conflict (Rose, 1959, p. 103;
McCagg, 1978, pp. 256–9, 282–4, 312; Spriano, 1985, pp. 284, 299;
Werth, 1971, pp. vii–xii, 96, 110–14).

What gave the British heart as this first period ended was the
growth of hostility not only between themselves and the Soviet
Union, but between the United States and Russia as well; they
sensed that there might be a special place for them in a global context
of Anglo-American leadership of the non-communist world. It at
least ceased to be necessary virtually to beg the American people for
support (Anstey, 1984, pp. 440, 443). While rejecting the idea of full
or exclusive partnership, predominant opinion in Washington
accepted to a considerable extent the British estimate of their role,
though for reasons that the British would not have found wholly
flattering. The first Joint Chiefs of Staff plan for war with Russia
(known as 'Pincher') in June 1946 postulated that America would
probably have to resign itself to the initial loss of most or all of
continental West Europe to the Red Army, but that Britain had to be
held at all costs (Herken, 1980, pp. 219–24). Britain's importance to
the United States in the Cold War depended to a great extent on the
simple fact that the country was an island. At all events, there was
now some justification for the government's retention of the
wartime military mission in Washington which, though absurdly
overstaffed, was by the summer of 1946 again doing business with
the US military on such matters as arms standardization and
weapons research, but not, needless to say, on nuclear weapons
(Anderson, 1981, pp. 127–9, 139–41; Colville, 1985a, p. 638).

Outside the strictly military field, the United States offered economic aid to non-communist Europe under the Marshall Plan, but here one must strike a double note of caution. The United States hoped that it would be able to sever its defence links with Western Europe once the area had recovered economically and could provide for its own defence needs, and once German statehood had been restored. Marshall aid was intended as the prelude to an American strategic withdrawal from Europe, not to a vastly stepped-up defence commitment (Ireland, 1981, p. 58). Specifically on Britain, the application of aid was marked by endless bad blood with the United States, from Bevin's initial failure to get US agreement that Britain should be treated as a special case in relation to assistance, to Britain's later 'success' in ensuring that the Organization for European Economic Co-operation, set up to administer aid, suffered, to quote its latest historian, 'complete political and economic emasculation' (Milward, 1984, pp. 61–3, 172–9, 184–5, 328–9, 469; Bullock, 1983, pp. 413–17). However, the United States swallowed its dismay at British opposition to an economically and politically integrated western Europe, and for long made concessions to British interests. For instance, the guarantees that Hugh Gaitskell as Chancellor of the Exchequer got for the sterling area in the European Payments Union negotiations of 1950 represented a British triumph (Milward, 1984, pp. 320–34; Williams, 1979, pp. 219–25; Roberts and Wilson, 1953, pp. 136–8).

American economic generosity resulted from the primacy of military and strategic factors, and it was the pre-eminence which the British also gave to these that caused their thinking about world affairs to be dominated by the concept of Atlanticism, to which even the Commonwealth became subsidiary. The key event in this process was the negotiation of the North Atlantic Treaty in 1948–9. It has been pointed out that the Brussels defence treaty with France and the Benelux countries in March 1948 was more than Bevin's stated 'sprat to catch the American mackerel' (Michael Howard, in Riste, 1985, pp. 16–17). Equally, there is no doubt that the British regarded the American connection as more important in ensuring that the Soviet Union, though apparently determined on 'all mischief short of war' (1950 Chatham House study group report quoted by Shlaim, 1978, p. 107), did not overstep that line, and resort to real war. The prospect of alliance with the United States also made Britain's own increased defence spending from 1947 meaningful as a contribution to a war that could be survived and won (Barker, 1983, pp. 99–102, 135–6, 154–5).

The British perceived great reluctance among policymakers such as George Kennan and Charles Bohlen, and probably among the majority of the American people, to enter into such a commitment. The Senate passed the Vandenberg resolution, but it was not lost on the British that the House of Representatives, which could be seen as standing closer to the grassroots of American opinion, did not pass any equivalent measure (Henderson, 1982, p. 32). In the end the administration was only able to carry the treaty through Congress with arguments about its limited significance, which one American historian has described as 'bordering on outright deception' (Ireland, 1981, pp. 120–1; Paterson, 1979, pp. 114–16, 121–6; Freymond, 1964, pp. 66–70). The British saw themselves as having been instrumental in securing this narrow victory; they acknowledged that Canada had played a useful role, but did not think that there would have been the remotest chance of negotiating a treaty acceptable to Congress without British leadership (Henderson, 1982, *passim*). All this coincided with the extremely close Anglo-American partnership in the airlift to relieve the Soviet blockade of Berlin, although Bevin was misleading himself in thinking that it was probably only his restraining hand that was preventing the United States from turning that crisis into one of actual war (Bell, 1985, *passim*; Bohlen, 1973, p. 294).

It is clear that in Bevin's later years at the Foreign Office Britain did play an immense role in bringing together the United States and Western Europe, and in relatively small matters as well as great, such as its mediation between the United States and the Netherlands over Indonesian independence in 1948–9 (Bullock, 1983, pp. 428–38, 457–65, 602–4, 660–1, 674–8, 821–2). Nevertheless, British officials acquired an exaggerated sense of their uniqueness and indispensability in the Western world. British leaders now saw themselves as the vital link between a Western Europe that was pusillanimous towards the Soviet threat, in need of constant rallying, and incapable of understanding America, and an America that was too inexperienced to comprehend how to handle either the West Europeans or crises in East–West relations. As a US Foreign Service officer put it in the early 1960s, Britain saw its 'role as keeper of the new transatlantic balance, the spokesman for a weakened Europe, and the Greece to a muscle-bound American Rome' (Steel, 1964, p. 90).

In the years around the mid-century US leaders were not totally dismissive of British wisdom and experience, and neither could they ignore the fact that Britain had some assets that they could not match. While, for instance, the Labour Party remained in office, Britain had special attractions for the non-communist left on the Continent. As a left-wing Italian historian has recently written: 'British Labourism had an international vitality that made it a pole of attraction for European socialists' (Spriano, 1985, p. 234; cf. Ovendale, 1985, p. 162). The Foreign Office noted the puzzling mixture of US behaviour towards Britain, sometimes highly considerate and sometimes that of a superior to an inferior, concluding that it was the 'resentments and humiliations that stay longest in mind' (F[oreign] O[ffice] to Oliver Franks, 20 December 1949, FO 371/ 74183/AN3854). To the United States, Britain's real importance was, as Hubert Humphrey put it in September 1949, 'the keystone to our North Atlantic defence system' (Manderson-Jones, 1972, p. 28). Britain was the piece of insular real estate that had to be held if the Red Army took the adjoining continent, and whose own forces had a vital role to play in naval defence in the North Atlantic and land defence in the Middle East. Following the signing of the NATO treaty the Joint Chiefs of Staff did agree to make a token effort to hold the Red Army along the Rhine, but expected it to fail (Riste, 1985, pp. 151–2). In the last resort British thinking also regarded the continent as expendable. A meeting of senior Whitehall officials in January 1949 agreed that 'We must in practice establish the position that the United States will defend us, whatever happens to the Europeans (*sic*)' (Clarke, 1982, p. 208). It was also the case that the British were capable of over-reaction. They formulated the domino theory independently of the Americans not only in the Far East, but, in addition, in the Middle East and Europe (in relation to the fall of West Berlin to communism) (Ovendale, 1985, pp. 50–3, 78–9, 148, 169–70). And a government that suspected a link between the communist coup in Prague and the Gold Coast riots in West Africa displayed something rather less than calm wisdom. Both events took place in February 1948; any further connection seems improbable (Fieldhouse, 1984, p. 112; Bullock, 1983, pp. 611–12).

Our second period was one of movement in which Britain played a major role, but not in convincing the United States and the continental West Europeans of the realities of the international situation. Ruling circles throughout the West came separately to the same conclusion: that the Soviet Union was hostile to the West, almost certainly irreconcilably, and was led by men who were not reckless or warmongering but whose ceaseless probing against Western interests might lead to conflict unless faced by the clearest and firmest (though not provocative) Western response. Britain's role lay more in its practical contribution to the forging of the Western Alliance. Yet even there Britain's vital part, if it ever had one, probably ended with the signing of the NATO Treaty. What completed the USA's transition to leadership of the alliance was not British diplomacy but two events over which it had no control. The first was the Soviet atom bomb test in 1949, which convinced the Truman administration, after a spasm of hope that US invulnerability could be restored by development of the hydrogen bomb, that the United States could no longer be defended relatively cheaply by a nuclear attack on a non-nuclear Russia that had started a war. It had been thought that this would force the Soviets to negotiate peace terms. The second was the outbreak of the Korean War, which Washington feared would be repeated in Europe with a surprise attack into West Germany or elsewhere. The Soviet bomb led to NSC 68 and US conventional rearmament, Korea to a dramatic abandonment of the earlier refusal to commit forces to Europe on condition that West Germany was rearmed so that it too could help. In late 1950 Eisenhower was appointed NATO commander in Europe, and in February 1951 Truman coupled the sending of a modest four US divisions to reinforce the two already in Germany with the more fateful decision that those forces should be integrated with those of the European NATO members (Ireland, 1981, pp. 125, 176, 183–95, 207–15, 226; Herken, 1980, pp. 278, 287, 298, 305, 327–9; Bullock, 1983, pp. 803–8, 828–9; Acheson, 1970, pp. 397–9, 435, 443–4; Barker, 1983, pp. 221–7; Riste, 1985, pp. 182–3; Shulman, 1963, pp. 148–50, 171–5; McGeehan, 1971, pp. 4–11, 21–3, 97–102).[3] Given their own rearmament and intense pressure not only from France but now also from West Germany for a serious effort to halt any Red Army advance in its earliest stages, American military planners abandoned the doctrine that the Continent would almost inevitably be lost in war (Riste, 1985, pp. 167–8, 199–200, 290).

The changes in American war plans involved some downgrading in Britain's importance, but this was less apparent to the British than were the plans' military advantages. In late 1949 the government had set up a committee on the implications of the Soviet atomic bomb on the assumption that it would eventually enable Russia to destroy the United Kingdom. In 1952 the Chiefs of Staff contributed the cheerful information that the Red Army had 51,000 tanks compared with a Second World War peak of 25,000 (minute by King, 8 December 1949, FO 371/77607/N9003; Hohler to Gascoigne, 31 January 1952, FO 371/100830/NS1026/3). Yet by then the new Conservative government had started to scale down the huge rearmament drive upon which the Attlee Cabinet had resolved after war broke out in Korea. Deterrence appeared to be working, though there were fears, among defence specialists if not among politicians, about what the Soviets would do after they had acquired the means to deliver nuclear weapons on to Western targets (papers by N. Wiggeshaus, pp. 201–2, and G. Warner and T. H. Etzold, *passim*, in Riste, 1985). In this dangerous, but not desperate, situation British leaders saw the Anglo-American special relationship as the mainstay of resistance to communism everywhere.

With the stakes believed to be so high, the Cold War became almost the sole preoccupation of British foreign policy in the early 1950s. It was so defined by one of the highest of Foreign Office officials, Gladwyn Jebb, in a confidential lecture to an audience of top-ranking military officers in 1950: 'Perhaps, if we are to think quite clearly, we may admit that the phrase 'cold war' so far as we are concerned, really involves the whole question of the maintenance of the United Kingdom's position in the world, and can therefore in the long run be equated with our general foreign policy' (lecture by Jebb at Imperial Defence College, 24 February 1950, FO 371/86736/NS1027/1). It is at least arguable that this frame of mind, in which the Cold War became almost a blessing to the extent that it enabled Britain to remain a great world power, caused British leaders to delude themselves into thinking that they could continue to play the same pivotal role that they had briefly played in 1948–9, and blinded them to the fact that there were other issues in foreign policy besides the Cold War, not least the question of a role in Western Europe. Probably what obscured reality more than anything else was the similarity in British and American thinking on the really important East–West problems. It is well known that Attlee's mission to Washington in December 1950 was an exercise in the unnecessary, because Truman had every intention of keeping the war limited and non-nuclear (see Morgan, 1984, pp. 427–31 for a

recent summary of the Attlee mission). This had been preceded
earlier in the year by unsuccessful British efforts to obtain commitments from the United States on the circumstances in which atomic
bombs might be dropped on to Soviet-bloc targets by US planes
based in England. Though an agreement was to be reached in
October 1951 and amplified by the new Churchill government three
months later, there were to be persistent misgivings in Britain about
whether its (secret) terms were 'watertight', especially whenever
American air power was involved in controversial incidents such as
those of the U–2 and RB 47 spy planes (the latter from a British base)
that were shot down over Russia in 1960 (Barker, 1983, pp. 192–3;
Macmillan, 1972, pp. 237–9). If the United States was reluctant to
accept any British control over its bases in Britain, it was clearly
unlikely to accept nuclear partnership with Britain in the Far East. It
was characteristic of the blunter tone of the Eisenhower administration that, in 1954, Dulles was to state specifically that the United
States reserved the right to decide for itself on the use of nuclear
weapons outside the NATO area without consulting other NATO
members (the focus of his attention was actually Korea in the event
of a resumption of war there) (Riste, 1985, p. 310).

   There was some complacency in British and US governing circles
because they considered that nuclear weapons were so terrible that
they had made war between the great powers unlikely. This applied
most strongly to Britain. Eden, as Churchill's postwar Foreign
Secretary, was convinced that a world war over Indo-China in 1954
would have been probable but for both the United States and Russia
having the hydrogen bomb; he looked forward eagerly to Britain's
acquiring its own fusion bomb in the hope that the weapon's
extreme destructiveness would go far to cancel out the disparity in
geographical size between Britain and the Soviet Union (Macmillan, 1969, pp. 620–1, 627–8; Avon, 1960, pp. 123–4, 368;
Carlton, 1981, p. 348; Churchill in H. C. Debates, 5 series, col.
1899, 1 March 1955). Likewise, if there were hawks and doves on
Cold War strategy in the United States, the same applied to some
extent in Britain where, as in America, disagreements tended to be
between civilian officials and the military. There seems to have been
a long-running clash between the Foreign Office and the Chiefs of
Staff about whether propaganda and subversion could be employed
to end communist rule in at least some of the East European
countries without provoking Russia into war with the West

(Barker, 1983, pp. 103–9, 177–9, 207–10, 228–30; Ovendale, 1985, p. 134). An exception to this conflict was Foreign Office readiness to use what it called 'special machinery' in Albania by consenting to train refugees and send them back to subvert the communist regime. This episode, which lasted from 1949 to 1953, was almost a caricature of the development of the Anglo-American relationship because it began as a British operation, with token American observers, and ended as a wholly American operation from which the British had dropped out. There was a similar, but much earlier, process by which Britain completely yielded Cold War leadership in Italy to the United States (Bethell, 1984, *passim*; Halliday, 1986, pp. 79–80, 329–30 for the Second World War origins of the Anglo-American obsession with destroying Albanian communism; Gladwyn Jebb at Russia Committee, 15 February 1949, FO 371/77623/N1727; Ellwood, 1985, *passim*).

Extreme counsels tended to fail as much in Washington as in London, even as the consensus on the hopelessness of trying to negotiate an end to the Cold War with the Soviet Union prevailed. By early 1949 Bevin was convinced that Western interests in the Cold War were best served by the existing immobility, although towards the end of his time at the Foreign Office (and of his life) he expressed interest in probing for a delimitation of the 'vital interests' of East and West, perhaps leading to 'an ideological and physical armistice or no man's land' (message from Bevin for British United Nations delegation, New York, 23 April 1949, FO 371/76583/C3382/23/18; minutes by I. Mallett, 1 and 2 December 1950, FO 371/86733/NS1023/48). While his successor, Eden, was ruminating that communist rulers were 'the primitive and ruthless priests of a modern religion' who could not be made to swerve from their ultimate goal of world domination, Dean Acheson on the other side of the Atlantic was proclaiming that talking to communism was as futile as talking to a river; if a river was causing problems, one could dam it or deflect it but not conduct a discussion with it (Avon, 1960, p. 431; Acheson, 1970, p. 379). Against such solidarity (tempered on the British side by occasional fears that American anti-communist policy might become so robust as to lead to war), Churchill's wish, almost obsession, to arrange a new East–West summit after Stalin's death in March 1953 was doomed to inevitable failure (Seldon, 1981, pp. 396–409; minute by Eden, February 1952, FO 371/100825/NS1023/9, for a typical expression of fear that American over-exuberance might lead to war).

There were almost constant quarrels in the Anglo-American relationship and personality clashes, of which the worst, before the temporary collapse of the relationship at the time of Suez, was probably that between Eden and Acheson during the last months of the latter's time as Secretary of State (Carlton, 1981, pp. 316–22). But these quarrels emphasize the point that '[A]ll the dialogue, all the diplomacy, took place within the blocs, not between them' (Morgan, 1974, p. 16). The foreign policy elites in both countries in the early 1950s saw most Anglo-American frictions as a thin layer on the cement of a fundamental unity caused by Soviet hostility to the Western world (Roberts and Wilson, 1953, pp. xiii, 221; memorandum by Denis Allen of the British embassy in Washington, August 1949, FO 371/74187/AN2671 for a characteristic statement of confidence in the solid foundations of the special relationship). It was tacitly accepted that total solidarity would inevitably have meant total British subservience to the United States (Frankel, 1975, pp. 213–16). It was believed that a fundamental aim of Soviet foreign policy was to divide Britain from the United States, and that this had to be resisted at all costs. Even so, Détente (referred to by that term) was always held to be desirable in principle if the Soviets would really change their ways (Gascoigne, ambassador in Moscow, to Hohler, 20 February 1952, FO 371/100838/NS1051/7; Hayter (Gascoigne's successor) to Foreign Office, 3 December 1953, FO 371/106535/NS1051/88; on Détente see memorandum by Northern Department of Foreign Office, 11 April 1950, FO 371/86766/NS1072/1). In the meantime, to reject Soviet overtures and divisive moves was not seen as requiring great skill because of their transparent purpose: they were 'a hook without bait' (Foreign Office brief for Hector McNeil, February 1949, FO 371/77611/N1381).

Partly, if not largely, because of a conviction of having a pivotal role in the Cold War, there was a degree of complacency in British foreign policy in the early and mid-1950s, which must provide some justification for Acheson's accusation that it was characterised by 'stubbornness bordering on stupidity' (Acheson, 1970, pp. 33–4). There was unwillingness to learn from Acheson's welcome to the Schuman plan for a coal and steel community in continental West Europe that might grow into an integrated unit that would almost dwarf Britain, and from Acheson's impatient rejection of a British document, for the first time formally mentioning the special relationship, immediately afterwards (Acheson, 1970, pp. 383–8; Bullock, 1983, p. 772; Charlton, 1983, pp. 95–7, 141–2). Instead, there were only such responses as Sir Paul Gore-Booth's lament that America too rarely gave Britain 'a pat on the shoulder' (Gore-Booth, 1974, p. 178). The newly-elected Eisenhower's insistence on holding a summit (at Bermuda: at least a British colony was chosen) with the French as well as British Prime Ministers was a cause for regret but not for reassessment (Colville, 1985a, p. 987, lamented that at Bermuda 'The real mistake was having the French with whom none of the things we mind most about can be discussed'). It seemed to require the leisure afforded by opposition for a leading politician to come to a more realistic estimate. This was achieved by Hugh Gaitskell, who wrote in 1952 that Britain sought a status based on the notion that the American–British power ratio was 2:1 whereas a truer figure would be 7:1 (Williams, 1983, p. 317).

A few years later Britain showed that it could play a role of first importance in Europe with its vital contribution to solving the issue of West German rearmament in the autumn and winter of 1954–5. However, for years longer British leaders still felt themselves to be 'in a different category' from the 'ruck of European countries', as Macmillan put it in a memorandum to his Foreign Secretary, Selwyn Lloyd, in December 1959 (Macmillan, 1972, p. 112). Between 1955 and 1959 Britain had actually boosted its great power claims by exploding a hydrogen bomb in the Pacific in 1957. This appears to have been seen by America as more truly taking Britain into the nuclear club than the atomic bomb test in 1952 (Spiers, 1981, p. 157). It paved the way for the final major British effort to play an ameliorating and semi-independent role in East–West relations between 1958 and 1960. That lies outside the scope of this paper, but the earliest harbinger of Détente, around 1955, had not been one in which Britain was a prime mover. The United States, if only because Russia had made great strides in building up its nuclear arsenal, had not then held back from seeking accommodation on a limited range of issues, such as an Austrian peace treaty, when the Soviets had shown a readiness to negotiate.

If we look for comparisons between the postwar decade and the mid-1980s, one obvious difference is that the first Cold War took place under the shadow of the Second World War. It had been an experience to breed pessimism. It had proved that the worst could and sometimes did happen. This helped greatly to produce the chronic fears of the first Cold War that the world was on the brink of a new war, though there was no fatalistic acceptance of such an outcome (Bullock, 1983, p. 486; Yergin, 1978, pp. 391–2; Dalton, 1962, p. 330). There were, of course, other factors, including the almost intolerable lack of 'hard' intelligence about Soviet intentions (cf. the inconclusive discussions of Soviet intentions by Foreign Office officials in February–March 1950, FO 371/86731/NS1023/ 11, and in September of that year, FO 371/86762/NS1053/27) and, more in the United States than in Britain, a deep-rooted anti-communism which, as George Kennan complained, caused many people to regard the Soviet Union as so self-evidently aggressive that the need to consider such evidence as there was about its motives and intentions did not arise (Kennan, 1968, pp. 497–500). At all events, after more than forty years of peace between the great powers there must be some risk of lapsing into complacency.

   In one important respect the shadow of war has lifted. Both the British and other West Europeans, and even some Americans, worried deeply after 1945 about future German threats to their security, and sheer hostility to the Germans, whether they posed a threat or not, was a factor (cf. Senator Vandenberg's remark on the NATO treaty in July 1949 in Riste, 1985, pp. 159–60, that, 'It would apply just as promptly and effectively to a German aggression as it does to a communist'). Between 1947 and 1950 such Americans as Kennan and Acheson were dismayed by the anti-German outbursts which they heard from the lips of British leaders, including Bevin (Acheson, 1970, p. 338; Bullock, 1983, pp. 763–4; Kennan's testimony in Urban, 1982, p. 390). As late as June 1959, Macmillan wrote to Eisenhower, at a time of acute East–West conflict over West Berlin, that if the Soviets pressed the issue it would be 'paradoxical, to use a mild term' to expect the British people to go to war 'in order to defend the liberties of people who have tried to destroy us twice in this century' (Macmillan, 1972, p. 73). It is surely impossible to visualize any recent British Prime Minister employing that kind of argument. By contrast, memory of the wartime alliance and of both Soviet casualties and the Soviet contribution to victory are probably a more potent influence now than in the 'high' Cold War when the sense of grievance against Russia – of having been betrayed –caused them almost to be forgotten. This tendency was aided by the Soviet Union's unwillingness until the 1960s to admit the scale of its wartime losses which even now – the famous figure of twenty million dead – it probably understates. In the early period, Attlee was typical in being briskly dismissive of the Soviets 'asking for everything on the grounds of their immense sufferings and so forth' (Tolstoy, 1981, pp. 280–4; Williams, 1961, p. 71).

Most obviously of all, there is Britain's decline from a power with worldwide economic, military and colonial positions in 1945 to a country largely without such positions now. Britain after the Second World War was in an ambiguous position. To quote Max Beloff's definition in 1961, it remained in 1945 'a power with world-wide interests and responsibilities, though no longer in the strict sense a world power' (Beloff, 1961, p. 15). The ambiguity has now gone, and was waning even in the early 1950s. More intangibly, there has been a decline in the passionate conviction of the early postwar years that Britain had unique assets of wisdom and experience in world affairs and, after the Cold War had set in, that Britain might be instrumental in the sort of crisis-management needed to prevent collapse into a war of atomic and later hydrogen bombs. In fact, as already argued, it is probable that the basic structure of the Western Alliance would have evolved even with a less active British role. The British for too long had a fixation with their spell of greatest influence at the end of the 1940s, and tried to make the temporary permanent. They often showed little sign of appreciating the prosaic reasons – the temporary weakness of the continental West European countries and the need for Britain as a sort of aircraft carrier if war did break out – that impelled the United States to accept the special relationship for a few years around the middle of the century. They might have done well to heed the words of General Eisenhower (as he then was) to the Labour politician Hugh Dalton in 1951 that for a time Britain could stay independent, but that 'maybe ultimately your choice is either to become the 49th state or to join the USE [United States of Europe]' (Manderson-Jones, 1972, p. 103). It was actually to take another ten years for British leaders to realize that there was an entire dimension of foreign policy outside the Cold War, and that the key to Britain's prosperity and at least some degree of international influence most probably lay in joining the integrationist moves of the six continental states instead of spurning them as in 1950 and 1955.

This can be asserted while accepting that it was completely illusory to postulate any option of Britain simply opting out of East-West conflict. The answer to that was given as long ago as 1947 by Bevin in a letter to Attlee: Britain might be able to convince Russia of its pacific intentions by destroying its defences, but that would create a vacuum which the Russians would suspect America of seeking to exploit in time of war (Bullock, 1983, pp. 350–1). He might have added that the Americans might equally have suspected Soviet intentions in such a situation. Either way, Britain would have been powerless and in danger.

To conclude with a broader look at how the two periods compare, the image of a coin with two sides might be used. On the debit side for the 1980s, the postwar world was surely wiser in seeing immense importance in the ideological chasm between East and West, something about which the communists have never been in doubt. Among all classes of the British people, though least among middle-class leftwingers, the conviction was widespread by the late 1940s that Soviet international behaviour, particularly as demonstrated in Eastern Europe, was 'flagrantly repulsive', as one observer put it, and constituted a menace that threatened to replace a no doubt imperfect society with one infinitely worse (Epstein, 1954, p. 97; Seton-Watson, 1977, p. 224).[4] Those who directed British foreign policy certainly derived confidence from the belief that their own intense dislike of the communist system and immunity to communist blandishments was shared by most of the British people in a way that would not have applied in France or Italy (cf. notes for House of Lords debate, March 1949, FO 371/77600/N2453, in which the new 'people's democracies' of Eastern Europe were declared to be 'a type of civilisation which is repugnant to every Western idea'; for the conviction that the British people supported Cold War foreign policy, see Mason to Gascoigne, 24 November 1952, FO 371/100831/NS1026/36).

It aided clarity that this was before the West European component of the communist movement had spawned the polycentrism of the 1960s or the Eurocommunism of the 1970s. If postwar British leaders wished to understand the challenge that faced them, they had only to look at the British Communist Party, whose academic intellectuals, of whom there was a significant number in the postwar decade, publicly endorsed in uncompromising terms the Leninist–Stalinist doctrine that a righteous end justified any means, and served notice that in a communist-ruled Britain freedom of speech and publication would be abolished on the grounds that: 'We cannot afford distracting or destructive influences, any more than a parent would allow a mesmerist to experiment upon his child' (Bernal *et al.*, 1947).[5] Where the present, and especially the West European component of the Western Alliance, scores over the first Cold War is in its greater readiness (knowing far more about Soviet history and society than did its predecessors of the postwar years) to recognize the role of competing interests, as well as ideologies, in East–West conflict so that such conflict does not preclude East–West dialogue (Moreton and Segal, 1984, pp. 5–6, 9, 77–9, 107–8).

Chapter 4: Notes

1 Eden had written that the most puzzling aspect of the postwar years was the way in which Stalin had needlessly squandered the wartime goodwill towards the Soviet Union; see Avon, 1960, pp. 6–7. A simple but convincing answer to this conundrum was suggested in 1949 by Violet Conolly of the Foreign Office in her observation that, faced by a choice between retaining Western goodwill and acquiring a new empire in Eastern Europe, Stalin had preferred 'the greater prize' (minute, 13 June 1949, FO 371/77604/N5832).

2 Elsewhere, Professor Watt has pointed out that United States policy-makers were intent on not becoming involved in such a conflict; see Watt, 1984b, pp. 103–5.

3 Whatever may be thought of the willingness to use nuclear weapons, original American peace terms for a Soviet Union forced to the negotiating table were liberal to the point of being other-worldly: the Russian state was to suffer practically no losses whereas the Communist Party of the Soviet Union was to be required to accept a multiparty system in the USSR! See Herken, 1980, pp. 275–6.

4 Professor Seton-Watson argued that the adverse effect on Western public opinion of what the communists were doing in Eastern Europe was so great that the Cold War on the Western side was primarily 'the yielding of Western States to the pressure of public opinion which was revolted by the information which got back to it'. Bullock, 1983, p. 689, quotes a study of Labour MPs who opposed Bevin's foreign policy, which concludes that they 'conformed strikingly to the popular stereotype of the socialist intellectual'. Bevin's dislike for leftwing intellectuals (for which, see Barclay, 1975, p. 77) had a rational basis. See also Rose, 1959, pp. 437–8, 480–3.

5 See especially lectures by John Lewis and Randall Swingler; for quotation from latter see Bernal *et al.*, 1947, p. 44. This booklet, which reproduces a

series of lectures by communist intellectuals sponsored by the London
District Committee of the Communist Party in 1946, makes in places
chilling reading.

PART III

Détente

5 Détente: A United States View

DAVID N. SCHWARTZ

There is probably no better way to start a fight at a Washington cocktail party than to bring up the topic of Détente. It is a subject on which almost everyone in that capital city has an opinion, and it is hardly surprising that disagreement is strong. Some view this period of US–Soviet relations, between 1972 and 1979, as a tragic sellout of US interests in pursuit of an illusory goal of accommodation with the Soviet Union. The party will liven up a bit when one of these pundits engages in conversation with someone who views the period as a series of tragically missed opportunities, one in which the noble goal of a stable peace was almost achieved.

The debate becomes a bit less intense as one travels away from Washington, into the heartland of the United States. In this part of the country – that is, the rest of the country – most people probably do not know what the word Détente means, much less how they actually feel about such esoteric matters as the Jackson–Vanik amendment or the SALT I interim agreement on offensive weapons. The American public is typically not preoccupied with foreign policy issues, for a wide variety of reasons, some perfectly understandable. But Americans in general are concerned about the relationship between Washington and Moscow. In this regard, most polling data shows that the vast majority of the American people harbour two distinct views of the Soviet Union: a basic distrust, and a desire for a lasting peace.

It is in this context – that is, a highly charged political environment in Washington, and a less intense, but equally divided stance among the broader American body politic – that policy-makers must chart a course for US policy towards the Soviet Union. It is understandable, therefore, that they often have difficulty. So the first observation should be that there really is no single American perspective on the subject of Détente. There are, in reality, many different perspectives, and the view set forth in this paper is only that of one observer of the US–Soviet relationship.

I

Much has been written about the 'conceptual structure' of the Nixon–Kissinger Détente, most of it on a rather grand, theoretical level. It is probably much more useful to think of the objectives of these two leaders in simpler, pragmatic terms. By the late 1960s it had become apparent that the Kremlin leadership had committed itself to becoming a superpower on par with the United States. This would pose new challenges for the United States, which had held a strategic advantage over the Soviet Union for some time. Since the Cuban missile crisis, the Soviet leadership had shown considerable caution when challenging US interests abroad, in part, we might assume, because of the nuclear supremacy of the United States and the apparent willingness of its leaders to use that supremacy if conditions compelled them to.

This could reasonably be expected to change once the Soviets caught up with the United States. The development of a huge Soviet nuclear arsenal might embolden the Kremlin leadership to become more aggressive in their challenges to US interests around the globe. The challenges of a newly aggressive Soviet Union might at first be manageable, but over an extended period of time they could lead to a deterioration of international stability and perhaps even to war. And war between the superpowers, armed as they would be with such huge nuclear arsenals, would entail unthinkable risks.

The task Nixon and Kissinger set for themselves, then, was to bring the Soviet Union to an understanding of the risks and responsibilities inherent in superpower status, which might serve to temper Moscow's perception of the opportunities this new status would present. The objective began fairly narrowly, to get an agreement to moderate the strategic nuclear arms competition. Later, the objective broadened a bit, to encompass an agreed (if only tacit) set of rules for behaviour in crisis or confrontation. If the two superpowers could establish such a basic framework for a relationship, then future crises, inevitable though they may be, need not deteriorate into war.

In light of statements at the time, and subsequent events, several observations are possible. First, and perhaps most important, the objectives behind Détente could only be realized through gradual, and somewhat ad hoc manoeuvring to create an intricate web of interests that would restrict Soviet ability to challenge US interests. Efforts to establish a dialogue on the strategic nuclear competition had already begun under the Johnson administration; these efforts, cancelled in the wake of the August 1968 invasion of Czechoslovakia, laid the basis for the initiation of the SALT talks in November 1969. Given the perception that it was the growth of the Soviet nuclear arsenal that had propelled the Soviet Union to its superpower status, and posed the greatest danger for world stability if left unchecked, it is not surprising that SALT became the first major effort to establish the Détente relationship. What is easy to forget is that, without the efforts of President Johnson and Secretary of Defense Robert McNamara to initiate these talks, in order to address not the political problem of the evolving role of the Soviet Union as a superpower but the more technical problem posed by strategic defences for the balance of terror, it may have taken longer for the Nixon administration to have set the process in motion.

As the relationship deepened in the strategic area, circumstances presented themselves to Nixon and Kissinger to broaden their strategy. The recurrent failures of the Soviet grain harvest during the early 1970s gave Washington a new lever with which to establish a framework of stability. During the latter half of the decade, it was this aspect of US strategy which was most obviously tested. The point here is perhaps too obvious to merit our consideration, but the fact is that, although the objective was perhaps fairly clear, the means of achieving that objective were dictated by circumstance in a more or less ad hoc fashion.

A second point here is that the originators of Détente were not profoundly ideological men. Both Nixon and Kissinger were comfortable with the 'realist' approach to foreign policy, in which international relations were dominated more by considerations of power and self-interest than belief in ideas. Rhetoric aside, they brought to policy-making an approach remarkably unencumbered by preconceptions about the 'evil' nature of the Soviet leadership that has dominated so much of US foreign policy-making both before and since. In retrospect, it is difficult to substantiate the charge that the Nixon–Kissinger foreign policy team harboured sanguine illusions about the nature of Soviet foreign policy, or the willingness of Soviet leaders to press for advantage wherever and whenever they prudently could. What perhaps is more open to question is whether they appreciated the difficulty of implementing a non-ideological foreign policy in the heated political environment of Washington.

II

Since the first focus of the process was nuclear arms control, any assessment of the decade of Détente must begin with an evaluation of this most important aspect of Détente.

It took two and a half years to hammer out the first SALT I accords. This achievement, acclaimed at the time, looks somewhat paltry from our current vantage point, but only because so little has happened since. At the time, it was clearly expected, perhaps even by both sides, that the Interim Offensive Agreement and the ABM Treaty were merely a prelude to further agreement and reductions on both sides.

The agreements themselves were simple by comparison to SALT II. The Interim Offensive Agreement basically stopped the build-up of ICBMs and SLBMs on both sides at the levels then existing. The ABM Treaty severely constrained both sides' ABM programmes, prohibiting in perpetuity the creation of nationwide ABM defences. The Administration argued that these agreements were the best that could be accomplished under the circumstances; most agreed, and the Treaty was ratified in the Senate. But even then, there were storm clouds on the horizon. For example, many observers wondered how long it would take to get an agreement on reductions from current levels, if it took more than two years to get an agreement that only froze missiles at current levels (and let bombers go unconstrained). Of greater concern to critics such as Senator Henry Jackson was the fact that a freeze at current levels left the Soviets at a numerical advantage; strict equality was the condition Jackson extracted for future agreements. The Joint Chiefs of Staff were not particularly enthusiastic about the notion of constraints on offensive forces either; they supported the Treaty on the condition that they would receive three major new strategic weapons systems, in addition to MIRV technology.

It is interesting that the ABM Treaty met with less hostility in the

Senate. True, there were some who were uncomfortable with the doctrinal dogmas pushed by some Treaty advocates regarding the 'stabilizing' nature of remaining naked before the enemy. But even these sceptics were aware that the US ABM programme was technically incapable of performing even the most restricted strategic defence missions, and thus were willing to go along with the Treaty. (Ironically, both supporters and detractors of the current SDI programme claim that the ABM Treaty was based on the belief that strategic defence was destabilizing; more truthfully, it was based on the apparently destabilizing nature of the rudimentary technologies available at the time.)

It took another seven years, and three Presidents, to achieve the next real arms-control breakthrough. This time-lag was itself one of the major problems facing the arms-control process. It was in part the result of a highly dynamic, changing political scene in the United States; each new President seemed committed to placing his own stamp on the process, even at the cost of significant delays. But, more important, the growing complexity of the problems being tackled by the negotiators in Geneva – MIRVed warheads, definitions of new types of missiles, cruise missiles, weapons on bombers, etc. – made them particularly resistant to quick solutions.

The extended delay had several dismal consequences. First, it allowed a great many events in other areas of the relationship to unfold and influence the public's receptivity to the Treaty, events that will be discussed below. Secondly, the extended delay led to an understandable anticipation of great things, not merely, in the words of the Carter administration, a 'modest but useful' addition to the nation's security. Proponents were not able to argue that it would result in significant cuts, or even changes, in the Soviet strategic arms build-up. What they fell back on was the argument that the Soviets could do even more without the constraints imposed by the Treaty – perhaps reason enough to support the Treaty, but certainly not, in the eyes of many, worth the seven-year wait. As a result, much support for the Treaty was tempered, even lost, during the ratification battle.

The complexity of the final document posed additional public relations problems. The first SALT Treaty and agreement had taken no more than ten pages of relatively straightforward language, easy for the interested layman to follow. The fifty pages of highly technical, dense jargon that made up the SALT II Treaty were enough to discourage even a reasonably interested layman from perusing the document.

It was mainly these two flaws that allowed opponents to develop a strong campaign against the Treaty. Their complaint was straight-forward: the Treaty was, in effect, too modest to be useful. Whether the public really understood the nuclear theology surrounding the charge that the Treaty did nothing to close the so-called 'window of vulnerability' mattered less than the fact that the opponents could argue that, under SALT II, the Soviets – far from being forced to cut back on their forces – could actually increase their warheads by a substantial factor.

Even then, however, the Treaty might well have passed the Senate (so argues veteran Capitol Hill defence expert Larry Smith) had not the controversy over the Soviet brigade in Cuba, and most critically the Soviet invasion of Afghanistan, overshadowed all other considerations. As it was, the withdrawal of the Treaty from Senate consideration effectively ended the decade of Détente.

III

The debate about SALT II was not merely a debate about an arms-control treaty. It was a debate about the broader nature of the US–Soviet relationship, prompted by events that had taken place during the previous five years. Most of these events centred not on the US–Soviet relationship directly, but on Soviet activities in regional conflicts, and the impact these had on the central relationship.

Nixon and Kissinger had hoped that progress in stabilizing the central strategic relationship would have a spill-over effect on to other areas of the relationship. There were several areas of concern. First was crisis-management. Perhaps crises were an unavoidable part of the superpower relationship; if so, might one develop 'rules of the road' for superpower behaviour during crises? These kinds of questions were initially addressed in a fuzzy, vaguely worded document of the Nixon–Kissinger period, the agreement on the prevention of nuclear war. Would it be possible to extend these principles – particularly the renunciation of unilateral advantage during a crisis – to areas outside the central strategic realm?

The first test came with the October 1973 Arab–Israeli War,

which found the United States and the Soviet Union on opposite sides of the fence for the first time since the SALT I agreements. Both sides were perhaps guilty of excessive posturing during the crisis in order to force the other to restrain its clients, but, in general, despite the melodrama of the US general nuclear alert at the height of the crisis, confrontation was avoided, and both sides eventually worked together to impose a cease-fire. More disturbing in retrospect was the revelation that Sadat had informed the Soviets of his intentions several days before the invasion, and the Soviets did nothing to dissuade him from moving ahead. If this betrayed a Soviet desire to gain unilateral advantage, however, certainly the principal outcome of the war – the freezing out of Moscow from the peace process – was an instance where the United States achieved a particularly significant unilateral advantage.

Hard on the heels of the October War, regional crises in central and southern Africa, as well as in the Horn of Africa, made it clear that the growth in Soviet military power had translated into a greater willingness to intervene (either directly or through Cuban, East German or North Korean proxies) in regional conflicts to gain political advantage. In each of these cases the regional disputes were largely of an internal nature, and almost certainly not caused by Soviet trouble-making; however, the Kremlin leadership seemed unafraid to insert itself into these conflicts, pick a side (or several sides, depending on the conflict) and hope for a positive outcome.

The American reaction to this new thrust in Soviet foreign policy was influenced by the relative novelty of such aggressive Soviet behaviour outside its immediate geographical area; by perhaps unrealistic expectations that the various 'carrots' offered to the Soviets, not only in the central strategic area but also in the more tangible economic and agricultural areas, would give the Soviets incentives not to expand influence into areas of opportunity; by the disastrous failure of the American effort in Vietnam; by increasing difficulties with US client states in the Third World, most notably Iran. As early as 1975, during the Ford administration, Détente had become a dirty word. (President Ford tried, unsuccessfully, to expunge it from the political vocabulary.) Certainly by 1979, the widespread perception was that Détente had completely failed to restrain Soviet behaviour around the world, that the carrot-and-stick approach had proved completely bankrupt, and that any of the products of Détente, particularly SALT II, were to be viewed with cynical contempt.

The most ambitious view of Détente came in the controversy about human rights in the Soviet Union. The case of Jewish immigration is a good example. Here, Nixon and Kissinger attempted, through quiet diplomacy, to link concessions on trade and finance to more liberal emigration policies on the part of Soviet officials for Jews who wanted to leave the country. Initially there was some success, but soon the issue was taken up in the US Senate, where Senators Henry Jackson and Adlai Stevenson jun. championed various measures to make the linkage explicit, public and legally binding. Once the White House had lost control of the diplomatic context in which the issue was addressed, Soviet flexibility on the matter quickly vanished, and Détente came in for some bitter attacks from those who believed that it should be used to force changes in the domestic political situation in the Soviet Union. Kremlin leaders would have none of that and, in a curious way, by expecting so much from Détente, far less was achieved than might otherwise have been the case.

IV

Most observers would agree that 1979 saw the end of Détente, at least as envisaged by Nixon and Kissinger some seven years earlier. December saw the death-knell, and three events are of particular note: the December 12 NATO decision to deploy new INF missiles in Europe (and to engage the Soviets in arms-control talks regarding these missiles); the Soviet invasion of Afghanistan; the withdrawal of SALT II from consideration by the Senate. Each deserves some comment.

The Soviets are quick to identify NATO's INF decision as the real turning-point in the relationship, the point at which US bad faith became apparent. If there is any merit at all in this position, it is superficial at best. Yes, the NATO decision was certainly an irritant in the relationship, but it was the result of several factors, for some of which the Soviets bear considerable responsibility. At a certain level, it was an attempt on the part of the United States to reassert political leadership over the Alliance after a sustained period of ineptitude in the early years of the Carter administration. But it was more than this. It was a response to a new strategic environment, dominated not only by the achievement of Soviet parity in the central strategic realm but by the sudden revival of Soviet efforts to target new, highly accurate, mobile missiles on to the European allies in NATO. The decision to respond to this new strategic environment was hardly sudden; in the two-year period during which NATO considered the decision, there was ample time for the Soviets to make their concerns known, and to take steps – such as offering to stop deployment of the SS-20 missile early on in the programme – which might have made the decision unnecessary. As it was, no such offers were made; indeed, given the subsequent Soviet charge that this decision was the real breaking-point in the relationship, it is odd to find that the first Soviet diplomatic initiative to address this concern came in October 1979, some twenty months after NATO began its deliberations, almost two years after the SS-20 force began to be deployed.

The Soviet invasion of Afghanistan is another matter entirely. In retrospect, it may be easy to see why the Soviets were concerned about the potential for instability in this small, backward country on its southern border. What is less easy to explain is the Soviets' apparent lack of regard for the Western reaction to the invasion. After all, the Carter administration had come to view this area of the world, the so-called 'arc of crisis', with an obsessive neurosis since mid-1978; the fall of the Shah, followed nine months later by the taking of US hostages at the American Embassy in Tehran, should have made the Kremlin aware of the probable reaction of the United States to the invasion. Here, we are struck with two equally lamentable possibilities: either that the Kremlin miscalculated, which says little for their understanding of the American political debate at the time, or that the Kremlin understood the probable reaction, and viewed it as worth risking given the importance of a stable, friendly Afghanistan. Some argue that this second possibility is more understandable, given the likelihood of SALT II's failure at the hands of the Senate.

But what was the likelihood of SALT II failure prior to the invasion? This question takes us into the realm of second-guessing history, but even so, there is a strong case to be made that the battle, however tough, was not decided at that point. The Administration had weathered the storm surrounding the alleged discovery of a

Soviet brigade in Cuba. The chairman of the Senate Foreign
Relations Committee, Frank Church, had shamelessly used this
'discovery' to demonstrate his 'hardline' credentials to his Idaho
constituency, at the cost of several months of lobbying for the
Treaty. But, by the end of the year, the tide was gradually turning in
favour of the Treaty. If the Administration had had several more
months to lobby on its behalf, it is not at all a foregone conclusion
that the Treaty would have died in the Senate. What made it a
foregone conclusion was the Soviet invasion.

V

So what went wrong? And who is to blame?

One is reluctant to venture definitive answers to either of these
questions. The US–Soviet relationship is highly complex, and no
development in the relationship can be traced to a single cause. But
there are certainly several factors that, while probably not completely explanatory, go some way towards a reasonable explanation.

One important factor seems to be the different expectations of
each side about the benefits and obligations inherent in a Détente
relationship. On the US side, expectations were that stability in the
central strategic relationship, combined with a 'carrot-and-stick'
approach in other areas of the relationship, would lead to less
aggressive Soviet behaviour around the world: less confrontation,
and more co-operation. Whether the policy-makers responsible for
implementing Détente in Washington really believed that Soviet
behaviour would change in a fundamental way is less important
than the fact that, through their own rhetoric, they encouraged
political expectations on the part of the public and Congress that this
would in fact be the case. When it wasn't, Détente became highly
vulnerable to attack from a broad spectrum of political opposition.

What Kremlin leaders expected from Détente is less clear, and that
in itself is a considerable source of tension. Soviet decision-making
takes place behind closed doors, without the benefit of the prolonged and open public debate that characterizes Western debates on
foreign policy. Who knows what they expected from Détente?
From their subsequent actions, we could make a convincing case
that they expected that superpower status in a period of Détente

permitted them to pursue global interests aggressively in areas such as Africa or central Asia without risking the central strategic relationship. Not that they would have a free hand: they probably expected US resistance in the Horn of Africa and other areas of competition for influence in the Third World. What they did not expect, it seems, is that this would gradually erode the basis for the central aspect of Détente.

One factor that looms large is the fractious domestic political environment of the United States during the turbulent decade of the 1970s. It was a decade that began with deep and continuing American involvement in Vietnam, and increasingly strong domestic opposition to that involvement; next came Watergate, and the crippling of the President upon whose shoulders Détente rested, followed by a caretaker Presidency, during the precise period when progress on the complex issues of SALT II was most vital; then the Carter years, marked by hesitancy, indecision, and at times true political ineptitude. It was not a good decade for the United States; we can hardly be surprised that sustaining political support for any policy, much less one as controversial as the US–Soviet relationship, became impossible.

Another factor was the technical complexity of the issues being addressed as the cornerstone of Détente, the central strategic relationship. The 1970s saw tremendous technological and military dynamism on both sides; it may have been too much to demand from our diplomats to keep up with these developments and address them in their carefully crafted treaties. That they largely did so is a tribute to their creativity; that it took them seven years, at the cost of considerable political momentum, is perhaps to be expected. But it made the prospects for political success rather dim. We probably expect too much of arms control; certainly, if we had set our sights lower, and not tried to address such complex questions as MIRVed warheads or cruise missiles, results could have been obtained more quickly.

What the decade of Détente may point to is a more sobering observation, that the areas of common interest are more circumscribed than we had hoped. Both countries share one very important common goal – the prevention of nuclear war. Efforts to reduce the likelihood of nuclear war have thus legitimately been the focal point of Détente and post-Détente diplomacy. But whether we share interest beyond this very important, but somewhat narrow, goal of avoiding nuclear war is open to question, at least on the basis of the record. We are tempted to compare the superpowers to elephants on a stage, wearing tutus and dancing to two different scores of ballet music. Even if they were dancing to the same tune, the result would not be aesthetically pleasing. As it is, we feel lucky if the stage remains standing.

But this is perhaps too neutral a stance. There was much merit in the original Nixon–Kissinger conception of Détente and, if it could have been achieved and implemented, the world would be a better place for it. Détente was an American initiative; it was driven by an admirable impulse, to stabilize superpower relations across a wide spectrum of issues. The tragedy is not that Washington's view was so broad, but rather that the Soviet view was so narrow.

VI

Where does that leave us today? What is the legacy of Détente?

The post-Détente years have been troubled ones for the US–Soviet relationship. The early 1980s saw a freeze in the relationship, occasionally thawing for a short period, only to plunge back into deep freeze. The low point, perhaps, was the KAL 007 incident, which ironically came at a time when Washington was in the midst of internal deliberations on how to change its arms control positions to a more accommodating stance. Since then, however, and particularly since the arrival of Mr Gorbachev on the scene, there has been a palpable warming of the relationship. A summit meeting in November 1985 has paved the way for modest progress on the arms-control front and for a revival of cultural exchanges that had been on the back-burner since the early 1980s. As of this writing (September 1986), a second summit has yet to be scheduled, but there are signs that both sides are eager for one, in spite of the momentary irritation of the Daniloff affair.

We hope that what is developing now is the basis for a sounder relationship, one based on the expectation that conflicts of interest will continue to exist; that the relationship will remain one primarily of confrontation, not co-operation; and yet that in certain areas of shared interest, particularly in the area of nuclear arms control, there is important work to be done. The experience of the 1970s may have lowered our expectations considerably; perhaps, in this frame of mind, we can accomplish more.

6 Britain and the Rise of Détente

BRIAN WHITE

The British contribution to the development of the Cold War has been well documented and is discussed in an earlier chapter of this book. Less noted and commented upon in the literature is the significance of a British role in the development of an East–West Détente. Assessments of the contribution of British diplomacy to moderating East–West conflict in the postwar period have concentrated on the negative side of the record, on the alleged failure of 'summitry' in the 1950s, for example, and the evident failure of Macmillan's Paris summit in 1960. British attempts to mediate between the superpowers have generally been regarded as both ineffectual and pretentious, a rather desperate attempt to prove that Britain could still wield influence on a global stage despite mounting evidence of a material 'descent from power'. Elizabeth Barker, for example, has argued that the British 'tended to fall between two stools' because they weakened the solidarity of the Western alliance by their persistent attempts to mediate, but they were not able to 'achieve a breakthrough in relations with the Soviet Union' (Barker, 1971, p. 144).

The late Professor Northedge, however, is one eminent scholar who consistently argued that successive British governments in the 1950s and early 1960s played an important mediating role between the superpowers and their respective blocs, by searching for 'tension-easing agreements' with Moscow and by seeking points of possible contact between the United States and China (Northedge, 1970, 1974, 1980). In one of his last publications, Northedge even declared that:

> the East–West détente, thought of, and denigrated, by most Americans as exclusively a superpower affair, was, as a matter of history, invented and advocated by the British, only to be

spurned in its early years by the United States, indeed by NATO in general – after the outbreak of the Korean War in June 1950, it was Britain who, above all her alliance partners, sought a rational negotiation of outstanding issues in the Cold War with the Soviet Union and her allies (Northedge and Wells, 1982, p. 124).

The Meaning of Détente

Any evaluation of the British contribution to Détente must start with some discussion of the meaning of Détente, because the concept has been used in a confusing variety of ways (see White, 1981). If, to take a conventional position, Détente is taken to denote tension-easing agreements between the blocs in the late 1960s and early 1970s, then it is unlikely that much significance would be attached to Britain's role. Joseph Korbel, for example, assumes that Détente was essentially a feature of that particular historical period and is thereby able to conclude that Britain's Détente policy 'requires no elaborate discussion' because British governments have not 'at least by deeds, demonstrated any intensive interest in détente' (1972, pp. 60, 66).

Other scholars, however, have argued that Détente is more appropriately conceived as a historical process of accommodation between the superpowers and their allies that has its origins in the 1950s (for a recent example, see Stevenson, 1985). Broadly, Détente as a process can be analysed either from a historical or a structural perspective. Historically, the development of an East–West accommodation can be traced over time, highlighting the more 'visible' manifestations of Détente such as summit meetings or arms-control agreements. A structural analysis, on the other hand, would focus more on the causes than the evidence of Détente, locating Détente within changing structures of international relations and resulting patterns of behaviour. If the Cold War is identified in structural terms with a bipolar distribution of power and the primacy of ideological and military-strategic alignments, Détente can be related to challenges to that structure of rigid bloc differentiation.

A structural analysis of Détente might be developed around four interrelated 'change' factors that have gradually weakened East–West ideological and military alignments and eroded a bipolar structure: the general impact of nuclear weapons and the specific impact of a nuclear stalemate; the growth of economic inter-dependence; the diversification and diffusion of power, and chang-ing interests and attitudes of international actors. These changes have produced, if not a recognizably multipolar system, at least a multi-levelled international system with interactions at different levels of activity on a variety of issues, not wholly constrained by an East–West ideological structure or limited to security politics.

If this conception of Détente is accepted, it can be argued that British diplomacy has been made a significant contribution to an important process of change in international relations and that, *pace* Northedge, the catalytic role of Britain in the 1950s and early 1960s has not received the attention it deserves. If the origins of Détente are identified by reference to specific 'landmarks' or 'turning points' such as the Geneva summit in 1955, the Eisenhower–Khrushchev summit in 1959 or the Partial Test Ban Treaty in 1963, linkages can be established between British policy and those key developments. If, on the other hand, Détente is identified structurally by reference to the piecemeal construction of contacts across the East–West ideological divide, the case for the catalytic role of British diplomacy in building and sustaining the momentum of such a process is even stronger. An investigation of British policy in this context, more-over, reveals some interesting insights into a distinctive British view of both the Cold War and Détente.

Britain, the Cold War and Détente

British attitudes towards Détente can usefully be traced back to the late 1940s when important changes occurred in American attitudes towards the Soviet Union and international communism. Given new American assumptions about the threat posed by a monolithic and nuclear-armed international communism, as detailed in NSC–68 published in May 1950, the object of containment was to build, in Secretary of State Dean Acheson's phrase, 'situations of strength' to match and counter the threat. Despite talk of eventual 'negotiation from strength', this object in practice excluded nego-tiation with the Soviet Union and its allies (see Gaddis, 1982). For the Americans, containment had effectively become an end in itself and the Cold War had come to mean political warfare between two

monolithic power blocs: on the one hand, strengthening and
increasing the cohesion of the Western block; and, on the other,
taking positive steps to undermine the cohesion of the communist
bloc.[1]

The British reaction to this hardening of American attitudes was
one of increasing concern. The central point to be developed here is
that the more pragmatic British could not wholly accept the
manichaeistic view of the world that had emerged in Washington.
Though the Attlee government played a major role in constructing a
'situation of strength' in Europe and elsewhere, the underlying
conception of containment and the Cold War remained close to the
original ideas of George Kennan (see Gaddis, 1982, chapter 2). The
Cold War, from a British perspective, could not be an end in itself:
the object remained the normalization of relations with the Soviet
Union and cutting off diplomatic contacts would fundamentally
undermine that objective. Indeed, it soon became apparent that
British policy-makers were committed to containing East–West
conflict not by confrontation or 'political warfare' but by a policy of
military strength combined with diplomatic accommodation. This
approach will be discussed in more detail at the end of this chapter.

Implicit Anglo-American differences concerning the nature of the
communist threat and, more significantly, appropriate responses to
that threat became an overt policy clash in 1949, when the precipi-
tating issue was China. For the Americans, the 'loss' of China
reinforced the notion of a monolithic communist bloc with which
negotiations were impossible. The British, for their part, infuriated
the Americans not only by recognizing the new Peking government
in January 1950 but by insisting that negotiations should be held
with Mao. The new Chinese leader was another Tito, they argued,
and should at least be talked to: the Chinese would not long remain
under the tutelage of the Soviet Union. Moreover, negotiations
with Mao would put pressure on the Russians to ameliorate their
hostility (see Boardman, 1976). The significance of British policy
here was that it was in line with the principle of keeping East–West
contacts open and it was an explicit rejection of the United States
conception of a monolithic international communism.

With the outbreak of the Korean War in June 1950, and the
possibility of open conflict between East and West, the dangers
posed by the NSC-68 version of containment soon became apparent
to the British government. Though the government loyally backed

the American line on Korea, the need to defuse the crisis persuaded Bevin to risk American displeasure by attempting to mediate. In July 1950, Bevin suggested to the Soviet government that they put pressure on the North Koreans to withdraw north of the 38th Parallel. This attempt to mediate was an embarrassing failure and military support for the war increased thereafter. But this initial failure did not signal the end of British attempts to mediate. The most significant diplomatic initiative was the November 1950 proposal to establish a demilitarized buffer zone in North Korea to separate the opposing forces (for details, see Farrar, 1983).

This plan was eventually overtaken by events, however, as MacArthur began his advance to the Yalu only to be repelled by a massive Chinese counter-attack. In the context of a rapidly deteriorating military situation, British attention switched from the demilitarization plan to trying to forestall a precipitate American response. Hints that President Truman was contemplating using atomic weapons to resolve the crisis were sufficient to send Attlee rushing to Washington, seeking assurances that they would not be used (see Bullock, 1985, pp. 820–4). Attlee's visit may not have been crucial in preventing a nuclear war in Asia, but the episode dramatically illustrates the extent of British concern about the direction of American policy and the state of East–West relations as a whole.

This concern was not restricted to the Labour government. By 1950, Bevin was openly sceptical of a diplomatic solution to East–West problems. The general election campaign of that year, however, brought Winston Churchill to the stump on this issue. In an important speech in Edinburgh, Churchill appealed for an East–West summit. Picking up this theme in the first foreign policy debate of the new parliament, Churchill argued that it was all very well to build up 'situations of strength' and then 'negotiate from strength' but, as he put it, 'time and patience – are not necessarily on our side'. The bipartisan nature of British concerns was confirmed after a Conservative government under Churchill was returned in October 1951. Churchill immediately returned to the issue of negotiations with the Russians. In a major speech at the Guildhall in London – to become a favoured venue for speeches about Détente – he talked in characteristically Olympian terms about the need to keep the giants from colliding.

The Americans, however, remained unmoved and 'uninfected' by what was becoming known as the 'English disease'. Calls for negotiations with the Russians were, after all, only to be expected from the man who had negotiated the 'spheres of influence' deal with Stalin. Nevertheless, there is some evidence that the Truman administration regarded Churchill's position on the desirability of East–West negotiations as a threat to American policy. The extensive preparations taken in Washington for Churchill's first visit as the new Prime Minister in January 1952 show how seriously the threat was taken. An interdepartmental steering group was set up to review all aspects of policy with the Soviet Union. The object was to enable the administration to justify its posture and, if possible, to persuade the Churchill government to align its policies more effectively. The specific concern was to show that there were no grounds for supposing that negotiations, particularly in a summit format, would achieve any positive results, although care was taken to 'avoid creating in the British mind any implication that we had abandoned the principle of negotiation with the Soviet Union'. These preparatory papers reveal, from an American perspective, the gulf that had emerged between British and American approaches to East–West relations and the extent of British fears about the longer-term direction of American policy.[2]

Britain as a Catalyst of Détente

Following his unsuccessful appeals for an East–West summit in 1950 and 1951, Churchill again took up the call for Détente (or, an 'easement of tension' as he preferred to call it) in a major speech to the House of Commons in May 1953. This time some progress was made in the form of negotiations between East and West on a number of issues during 1954–55. Negotiations began in January 1954 with a four-power foreign ministers meeting in Berlin, the first attempt since 1949 to reach a negotiated East–West agreement. No progress was made towards resolving the central problem of a divided Germany, but the conference did agree to include China in a five-power conference on Korea and Indo-China to be held in Geneva. This was significant because, although the Berlin conference had confirmed an East–West stalemate in Europe, the Cold War in Asia had reached another dangerous phase. The prospect of a French defeat in Indo-China had again highlighted the possibility of a general war. Foreign Minister Anthony Eden refused to back

Dulles's attempts to internationalize a military intervention, however, and he skilfully guided the Geneva conference to a negotiated settlement of the Indo-China problem (see Carlton, 1981).

Eden was also centrally involved in resolving the German rearmament issue and the Formosa Strait crisis, which cleared the ground for a four-power summit meeting in Geneva in 1955. At the summit, both sides took up fixed positions and no progress in the form of substantive agreements was forthcoming. But the Geneva meetings did not simply represent a continuation of the Cold War 'by other means'. The absence of a dramatic breakthrough in East–West relations did not mean that there were no important outcomes related to a Détente process. The so-called 'Spirit of Geneva' was not a figment of collective imaginations. It may have been a handy metaphor, but the new international atmosphere it was used to describe was real enough while it lasted. That a first summit since 1945 could be held at all without apparent rancour was a reflection of a new atmosphere, which in turn was underpinned by tangible settlements – the ending of the wars in Korea and Indo-China, and the signing of the Austrian State Treaty.

The most significant outcome of Geneva was the general perception that, as a result of the summit, a world war involving nuclear weapons had become less likely. There was a sense in which the leaders meeting together for the first time at Geneva were also coming to grips for the first time with the realities of a thermo-nuclear world in which both sides of the ideological divide now had the means of inflicting unacceptable destruction on the other. It was not only accepted on all sides that thermonuclear weapons could not be rational instruments of policy. Perceptions of a diminished likelihood of war were also powerfully affected by the more positive assumption that if a *modus vivendi* could be established and maintained between East and West, mutual possession of nuclear weapons could actually keep the peace, a *pax atomica*.

These perceptions were reinforced by the fact that the summit did produce the tentative beginnings of an East–West accommodation. The summit had precisely the effect that Dulles feared. It did involve on both sides a tacit recognition of the territorial status quo in Europe, and to that extent Soviet control of Eastern Europe had ceased to be a *casus belli*. Coral Bell makes this important point: 'War had become less likely, not because the two dominant powers had reached a negotiated accommodation, but because there had been an unspoken recognition of spheres of influence and the prospective penalties of disturbing them' (Bell, 1962, p. 130).

If the 'summitry' of 1955 can be appropriately described as a landmark in the Détente process, Britain deserves most of the credit on the Western side for the diplomatic activity culminating in the Geneva conferences. There was a striking continuity through the governments of Churchill and Eden in the British voice calling for a normalization of relations with the Soviet bloc, and for much of this period that voice belonged literally to Churchill. While the Americans were doing everything possible to avoid East–West negotiations, the French were preoccupied with Indo-China and the EDC, and Adenauer with securing sovereignty for the Federal Republic, Churchill contributed his international stature and his anti-communist credentials to the call for negotiations.

It was Churchill who responded to popular hopes of reduced tensions that followed the death of Stalin, just when those hopes were beginning to crumble. His May 1953 speech, with its piecemeal approach, recognition of the legitimacy of Soviet inter-ests and willingness to reconcile Soviet and West European security, received a favourable response from many quarters, including Moscow. It was Churchill again in 1954 who responded to and reinforced growing fears about the destructive power of hydrogen bombs and the dangers of their use, by renewing the call for an accommodation between East and West. His speeches on the 'balance of terror' theme also underpinned the *pax atomica* idea, which so influenced the international atmosphere of 1955.

Given the constraints on his freedom of action, it would be difficult to suggest what else Churchill could have done to promote Détente. With his speeches and his threats to meet Malenkov, with or without the Americans, he repeatedly risked a rift with Wash-ington despite the fact that the Anglo-American alliance had long been the cornerstone of his foreign and defence policies. He unashamedly used his wartime friendship with Eisenhower to press for a meeting with the Russians on every available opportunity. If Churchill was frustrated by American intransigence, he was also constrained by the limits imposed on Western diplomacy as a whole by the German reunification issue so adroitly promoted by Adenauer. What was undoubtedly the most galling constraint for Churchill, however, was the unwillingness of his Cabinet colleagues, and Eden in particular, to provide a united governmental front (see Carlton, 1981). This could not but weaken his position and detract from his efforts to press for a summit.

But if the question of the desirability of a summit bitterly divided Churchill and Eden (until the latter became Prime Minister), their common fears about the dangers of nuclear war linked the Prime Minister's efforts and the arguably more practical contribution of his Foreign Minister. To the extent that the 1955 Détente was built upon the foundation of agreements that resolved certain East–West conflicts that might have resulted in nuclear war, Anthony Eden made a significant contribution. Thus, both Churchill and Eden in their different ways played an important role in the Détente process. By 1955, it must be said, the British government was not alone in pressing for a Détente, but no other Western state matched the British commitment to a normalization of East–West relations in the first half of the 1950s.

Macmillan and Détente

The contribution of the Macmillan government to the next phase of Détente was even more distinctive. By the late 1950s, no other state on either side of the Iron Curtain was pursuing Détente with the persistence and the determination shown by the British govern-ment. During the Macmillan period as a whole, the centrepiece of British efforts to ameliorate East–West tensions was the patient diplomacy between the end of 1957 and the spring of 1960, which culminated in the Paris summit. Of more practical and immediate significance, however, as in the earlier period, were British efforts to play a conciliatory role in East–West crises. British policy in the Middle East, Berlin and Laotian crises between 1958 and 1961 illustrates the positive role of British diplomacy in reducing the possibility of military conflict between East and West.

With hindsight, the NATO Council meeting in December 1957 marked the revival of a persistent British advocacy of an East–West summit during the next two and a half years, which, given the restored relationship between Britain and the United States after Suez, could scarcely be ignored by the Eisenhower administration. If the pressure on Washington slackened in the spring of 1958 as attention was diverted to the test ban issue, it was resumed in the summer in the context of the Middle East crisis. Macmillan's positive response to Khrushchev's call for an immediate summit effectively took the initiative away from Washington. The Americans had only been prepared to agree to a foreign ministers' meeting that could be controlled by Dulles but, as Coral Bell argues, the Secretary of State was 'obliged to acquiesce by the tone of Macmillan's letter to Khrushchev and the necessity of avoiding the appearance of another rift with Britain' (Bell, 1962, p. 176).

With the onset of the Berlin crisis at the end of 1958, British Détente policy entered one of its most important phases. During the next twelve months, British diplomacy played a major role in relieving the tensions of the crisis and in so doing paved the way to the Paris summit. The achievement of British diplomacy during this period was to develop and sustain a momentum that transcended the immediate crisis and carried the other major states towards a summit meeting that none of them, certainly none of Britain's allies, wanted. To put it another way, British policy linked the chain of diplomatic developments in 1959 – Macmillan's visit to Moscow, the foreign ministers meeting in Geneva and the Eisenhower–Khrushchev summit at Camp David – that culminated in Paris in May 1960.

From this perspective, Macmillan's visit to Moscow in February 1959 was crucial. At the heart of the Berlin crisis was Khrushchev's ultimatum. Until that was lifted, it was difficult to see how there could be a negotiated settlement of the Berlin problem or a solution to broader East–West differences. Such blatant coercion, it might be argued, could only produce a united but negative Western response: meanwhile, tensions mounted as the Soviet deadline approached. Mikoyan's visit to the United States may have eased tensions somewhat and may even have put negotiations at some level back on the agenda, but the time-limit remained operative. It was Macmillan's dramatic initiative the next month that produced the lifting of the ultimatum by persuading Khrushchev to accept the idea of an interim foreign ministers' meeting to discuss Berlin. The Prime Minister still had the difficult task of persuading the allies to agree to that meeting, but the Moscow visit had succeeded in setting in train a process of negotiation and had effectively stabilized a very dangerous and unpredictable situation.

Having secured general agreement to the foreign ministers' meeting, Macmillan wanted the allies to regard that meeting as a preliminary to a summit. Eisenhower made an important con-cession to this view by agreeing publicly to this sequence, though he insisted on making his agreement to attend a summit conditional upon progress at the foreign ministers' meeting. Little was achieved of a substantive nature at the Geneva meetings and a diplomatic stalemate soon prevailed, but the fact that high-level talks were taking place seemed to make a further contribution to a reduction of tensions. More important in terms of the continuing impact of British policy, sufficient progress was made towards an interim Berlin settlement to enable Macmillan, in his correspondence with Eisenhower, to maintain the pressure on the President to follow through on his commitment to a summit. The unexpected outcome of this build-up of British pressure was the invitation to Camp David.

The Eisenhower–Khrushchev meeting in September 1959 restored the momentum of the negotiating process. The two leaders agreed to continue negotiations about Berlin without a specific time-limit hanging over the proceedings. Sufficient progress was made at Camp David for Eisenhower to declare that many of his objections to a four-power summit had now been removed. Thus, the meeting resolved the question of whether or not a summit would take place, even if important issues of timing and agenda remained to be discussed. The significance of this meeting, however, went beyond the fact that it led to another temporary improvement in the international atmosphere. From an American perspective, as Gaddis notes, the Camp David meeting 'served to legitimize the idea that negotiations were an appropriate means of dealing with Moscow, and that they could be undertaken without risking the unravelling of alliances or the appearance of appeasement' (Gaddis, 1982, pp. 195–7). This 'legitimization' of negotiations provided an important legacy that Eisenhower's successors could build upon.

The Macmillan government could claim much of the credit for this crucial meeting, not least because the Prime Minister's trip to Moscow had provided a recent precedent for a heads of government meeting. As Macmillan himself succinctly put it, 'the British broke the ice' (Macmillan, 1972, p. 81). It can certainly be argued that the February meeting encouraged Eisenhower to send and Khrushchev to accept the invitation to the United States. To the extent that unremitting British pressure on Washington was responsible for

Camp David, however, the government had been almost too successful. In the longer term, the more the leaders of the United States and the Soviet Union got into the habit of consulting directly, the less they needed Britain's services as an intermediary. Direct contacts were bound to limit the ability of third parties to influence the Détente process. In this sense, the Camp David meeting rather than the failure of the Paris summit six months later marked a turning point for Britain. Thereafter, British diplomacy as a major influence on the direction of East–West relations began to assume less significance.

But if Macmillan had lost the initiative several months before the Paris *débacle*, his government still managed to play a significant role in reviving and sustaining the Détente process after the collapse of the summit. The Prime Minister personally played a statesmanlike role in keeping open East–West contacts in the last six months of 1960, as dangerous and unpredictable a period in East–West relations as any since 1956. Continuing British attempts to promote Détente extended into the Kennedy period, illustrated by the extensive efforts to bring the 1961 crises in Berlin and Laos to a diplomatic solution. The British contribution to the Test Ban negotiations between 1959 and 1963, however, provides the best illustration of the catalytic role of British diplomacy during this period.

Britain and the Test Ban Negotiations

The Macmillan government had been ambivalent at best about the idea of negotiating a ban on nuclear tests, but once the Geneva talks were in progress a series of British initiatives played an important role in keeping them going and eventually reaching a successful conclusion in the form of the Partial Test Ban Treaty (see Wright, 1964). These initiatives helped to keep the Test Ban talks going at critical times, but they were arguably less significant than the sustained pressure on both superpowers, and on the Americans in particular, for an extended period. As one British negotiator put it, 'the initiative was in forcing the issue in private with the other two. We looked at Britain as being in a position of being able to bring the two sides together' (quoted in Nunnerly, 1972, p. 109).

What the Macmillan government managed to do remarkably

successfully was to influence domestic political processes in the United States and, to a lesser degree, in the Soviet Union. The existence of powerful lobbies in Washington and Moscow, who were actively opposed to any sort of Test Ban Treaty, meant that the respective leaders had very little room for manoeuvre. The well-timed meeting or more often a letter from Macmillan were only the most obvious manifestations of a sustained attempt to reinforce the often embattled positions of those who were fighting for a treaty. Leadership links and personal friendships, ministers, diplomats and scientists on the ground in Geneva were all used to maximize British influence. The fact that open disagreements with the United States were usually avoided and the semblance at least of a unified Western negotiating position maintained at Geneva only served to increase the effectiveness of British diplomacy.

Of the specific British initiatives, the most important in terms of affecting the outcome was Macmillan's March 1963 proposal that personal emissaries should negotiate directly in Moscow rather than in Geneva. The Cuban missile crisis had finally impressed upon both Kennedy and Khrushchev the need to make common cause as far as a Test Ban Treaty was concerned. But the extent of domestic opposition to a treaty that surfaced in Washington and Moscow in the early weeks of 1963 produced an *impasse* in Geneva and made it impossible for either leader to make any further moves to break the deadlock. Hence Macmillan's initiative, which triggered what turned out to be the final talks in Moscow four months later, was crucially important and perfectly timed (Seaborg, 1981).

The Prime Minister himself had no doubts about the significance of a Test Ban Treaty. In an interview given shortly before the Moscow talks, he maintained that there had been an East–West Détente since 1959 'not in treaties or documents but in tone'. If a Test Ban Treaty could be secured, he was convinced that 'one actual agreement would symbolise the detente which everyone knows has taken place but which it is difficult for any of us to grasp' (quoted in Sampson, 1967, pp. 232–3). Macmillan was not alone in explicitly linking the achievement of a Test Ban Treaty to Détente. Kennedy, and increasingly Khrushchev, particularly after the Cuban missile crisis, shared his sense of urgency about the need to establish a political climate in which the arms race could be controlled and other states prevented from acquiring nuclear weapons.

It can be argued, with hindsight, that the rather exaggerated hopes and expectations associated with the Test Ban Treaty were scarcely realized. Nevertheless, the Treaty was an important landmark in the Détente process. From an arms-control perspective, the Treaty was the first example in the nuclear age of a detailed and complex arms-control negotiation resulting in a positive outcome. As such, it provided a breakthrough, demonstrating that successful East–West arms-control negotiations were possible. The negotiations provided an important learning experience and the confidence to make further progress in other areas: the Treaty generated the necessary impetus for the series of arms-control agreements that followed in the late 1960s and early 1970s.

The structural link with the process of East–West Détente derives from the extent to which the treaty 'hastened the dilution of bipolarity' (Jacobson and Stein, 1966, pp. 500–1). Though both superpowers were clearly alarmed at the threat to their control of international relations posed by the proliferation of nuclear weapons to allied states, and this provided a powerful incentive to negotiate a Test Ban Treaty, paradoxically the signing of the Treaty only served at one level to hasten the diffusion of power in the international system, demonstrating as it did that neither bloc was monolithic. The Treaty helped to seal the rift between Moscow and Peking, and it further alienated France from the Western allies.

A British Approach to Détente

This brief overview of British policy in the 1950s and early 1960s suggests that there is substance to the Northedge argument that the positive British contribution to Détente has not received the attention it deserves. Whether or not Britain 'invented' Détente, British diplomacy certainly played an important catalytic role in the process of East–West accommodation during this period. The persistence and determination of British efforts despite constraints and setbacks contrasts favourably with the halting efforts of other major states to promote Détente. Moreover, from a structural perspective, the way in which successive British governments used Détente to create leverage and flexibility in an hegemonial system dominated by the United States would appear to provide a model for later French and West German Détente policy, analyses of which have received much more scholarly attention. Given also the significance of the British contribution to the development of the Cold War, however, it would be useful to conclude this chapter with some discussion of British attitudes towards Détente and Cold War, which will include an attempt to establish the historical antecedents of a distinctive British approach.

The attempt here to identify a British approach to Détente began by contrasting British and American attitudes to the Cold War in the late 1940s. While the Americans were beginning to see the Cold War as an end in itself, it was suggested that the British continued to regard the containment of the Soviet Union as a means to an end: the object remained the normalization of East–West relations. If, for the Americans, 'Cold War' and 'Détente' represented antithetical approaches to East–West relations, the British seemed to regard them as complementary, with Détente viewed as 'normal diplomacy'.

At first sight, British Détente policy in the 1950s seemed to reflect a preoccupation with summitry: normal diplomacy appeared to be synonymous with summit diplomacy. In November 1955, for example, Foreign Minister Harold Macmillan related the 'Spirit of Geneva' to what he called 'a return to normal human relations', by which he meant it represented flexibility, 'give and take', a readiness to discuss and negotiate (Frankland, 1958, p. 73). By implication, more 'Genevas' would bring about a normalization of East–West relations. But there are indications that there was more to a British view of Détente than 'mere' summitry. Churchill's idea of a new approach to East–West relations in 1953–54 consisted not only of restoring and expanding politico-diplomatic contacts but also of developing as many commercial, social and cultural contacts as possible (see Colville, 1981, p. 107).

Macmillan as Prime Minister worked hard to institutionalize summit meetings, but he clearly located summit meetings within a regularized cycle of negotiations. Reflecting on the Geneva experience, he now assumed that summit meetings would be more effective in terms of producing practical results if preparatory work were undertaken by lower level meetings. For Macmillan, Détente as normal diplomacy connoted permanent East–West contacts, interspersed by meetings of ministers, and regular if less frequent meetings of heads of government/state (see Macmillan, 1971, pp. 588–9). Speeches by his Foreign Minister, Selwyn Lloyd, in 1959 and 1960 suggest that the Macmillan government shared

Churchill's 'open contacts' view that normalized diplomacy of itself would not 'normalize' East–West relations; it was necessary to buttress political contacts by developing contacts across the spectrum of non-governmental relations. The object of British Détente policy, according to Lloyd, was nothing less than 'evolving a system of regulating international affairs' which would 'avoid a constant atmosphere of crisis'.[3]

If 'normal diplomacy' and 'open contacts' capture the essence of a consistent British view of Détente during this period, this provides a basis for locating attitudes towards Détente within traditional attitudes to war and peace that might in turn define a British conception of 'normal' international relations. British attitudes towards Détente, it can be argued, have their origins within traditional attitudes to diplomacy. Persistent efforts to mediate between the superpowers, like the policy of appeasement in the 1930s, illustrate what Lord Strang called the 'conciliatory quality' in British diplomacy (Strang, 1961, pp. 359–60). Historically, this distinctive quality was a product of two major factors: long experience of playing a leading role in the European diplomatic system and assumptions, dating from the nineteenth century, about how to maintain Britain's global position in the face of growing challenges to that position.

The idea of Détente as normal diplomacy suggests a link with a historically familiar European system, where conciliation was the important norm of diplomacy. Macmillan's description of a return to 'normal human relations' positively evokes that system, which, in contrast to the inflexibile bipolar system of the postwar period, was characterized by flexible, shifting alliances, shared interests in maintaining the system and the absence of ideologically oriented confrontation politics. If attitudes learnt over more than two centuries of experience in the pragmatic European school of diplomacy reappeared in attitudes towards Détente, those attitudes also reflected traditional assumptions related to the maintenance of Britain's global interests. It had long been assumed, certainly since the middle of the nineteenth century, that the preservation of peace was crucial to the protection of global politico–economic interests. The new Liberal orthodoxy argued that Britain's position of pre-eminence could best be maintained by pursuing a policy of 'free trade', which in turn necessitated the preservation of peace by conciliatory diplomacy.

It is important to note, however, in terms of trying to establish the historical roots of British attitudes to Détente, that it was never assumed, even by the most radical Liberals, that peace could be maintained solely by conciliatory diplomacy. It is useful in this context to differentiate between what may be called liberal and conservative approaches to problems of war and peace, which can be identified in nineteenth-century Britain (see Kennedy, 1981). Briefly, the liberal approach stressed the need for a foreign policy that was pragmatic and conciliatory but, suspicious of government-to-government diplomacy, tended towards the view that peace could best be maintained by expanding non-governmental contacts. The classic liberal belief in a natural harmony of interests that underpinned this view, however, was rejected by conservatives who, though not opposed in principle to conciliatory diplomacy, tended towards the older Realpolitik position, which held that conflict rather than harmony was the natural state of affairs. The conservatives believed that the necessary defence of national interests required firmness and resolution as well as conciliation. From this perspective, indeed, war could only be avoided by combining conciliation and strength, diplomacy and defence.

Elements of both traditions of thought, it can be argued, reappear in attitudes towards Détente and help to explain the relationship, from a British perspective, between Cold War and Détente. The notion of Détente as open contacts can be traced back to nineteenth-century liberal ideas, associated in particular with Richard Cobden. There was, as Geoffrey Goodwin has noted, a 'deep streak of Cobdenism in much of British thinking' in the postwar period (Leifer, 1972, p. 43). Conservative governments in the 1950s scarcely accepted Cobden's radical philosophy in its entirety, but Churchill's belief in trade as the 'great Mediator', for example, echoed Cobden's view of commerce as the 'great panacea'. The common assumption was that the extension of trade would act as a solvent of political differences and serve as an alternative to war.

If elements of liberal thinking about the relationship between commerce and peace reappear in attitudes towards Détente, the view of Cold War and Détente as two sides of the same coin reveals the continuing impact of British policy of the more conservative Realpolitik tradition, particularly with respect to the assumed linkage between the avoidance of war and a balanced relationship between diplomacy and defence. Collective security in a North

Atlantic context may have replaced a 'balance of power' role in Europe, but the assumption persisted that conciliatory diplomacy, however desirable for all the reasons touched on here, would only be effective if wedded to a credible structure of defence or, in a nuclear context, deterrence. Notions of balance and complementarity pervade descriptions of a proper relationship between the political and military components of British foreign policy during this period. Two examples will serve to illustrate. At his meeting with Eisenhower in Bermuda in December 1953, according to John Colville's account, Churchill advocated a policy that linked simple notions of Détente and deterrence and seemed to go to the heart of Churchill's conception of Détente

Both at the Plenary Conferences and in private Churchill advocated what it amused him to call his policy of 'double dealing'. This he described as a policy of strength towards the Soviet Union combined with holding out the hand of friendship. He said that only by proving to our peoples that we should neglect no chance of easement could we persuade them to accept the sacrifices necessary to maintain strong armed forces (Colville, 1976, p. 240).

Exactly four years later, in December 1957, Macmillan expounded on a similar theme. On his return from the NATO Council meeting in Paris he summed up the British position to the House of Commons. 'Our policy . . . is really two-fold, and I think in essence simple. It is a firm and powerful NATO, from the military point of view, but always ready to discuss and negotiate on a practical basis to obtain practical results.' In his memoirs Macmillan adds: 'in a single phrase it could be described as "arm and parley" (Macmillan, 1971, p. 340).

It is appropriate that the final word should be left with Northedge. He maintains that there was nothing inconsistent about British policy-makers advocating collective defence within NATO and Détente with the Soviet Union. It was, he argues, 'the continuation of a long-standing British principle of foreign policy, which Lord Templewood, the Sir Samuel Hoare of the 1930s, called the "double line" – a strong defence posture combined with the energetic search for accommodation' (Northedge, 1980, p. 21). Moreover, Northedge argues elsewhere, with the exception of the (first) Thatcher government, 'British policy towards the Soviet Union since 1945 has followed a consistent course of armed vigilance against aggression, coupled with a search for détente and all manner of agreements to ease international tension, as and when opportunities for making these presented themselves' (Northedge and Wells, 1982, p. 133).

Chapter 6: Notes

1 A clear statement of this position occurs in an interdepartmental steering committee paper prepared for the forthcoming visit to Washington in January 1952 (Truman, 1952, Steering Group Negotiating Papers, 6 January TCT D–1/5A 108B).
2 Truman, 1951, 1952, Steering Group Negotiating Papers, 28 December 1951, TCT D-1/3A 92C; 29 December 1951, TCT D-1/4A 93A; 6 January 1952, TCT D-1/6 93B.
3 The relevant extracts from Lloyd's speeches can be found in King, 1963, pp. 69–94 and in Goff *et al.*, 1964, pp. 2–3.

7 The United States and Détente: A European View

PHIL WILLIAMS

It is sometimes claimed that nostalgia is not what it used to be. The same could be said about the East–West Détente of the 1970s.[1] Détente looks very different now from the way it appeared in the early 1970s. In 1972 and 1973, it was the United States, under Nixon and Kissinger, that was most enthusiastic about Détente. The West Europeans, in contrast, were more cautious and more sceptical. Although the Federal Republic pursued its Ostpolitik with considerable vigour and enthusiasm, elsewhere in Europe there was greater ambivalence. Europeans welcomed the reduction of tensions, but there was apprehension about the improvement in superpower relations. It was feared, especially in France, that Soviet–American Détente might lead to superpower condominium – at the expense of America's allies. This concern over collusion was perhaps most evident in the European reaction to the Prevention of Nuclear War Agreement of 1973. Critics of the accord claimed that the United States was subordinating its obligations to allies to the desire to establish agreed codes of behaviour with Moscow. The French, in particular, castigated the agreement as an attempt by the superpowers to ensure that if an East–West conflict occurred in Europe it would be limited in ways that maintained both the Soviet and American homelands as sanctuaries. Such fears tended to caricature an agreement that had been drafted in part by a senior official in the British Foreign Office, Thomas Brimelow (Kissinger, 1982, pp. 278–82). Nevertheless, they symbolized the ambivalence that existed in Europe about Détente. This ambivalence continued even during the latter half of the 1970s, when many Europeans expressed reservations about certain aspects of the proposed SALT II Treaty, and it took a major effort by the Carter administration to assuage Allied concerns.

The other important element in West European attitudes to

Détente was what might be termed a cautious scepticism. Détente was not regarded as the resolution of fundamental differences between East and West, but simply as an attempt to move towards an international order in which differing ideological and political systems could safely coexist. Détente was seen simply as a means of stabilizing East–West relations and rendering them less dangerous and less acrimonious than in the past.[2] It was hoped that increased commercial and cultural contacts would be facilitated by the relaxation of tension, and that this in turn would feed back into the process and encourage a further relaxation. Yet it was precisely because Détente was viewed as a process that Europeans did not develop excessive expectations about it. They recognized that it could be stopped or even reversed. Many officials also remained highly sceptical about Soviet motives and objectives, believing that Détente, although to be welcomed, might prove to be little more than a shift in Soviet tactics.

The United States, in contrast, seemed much more euphoric about Détente in the early 1970s. President Nixon talked about building a 'new structure of peace', and at times Détente was portrayed as marking the end of superpower rivalry. If Détente was oversold by the Nixon administration, it was also overbought by a public and Congress weary of the burdens of the Cold War. Although both Nixon and Kissinger essentially saw Détente in sepia tones as a way of managing the rise of Soviet power and disciplining Soviet behaviour in a period when the United States was constrained by the domestic reaction against the Vietnam War, their public presentation was in bright Technicolor. The expectations that were generated were inevitably doomed to disappointment. Indeed, one of the ironies is that, as the United States began to reappraise and then to reject the policies of the early 1970s, the West Europeans were left in a position where they became the major advocates for continuing Détente. Their expectations about Détente may have been limited, but the gains were nevertheless very real. The growth of East–West trade, the lowering of barriers to human contacts and the general relaxation of tensions gave the Europeans a vested interest in the maintenance of Détente. It was not surprising, therefore, that, in the aftermath of the Soviet invasion of Afghanistan, the Europeans claimed that Détente was 'divisible' – Soviet activities in the Third World should not affect the continued normalization of relations in Europe itself. The United States, with a global perspective, was not willing to differentiate policy towards the Soviet Union in this way.

Indeed, the dominant image of the Soviet Union in the United States in the later 1970s was similar to that which had prevailed in the 1950s and had once been characterized by Kissinger as an 'inherent bad faith model'. Although President Carter resisted the pressure to base his policies on such an assessment, the Soviet invasion of Afghanistan led him to admit that his more benign appraisal of the Soviet Union had been badly wrong. Afghanistan was widely seen in the United States as the culmination of a Soviet offensive in the Third World that had started in 1973 in the Middle East, had involved the use of Cuban proxies in both Angola and the Horn of Africa, and had given the Soviet Union considerable gains in countries as diverse as South Yemen and Vietnam (see Porter, 1982). This Soviet activism and assertiveness was linked by some commentators to a shift in the strategic balance. American superiority had given way to parity and, in the view of critics such as Paul Nitze and other members of the Committee on the Present Danger, to inferiority. The United States, as a result of Vietnam, had allowed its military position to deteriorate in what was subsequently characterized as a 'decade of neglect'. The idea of a 'window of vulnerability', whereby the Soviet Union could destroy a large proportion of American land-based missiles and deter any retaliatory strike by Washington because of the continued threat to American cities, became a dominant theme in the American debate towards the end of the 1970s. It was claimed that a superpower confrontation would result in a Cuban missile crisis in reverse, with the United States compelled to back down as a result of Soviet strategic superiority (Tyroler, 1984, p. 41). A direct connection was made between the strategic balance and Soviet geopolitical behaviour, and it was alleged that the 'window of vulnerability' would provide Moscow with a 'window of opportunity' in which it could further enhance its position in the Third World at the expense of the United States.

The implication of this analysis, of course, is that the Soviet Union alone was responsible for the demise of Détente. Soviet behaviour had revealed that Détente was no more than a tactic to lull the United States into a false sense of security while Moscow engaged in a sustained and calculated effort to outflank the West in the Third World. Afghanistan was simply another, if more brutal and direct, manifestation of the fundamental Soviet impulse to establish global predominance. It was particularly disturbing, though, because of its proximity to the Persian Gulf. Fears were aroused that Moscow would be able to threaten Western access to vital oil supplies.

The Europeans, while not oblivious to the dangers, did not fully share the American appreciation of the new Soviet threat. Nor were they happy with the American reaction. The last year of the Carter presidency and the first two years or so of the Reagan administration was a period of considerable tension and turmoil in Atlantic relations. The differences concerning both the nature of the threat to Western security and the most appropriate response were intensified by the imposition of martial law in Poland – a development that led to a major row between Allied governments and Washington over the imposition of sanctions against the Soviet Union and the question of extra-territorial jurisdiction.

The effect of these splits, which have continued, albeit in more muted form, into the second half of the 1980s has been far-reaching. Some members of the Reagan administration as well as members of Congress have concluded that the European Allies have little backbone and are unable to take the hard decisions that their security requires. For their part, the Europeans have become apprehensive about what is seen as American belligerence and unilateralism. The result has been that the Western Alliance tends to suffer continually from the politics of symbolism: issues confronting the Alliance tend to be elevated by Washington into texts of European fidelity to the Alliance and to be viewed in European capitals as tests of American wisdom and restraint. Although the differences have now taken on their own momentum, the underlying source can be found in contrasting interpretations of the experiences of the 1970s. Put very crudely, the orthodoxy in the United States offers what might be termed a 'purist' interpretation of the decline of Détente and of subsequent events, while European assessments tend to reject this in favour of more complex and mixed explanations. This is not to suggest that there is a single European assessment of the decline of Détente. There are many views of what went wrong. Some on the right tend to sympathize with the Reaganite attribution of responsibility to the Soviet Union, while some on the left tend to see the United States as the major villain. From an analytic point of view, however, neither position is satisfactory. Indeed, the major concern should not be with identifying villains but with pinpointing causes. In some respects it is easier to do this from Europe than from the United States, where challenges to the conventional wisdom tend to be dismissed as soft on the Soviet Union.

The thesis offered here is intended to be analytical rather than polemical. The main contention is that Détente resulted from a coincidence of interests between the superpowers that was only temporary, that the inherent tensions and potential contradictions between Soviet and American conceptions of Détente made it unlikely that it would be sustainable, and that the changes in American domestic politics interacted with Soviet behaviour in the Third World in ways that made the demise of Détente inevitable.[3] Throughout the analysis the focus is on American domestic politics, as neither the rise nor the fall of Détente can adequately be understood without taking this into consideration.

The Détente of the 1970s can be traced back to the change in Soviet–American relations that occurred after the Cuban missile crisis. The confrontation over Soviet missiles in Cuba had under-lined the common interest of the superpowers in avoiding nuclear war. While this prompted moves towards a relaxation of tension, however, it was not sufficient to generate more than a very limited Détente. The transition from a limited to a full-blown Détente occurred in the late 1960s and early 1970s because other interests of the United States and the Soviet Union coincided. Both super-powers concluded independently that moves towards a more restrained and less acrimonious relationship would be advan-tageous. Their reasons for this conclusion, however, were not only very different but were in many respects antithetical. It is even possible to discern what can be termed an opportunities–constraints dichotomy: what were seen as problems or constraints by one superpower were seen as opportunities by the other.

There was a series of issues on which this was the case. The Sino–Soviet split, for example, was a problem for the Soviet Union but opened up new opportunities for triangular diplomacy by the United States. Similarly, the Soviet economy made the Soviet leadership look to the West for trade and technology transfer; this was seen by the United States as an opportunity to exert greater influence on Soviet behaviour through the linkage strategy devised by Kissinger. Conversely, the emergence of a government in the Federal Republic of Germany that was committed to improving relations with Eastern Europe offered new opportunities for Moscow, but was seen as a problem by Kissinger and Nixon, who were concerned about the divisive effect of a fragmented Détente. Indeed, one reason why Kissinger became such a strong proponent of Détente was that he hoped American involvement in the process of normalization in Europe would enable the Nixon administration to determine the pace and scope of change.

Even more important was the Soviet attainment of strategic parity. This was viewed as a problem by the United States, but was regarded in Moscow as a considerable achievement that should bring with it recognition of political parity by the United States. Having made great sacrifices to overcome its position of strategic inferiority, the Soviet Union wanted and expected to be acknowledged as an equal by the United States and accredited with the same rights and responsibilities that normally accrued to Washington. Yet such recognition would not be granted easily by a United States that had become accustomed to primacy in the international system and that had accepted the limits of power in Vietnam only with great reluctance. Indeed, it was Vietnam that provided the final opportunity – constraint dichotomy. Not only did the United States want Soviet assistance in extricating itself from the war but it also wanted Soviet co-operation in ensuring that the consequences of this for the American position in the world were manageable. In other words, the limits on American power and will as a result of the war in Vietnam impelled the United States towards a more regulated relationship with the Soviet Union. Yet these same limits offered new opportunities for Moscow to implement policies fully consonant with the Soviet status as a superpower.

In view of all this it is hardly surprising that there were very different conceptions of Détente in Washington and Moscow. Each side promoted a conception of Détente that promised to advance its interests and, although there was some acknowledgement of the basic common interest of the superpowers in the avoidance of war and crises that could lead to war, in practice it was the divergent interests and contrasting priorities that were most evident.

The Soviet leaders saw Détente as both an extension of the peaceful coexistence strategy and an acknowledgement of the new Soviet status as a superpower. It was emphasized in Soviet pronouncements that Détente did not mean an end to the class struggle and would not prevent the Soviet Union continuing to support wars of national liberation. These notions ran counter to an American conception of Détente that was concerned predominantly with regulating Soviet behaviour and encouraging Soviet restraint. Indeed, Kissinger saw Détente as a means of inducing Soviet 'self-containment' when the United States was no longer able to enforce containment through traditional military means (Hoffman, 1983, p. 90). The emphasis on regulation and restraint was a tacit recognition by the United States that, for the moment at least, it could not compete effectively in an unrestrained competition. Yet Soviet restraint could not simply be taken for granted. It had to be encouraged. This was to be done through Kissinger's linkage strategy, which emphasized inducements for Soviet good behaviour and penalties for Soviet misdeeds. The idea of enmeshing the Soviet Union in a web of interdependence that would give Moscow a stake in restraint was predicated on the assumption that the United States, for all its handicaps, was still the dominant power in the relationship and could still determine the rules under which the game would be played. The problem, however, was that this strategy was never fully executed because of domestic impediments.

One of the ironies of the Nixon–Kissinger concept of Détente is that the domestic problems that had made it necessary also made it impossible to implement in the way its proponents wanted. The breakdown of the foreign policy consensus and the loss of confidence by the traditional policy-making establishment, which provided an important backdrop to the adoption of Détente, caused difficulties for the new policy. Vietnam was a crucial factor in the promulgation of Détente and in its failure. The centrifugal influences in American political life unleashed by the Vietnam war were not easily contained, and the congressional resurgence – which was precipitated by Vietnam and facilitated by Watergate – undermined a linkage strategy that depended for its success on strong centralized control.

The resurgent pluralism in US foreign policy also provided opportunities for the critics of Détente. Henry Jackson, aided by a powerful staff in which Richard Perle and Dorothy Fosdick were both prominent, was unhappy about Détente virtually from the outset. And, in his attempt to destroy what was seen as a one-sided relationship, Jackson had several assets. His network of supporters went well beyond Capitol Hill and even included key figures in the administration such as Secretary of Defense, James Schlesinger.[4]

One commentator has even described Schlesinger as 'Jackson's man' in the national security bureaucracy (Cox, 1976, p. 144). Although this is an exaggeration, there was clearly a close affinity of interest and outlook between the two men, an affinity that was strengthened by the personal antipathy they shared towards Henry Kissinger. Other key figures in the Jackson network were Fred Ikle at the Arms Control and Disarmament Agency (ACDA) and Admiral Zumwalt, while it was given added power by Jackson's close relationship with George Meany, head of the United States Trade Union movement, the AFL-CIO (see Stern, 1979). Furthermore, the objections to the administration's policy found a ready and sympathetic outlet in the Evans and Novak column in *The Washington Post*.

Through the use of this network, Jackson was able to conduct a campaign of guerrilla warfare against the SALT process, a campaign which was made easier by the ambiguities of SALT I (see Garthoff, 1985, pp. 169–74). Through this campaign Jackson did much to erode the support for arms control with the Soviet Union. It was not arms control, however, but the issue of Jewish emigration that enabled Jackson to move to a more direct assault on the legitimacy of Détente. By focusing on a specific form of human rights violations, Jackson was able to combine an appeal to conservatives who disliked Détente with an appeal to liberals who disliked repression. Furthermore, he was able to invoke the rich vein of crusading moralism that had been temporarily obscured by the reaction against the Vietnam war but which remained a powerful impulse in the American approach to international politics, and which was fundamentally antithetical to the amoral Realpolitik stance adopted by Henry Kissinger. Jackson's campaign against Soviet restrictions on Jewish emigration also won the support of the Jewish community in the United States, especially in the aftermath of the Middle East War of 1973. Although Kissinger argued with some justification that Détente had made it easier to avoid a superpower confrontation, it was Jackson's assessment of Soviet behaviour as being wholly inconsistent with Détente that predominated. Indeed, George Will claimed that, in the aftermath of the 1973 war, anti-communism became respectable once again (*Washington Post*, 19 February 1974).

The implication of all this is that the fragmented political system and the skill of his political opponents made it difficult for Kissinger to mobilize a consensus behind his Détente policy. The campaign on Jewish emigration also affected his policy in a more direct way, however. In the administration's conception of Détente, the carrot for Soviet restraint was increased Soviet–American trade. An agreement to facilitate this had been reached in October 1972. Among the package of measures was an American commitment to grant the Soviet Union 'Most Favoured Nation' (MFN) status and to provide substantial credits for Soviet purchases from the United States. The Jackson–Vanik Amendment, however, linked MFN status to the liberalization of Jewish emigration (Stern, 1979). This was facilitated by the fact that Kissinger himself had espoused the notion of linkage, thereby providing it with a degree of legitimacy. What Jackson did was to extend its applicability from Soviet foreign policy to domestic policy and to take it from the realms of quiet diplomacy and transform it into a much more overt and public weapon. The Soviet Union could hardly fail to reject such an approach, especially after a series of private concessions only encouraged Jackson to increase his demands. Perhaps even more disappointing to the Soviet Union, however, was the Stevenson Amendment, which established restrictions on the amount of credits available to Moscow. Although the Stevenson Amendment was at one stage a possible substitute for the Jackson Amendment, the fact that they were running on parallel tracks, and Kissinger's relative neglect of the credits issue, led to the passage of both pieces of legislation.

For the Soviet Union the whole episode was both distasteful and disappointing. Not only had Moscow been subject to public pressure but the United States had failed to deliver on part of the Détente bargain. It has even been suggested that it was in the aftermath of the Jackson–Vanik and Stevenson Amendments that the Soviet Union decided to embark on a more assertive and expansionist policy in the Third World (Gelman, 1985, p. 58). Whether or not a conscious decision to this effect was taken is not entirely clear. It does seem likely, however, that the episode, and Kissinger's 'exclusionary diplomacy' in the Middle East, led some Soviet decision-makers to conclude that Détente was a one-way-street in America's favour and that the Soviet Union should not, therefore, ignore any opportunities that opened up in the Third World. What the Politburo did not seem to realize was that Soviet activities in the Third World would feed back into the American debate and strengthen the arguments of Jackson and his associates.

The restrictions on trade were also important in revealing the future direction of American policy. In retrospect, Jackson's actions can be understood as a reassertion of the moral impulse in US foreign policy. They represented the beginnings of a moral rehabilitation of US foreign policy that was to lead through the Carter emphasis on 'human rights' and culminate in Reagan's 'evil empire' statement.

The Jackson campaign and subsequent developments revealed clearly that the United States was never very comfortable with Détente. This is not entirely surprising. The concept of Détente itself is a European notion and has an abstract quality that was alien to many Americans. Furthermore, the depth and extent of US antipathy towards the Soviet Union militated against the ready acceptance of a mixed relationship in which continued competition went hand-in-hand with unprecedented attempts at co-operation on issues such as arms control. The Cold War had a clarity and simplicity that were lost in Détente. The difficulties the United States had in coming to terms with the mixed relationship were evident in the debate that took place about the linkage between arms control and Soviet geopolitical behaviour. The contrast with the Soviet approach could hardly have been more stark. During the SALT I negotiations, the fact that members of the Soviet delegation did not mention the American invasion of Cambodia, convinced their American counterparts, perhaps for the first time, that the talks were serious (Smith, 1980, p. 137). This willingness to compartmentalize relations was even more apparent in the spring of 1972, when the American mining and bombing of Haiphong Harbour did not prevent the Moscow Summit going ahead.

Because of the centralized control, of course, it is relatively easy for the Soviet Union to adopt a compartmentalized approach in which competition in some areas coexists with co-operation in others. Acceptance of the mix is also made easier by a Soviet approach that sees developments in terms of the dialectic of history. For the United States, with an absolutist approach to foreign policy, this is much more difficult.

Indeed, the great advantage that Jackson and other critics of Détente had was that they appealed to principles and values that were deeply entrenched in American history and tradition. For a nation founded on competitive individualism and the protestant ethic, the Soviet system was anathema. It appeared even more so because it was embedded in a state that, in the 1970s, seemed to be augmenting its military power and expanding its influence with remarkable success. The antipathy towards Moscow was so deeply rooted in American political life that policies based on a moderate, albeit still tough-minded, appraisal of the Soviet Union could not easily gain acceptance. It is difficult, therefore, to argue with the conclusion of one analyst that the architects of the new approach failed to 'relate the policy of Détente to important American beliefs and values' (Caldwell, 1982, p. 98).

For all this, it should not be assumed that Kissinger was soft on the Soviet Union. His own assessment of Soviet behaviour was not as far removed from that of Jackson as is sometimes suggested. The concomitant of this, of course, is that the United States did not cease to compete with Moscow either in terms of strategic armaments or geopolitical competition. The contention that the 1970s was a 'decade of neglect' has some relevance to conventional forces. Yet even here the problem was related not so much to Détente as to the Vietnam War, which had distorted priorities within defence and delayed the modernization and re-equipment of American general-purpose forces, especially those of the navy. At the level of strategic forces, however, the 'decade of neglect' is pure fiction. The Reagan administration has virtually suggested that, during the 1970s, the United States opted out of the strategic arms race. The facts are very different. Although it is true that the United States did not deploy new families of ICBMs in the way that the Soviet Union did, this was the result of differing procurement philosophies and moderniz-ation programmes. United States strategic modernization took the form of MIRVing both land-based and sea-based missiles. During the period when SALT I was in force, the United States deployed an average of three new warheads every day. In addition, the United States had a highly effective research and development process that produced the strategic cruise missile capable of being launched from platforms on land, at sea or in the air. As one study has noted, 'when it became apparent that the cruise missile would be a supremely elegant weapon and one that clearly reflected US superiority in the relevant technologies, there emerged a strengthening determination to find a slot for it in the strategic arsenal' (Huisken, 1981, p. 186). This was reinforced by the desire to demonstrate that the United States was able to compete effectively against the Soviet Union despite the domestic problems resulting from Vietnam. In short, the very concerns that the United States might be on the verge of a decade of neglect played a large part in ensuring that the 1970s were anything but this in terms of the American strategic arsenal.

Nor did Détente involve a one-sided competition in the Third World. Nixon and Kissinger were aware that they could not compete with the Soviet Union in terms of military intervention. But this did not prevent them from competing by other means. In the Middle East, in particular, Kissinger's overriding goal was to exclude the Soviet Union. This was the major element in his approach before, during and after the October 1973 War, and one that succeeded brilliantly. Strategic parity was not to be accompanied by political parity in the Middle East or elsewhere. Indeed, although there were aspects of Soviet behaviour during the war that were disturbing, it was Kissinger's insensitivity to the fate of the Egyptian Third Army in the face of the Israeli cease-fire violations that gave Moscow little alternative to making threats to intervene. Far from perceiving an opportunity for enhancing its position, the Soviet Union was engaged in an exercise in damage limitation and attempting to prevent the complete defeat of one of its most important clients.

Kissinger's approach to the Yom Kippur War reveals clearly that his embrace of Détente had not led to an abandonment of cold war thinking. Indeed, both Nixon and Kissinger displayed a marked tendency to see events in the Third World through a bipolar lens and to attribute more responsibility to Moscow for unfavourable developments than was warranted. This was evident during the Jordan crisis of 1970 and the Indo-Pakistan war of 1971. After Watergate, Kissinger became even more neurotic about the Third World, so much so that American interests in a particular region were identified almost completely in terms of Soviet involvement. If Moscow were involved, then this was seen as a challenge requiring a decisive response to demonstrate that, despite its domestic problems, the United States could not be trifled with.

The clearest case of this was Angola in 1975. Although the Soviet and Cuban involvement in Angola is widely seen in the United States as an example of Soviet behaviour that contravened the rules of Détente, this interpretation is wrong on two counts. In the first place, it overlooks the differences between the US and Soviet conceptions of Détente, differences that rendered the rules ambiguous if not irrelevant. The Soviet Union had not accepted that the principle of restraint should take priority over its support for national liberation struggles. Secondly, by suggesting that the Soviet Union alone was being interventionist is to distort a situation in which both sides played a highly competitive game. Becoming involved in this game was a major tactical error by Kissinger, who, unlike the Soviet leadership, had to operate in a domestic environment hostile to covert activities or overt military intervention in the Third World. Indeed, it is hard not to sympathize with Nathaniel Davis, the Assistant Secretary of State for African Affairs, who resigned in July 1975 because his proposals for finding black African solutions to an African problem were disregarded by Ford and Kissinger in favour of escalating American involvement. Although it is not certain that the course advocated by Davis would have been more successful than the Kissinger policy, there are strong grounds for suggesting that, in the circumstances of 1975, it was a more sensible option. Kissinger's policy combined the worst of all worlds. It involved a competition that the United States Congress, because of concerns about another Vietnam, was unwilling to support. Yet, by backing the same factions as South Africa, and possibly even engaging in tacit co-operation with Pretoria, the United States helped to legitimize the involvement of the Soviet Union and the introduction of Cuban combat forces in support of the MPLA. Indeed, it was only after Congress had refused to provide further aid for the American-backed factions that Kissinger began to emphasize that the Soviet Union was not playing by the rules. By this stage, however, such assertions seemed to suggest simply that Kissinger was a bad loser, and a hypocrite to boot.

Kissinger's somewhat belated denunciations of Soviet behaviour were also counter-productive in that they strengthened the position of the critics of Détente. In 1976, these critics could be found not only among the Jackson Democrats but also among the right wing of the Republican Party. In order to protect himself from the Reagan challenge for the Republican nomination, President Ford banned the word Détente from his political vocabulary. Even so, the policy towards the Soviet Union that had been developed by Nixon and Kissinger and maintained by Ford was subjected to ridicule. Reagan claimed that its principal accomplishment was 'the acquisition of the right to sell Pepsi-Cola in Siberia', while on the debit side the United States had become 'Number Two in a world where it is dangerous – if not fatal – to be second best' (quoted in Ford, 1979, p. 373).

Although Ford was able to stave off the Reagan challenge, he was unable to defeat that mounted by Jimmy Carter.

When Carter arrived in the White House in January 1977, Détente was in limbo. It was not clear in which direction US–Soviet relations would move. If Détente was to be revived and sustained then the Soviet–American relationship would require very careful management. This was something that the Carter administration was ill-equipped to provide. There were times when it seemed to walk away from the superpower relationship in favour of an emphasis on North–South relations. And when it did attempt to provide a degree of management, its efforts appeared improvised, confused and ultimately counter-productive. The result was that an administration, which began with a commitment to 'world order' issues, and which in 1977 and 1978 saw the Soviet–American relationship as only one dimension in a new approach to international politics, became increasingly preoccupied with the Soviet challenge and pressured into adopting a firmer stance against Moscow. The attempt to transcend containment, establish a new agenda to manage interdependence, and reassert a managerial form of American leadership was dropped in favour of the restoration of traditional policies that once again exhibited the obsession with Moscow that Carter had been so anxious to end.

Indeed, the late 1970s was a period in which there was a vacuum in US foreign policy and one that the Carter administration was unable to fill. The President's own preferences ran up against a rival set of prescriptions put forward by the Committee on the Present Danger (CPD). The CPD was a bipartisan group, albeit one in which disaffected Democrats loomed large. Its members believed that Carter represented the McGovern wing of the party rather than the Jackson wing and was insufficiently sensitive to the Soviet peril. The CPD contended that 'the principal threat to our nation, to world peace, and to the cause of freedom is the Soviet drive for dominance based upon an unparalleled military build-up' (Tyroler, 1984, p. 3).

This theme and the CPD campaign in general struck a responsive echo in a United States increasingly frustrated at what was seen to be a decline in power. Its message was a simple one – in contrast to Carter's more complex approach to foreign policy – and appealed to deep-rooted American attitudes. The very things that had made it difficult for Nixon and Kissinger to establish a consensus in favour of Détente facilitated the attempt by the Committee on the Present Danger to re-establish the old cold war consensus.

The Committee was assisted in this by several factors. The Carter administration's own ineptness and several key decisions such as the cancellation of the B–1 bomber created a widespread impression that the President was unreliable on national security issues. Furthermore, the Committee had a tacit ally in the administration in National Security Adviser, Zbigniew Brzezinski. Indeed, Brzezinski argued very vigorously that arms control with the Soviet Union should be made dependent upon Soviet geopolitical restraint. Although Secretary of State Vance contended that arms control was too important to be held hostage to events elsewhere, Brzezinski's arguments helped to legitimize the use of linkage by those who were hostile to the SALT process (Marder, 1981). Indeed, Soviet activities in the Horn of Africa and the introduction of a large contingent of Cuban troops seemed to reinforce the arguments of the CPD that the Soviet Union was engaged in a relentless expansionism that posed a major threat to American security.

The Committee on the Present Danger also found a sympathetic audience because of the general trend towards conservatism in American politics. This trend had several distinct but mutually reinforcing strands, ranging from the rise of the populist new right, through the emergence of the more intellectual neo-conservatives to the resurgence of religious fundamentalism, and was reflected in the emergence of an extreme right-wing group in the Senate led by Jesse Helms. Indeed, by the late 1970s, the Senate, which in the first half of the decade had been the most liberal institution in the American government, had become the most conservative. After 1976, Republican Senators were no longer constrained in their criticism of Détente by loyalty to a Republican President. Furthermore, Carter was an easy target for their attacks.

Ironically, Carter himself may have contributed to the resurgence of anti-Soviet sentiment with his human rights campaign. By replacing Kissinger's amoral approach to foreign policy with an ideological approach, Carter prepared the way for the restoration of American strength. Self-righteousness only made sense if combined with American military power. Soviet tyranny could not go unchallenged, and Soviet expansionism could not go unopposed. This tendency to focus on the Soviet threat was reinforced by what might be termed the scapegoat factor. The 1970s was a very traumatic decade for the United States. It had, for the first time in its history, lost a war, and there was a strong feeling that American power and will had declined – a feeling intensified by Carter's claim that the United States was suffering from 'malaise'.

The result of all this was that the Carter administration itself began to change. After a year or so in which 'world order' themes had predominated, the administration began to focus much more of its attention on the competition with the Soviet Union. Largely through the initiatives of Brzezinski, the United States through 1978 normalized relations with China, thereby fulfilling the logic inherent in the Kissinger notion of triangular diplomacy. In 1979 Carter announced that he would go ahead with deployment of the mobile MX missile. For the President himself this decision was anathema. Nevertheless, Carter recognized that it was a political necessity if the SALT II Treaty, which was concluded in June, was to stand any chance of obtaining Senate approval. By this stage, SALT was all that was left of Détente. Subsequent events demonstrated, however, that arms control could not stand apart from the overall Soviet–American relationship. Brzezinski's later comment that 'SALT Two was buried in the sands of the Ogaden' was astute (Brzezinski, 1983, p. 189). Linkage was a fact of life in the American political system – albeit one that had been nurtured by Brzezinski himself.

The opposition to SALT II was significant for several reasons. It reflected a lack of confidence in the Carter administration's handling of foreign policy, and a lack of faith in the Soviet Union as a reliable partner in Détente. It was also an expression of disquiet at the stage of the strategic balance – the campaign by Paul Nitze and the Committee on the Present Danger had found a receptive audience. In political terms, it marked an alliance between the Democratic right led by Perle and Jackson and the New Right symbolized by Helms and such groups as the American Conservative Union and the Conservative Caucus. Nor was the campaign for SALT ratification helped by the Carter administration's tardiness in mobilizing support for the Treaty.

Nevertheless, the Carter administration did begin to generate support for SALT II by combining it with a tougher stance towards Moscow. At one stage it appeared that the Treaty might receive Senate approval as part of a package that also consisted of a 5 per cent increase in the defence budget and the NATO decision to deploy Cruise and Pershing missiles in Europe. By its actions in 1979, however, the administration had gone a long way towards accepting the assessment of American security needs offered by the Committee on the Present Danger. In view of this, its own actions seemed to be too little too late. This was especially the case after the issue of the Soviet combat brigade in Cuba exploded. Essentially this was a fabricated issue, used by the conservatives to undermine support for SALT II and by the liberals to demonstrate that they too could be tough on the Russians. It also showed the lack of institutional memory in the American government. The overall result though was to delay SALT consideration on the Senate floor. Consequently, the Treaty was overtaken by events. The Iran hostage situation – which appeared to underline once again American weakness – and the Soviet invasion of Afghanistan ended what remaining chance there was of SALT's being approved. The President requested that further consideration of the Treaty be deferred indefinitely. Even without Iran and Afghanistan, however, it is far from certain that the Senate would have consented to ratification. At the very least, it seems likely that SALT II would have been amended in ways that might have required renegotiation.

Afghanistan was significant because of its effect on Carter. The President acknowledged that he had learnt more about the Soviet Union from the invasion than from the previous three years of dealing with Moscow. Accordingly he made clear that the United States had vital interests in the Persian Gulf, which it would be prepared to defend if Moscow attempted to go any further. However, for those who saw the Soviet action not as an isolated incident but as the culmination of the Soviet offensive in the Third World that had started in the mid 1970s, Carter's admission was simply one more example of the naïvety of a President who, although he now rejected Détente, was neither an effective nor an enthusiastic cold warrior.

Even without Afghanistan it is unlikely that Détente could have survived the changes in American domestic politics that were taking place throughout the 1970s – not least because Détente became associated too closely with American decline. The Reagan Presidency can be understood in terms of an attempt to reverse this decline and restore American strength, credibility and will. This has not been a comfortable process for either America's allies or the

Soviet Union. There is a tendency to believe that under Reagan's successor it will all be different. What this ignores, though, is that Reagan is in the mainstream of postwar United States foreign policy. It was Kissinger with his amoral foreign policy and Carter with his reluctance to accept the 'inordinate fear of communism' who were the anomalies. The Détente developed in the early 1970s was an aberration in United States foreign policy. The short-term reappraisal provoked by Vietnam has given way to a long-term reaffirmation of the major themes in American foreign policy established by the Truman administration. Negotiation from strength is the only game in town!

Chapter 7: Notes

1 For a comprehensive analysis of Détente, see Garthoff (1985).
2 For a fuller analysis of British attitudes, see Williams (1986).
3 This notion, together with much of the subsequent analysis, is developed more fully in Bowker and Williams (1987).
4 This idea of networks was suggested to the author by Larry Smith.

8 The Soviet Union and Détente

MIKE BOWKER

The United States soon became disillusioned with the process of superpower Détente. Support was badly shaken when both the superpowers threatened direct intervention in the Arab–Israeli war of 1973. Three years later, this disillusionment had reached such a level that President Ford prohibited the use of the word Détente during his election campaign. President Carter made some attempt to revive the concept – albeit in a rather different form – but, because of the continued military build-up and Soviet actions in the Third World, the revival was shortlived. After the invasion of Afghanistan in December 1979, Carter did not even try to get Senate ratification for SALT II. By the turn of the decade, Détente was dead in the United States. Even the majority of liberals viewed Détente as an experiment that had failed.

This attitude contrasts sharply with the Soviet experience. In Moscow, Soviet leaders have consistently expressed support for the process of Détente. Some in the West thought this commitment might be a result of Brezhnev's close identification with the policy. But it seems to have been more than that. For, although Brezhnev has been heavily criticized for many things, Détente has remained firmly on the political agenda. The latest Party Programme stated quite categorically that the 'party will seek the development of the process of international détente' (*Pravda*, 26 October 1985).

How can this asymmetry of attitudes towards Détente be explained? The Soviets say the reason is simple – Moscow is more genuinely committed to peace than is Washington. America, they argue, had difficulty in coming to terms with the emergence of the USSR as the military equal of the United States. As a result of the Soviet Union's growing military strength, the United States was no longer able to dominate the international scene to the extent to which it was accustomed. This decline was exacerbated by a series of crises that had nothing to do with Moscow: the Vietnam war, the Watergate scandal, and the economic recession in the West. Nevertheless, the Soviet Union became a scapegoat for the American loss of confidence. In an atmosphere of growing paranoia, the military–industrial complex, accompanied by the New Right, gained in influence, and this conservative coalition was able to undermine support for Détente.

The Soviet view has much to commend it. American domestic politics was certainly an important factor in explaining the demise of Détente. Nevertheless, the Soviet case is weakened by its pious self-righteousness. The USSR seemed slow to appreciate that its military build-up and Third World policy created genuine fears, not only in the United States but throughout the world. Although these aspects are frequently exaggerated in the West, there is no doubt that they are important factors in any analysis of the fall of Détente.

Unfortunately, however, the current US administration is equally one-sided in its apportionment of blame. Détente, according to the present Reagan administration, was little more than a one-way street in favour of Moscow. In such circumstances, it was scarcely surprising that the Soviet leadership favoured the policy. In this view, Moscow entered into Détente merely as a tactic to further its long-term foreign policy aims. As a result, Détente, from the American perspective, was a mistaken policy from the start. But what are the Soviet long-term foreign policy aims? And to what extent can we talk about Détente being a one-way street?

There are two long-term aims of Soviet foreign policy that are readily identifiable. The first, the desire to avoid superpower conflict, is rarely mentioned by the US administration in this context. The reason is not difficult to surmise, for this goal is entirely consistent with Western interests. Khrushchev, back in the 1950s, declared nuclear war was unwinnable, and this message has been taken up by his successors. The second, the inevitable victory of international communism, on the other hand, is frequently cited in the United States as a threat to Western interests. In fact, Marxist–Leninist dogma such as this always leaves considerable room for interpretation. No doubt there are those in the Soviet Union who see it as a call to revolutionary action. The opposite, however, is also true, for the fact that the victory is inevitable could justify the Soviets adopting a relatively passive posture in world affairs. Although it could not explain the heightened activity of the

USSR in the Third World from the mid-1970s, it might explain Moscow's relaxed attitude towards setbacks, such as in Chile, Egypt and Somalia. Perhaps this aspect of the ideology is better equipped to adopt the philosophy of 'you win some, you lose some' – or, in Leninist terminology, 'two steps forward, one step back'.

The Soviet ideology also stresses consistently that communism will not come about through the 'export of revolution'. Gorbachev was most explicit on this point at the 27th Party Congress, when he said: 'Today we are firmly convinced that pushing revolutions from outside, and doubly so by military means, is futile and inadmissable.' (*Pravda*, 26 February 1986) This statement reflected the view that the dynamic of socialist revolutions is not military but economic and social. This aspect of the ideology seems to be one not so much to be feared by the West as to be encouraged. After all, it is only in the military sphere that the Soviet Union can effectively compete with the West. In economic terms the USSR is becoming a less attractive model for the Third World.

It should be noted, however, that the Soviet Union, as Brezhnev clearly expressed it at the 26th Party Congress in 1981, also reserves the right to defend states from the export of counter-revolution (Communist Party of the Soviet Union, 1981, p. 81). This seems to be fairly flexible terminology, when it is remembered that those words were used to justify the invasions of Hungary in 1956, Czechoslovakia in 1968 and Afghanistan in 1979 (Arbatov, 1973, p. 262; *Pravda*, 24 February 1981).

All this only serves to show that Marxism–Leninism allows a wide variety of interpretation on foreign policy matters. A close reading of ideological texts will, therefore, have no more than peripheral value in understanding policy actions. The ideology has elements that can justify non-antagonistic as well as antagonistic relations with the West. This also applies to the Soviet concept of Détente.

Was Détente a one-way street in favour of the Soviet Union? There can be no doubt that the Soviet leadership believed the policy of Détente brought advantages, but this is hardly sinister. No government would ever consciously pursue a policy it deemed contrary to its interests. Benefits included the regularization of the superpower competition, the stabilization of relations between the two military blocs in Europe, an increase in East–West trade, as well as certain gains in the Third World. Nevertheless, it is simply incorrect to describe Détente as a one-way street. The Soviets, as will be shown throughout this chapter, also suffered setbacks during the 1970s. Indeed, by the time of Brezhnev's death in 1982, his Détente policy looked in disarray: East–West relations were at a low ebb, arms control was moribund, trade sanctions had been imposed on the Eastern bloc after Afghanistan and Poland, and renewed fears of encirclement had arisen in the late 1970s when China signed treaties with Japan and the USA.

Yet despite these, and other setbacks, the Soviets managed to maintain a consensus in favour of Détente. How was this done? The nature of the political system makes organized opposition to the government impossible, and this contributes to stability and continuity in Soviet policy. Nevertheless, debates do occur and these have produced reform and changes in other policy areas. Systemic factors are important, but they can only provide a partial explanation for the Soviet commitment to Détente.

More positively, Brezhnev was successful in formulating policies that gained the consent of a broad-based coalition, including reformist and orthodox elements in the Soviet elite. When problems arose, this coalition, unlike the one in the United States, proved strong enough to survive and prosper. The natural supporters of Détente may have been the more reformist members of the elite, but it was important for Brezhnev also to gain the acquiescence of the more orthodox. To this end, assurances were given to the party apparatus, and to the military in particular. The party was told that the commitment to the Third World would not cease, and that the ideological struggle with capitalism would continue. As Brezhnev said at the 24th Party Congress in 1971, when he unveiled his so-called 'Peace Programme': 'We declare that, consistently pursuing a policy of peace and friendship among peoples, the Soviet Union will continue to wage a resolute struggle against imperialism and will administer a firm rebuff to the intrigues and sabotage of oppressors. We shall continue, as in the past, steadfastly to support the struggle of the peoples for democracy, national liberation and socialism' (*Current Digest of the Soviet Press*, 1971, p. 13). The military was also placated by guarantees of parity with the United States. Therefore, Détente did not mean that the USSR envisaged a smaller role in international affairs. On the contrary, the Soviets believed that they had the right to participate in world affairs as the equal of the United States. They further believed that, with the

acceptance of military parity, the United States had also acknowledged that fact. The US administration was, therefore, correct in
perceiving competitive elements in the Soviet concept of Détente.
However, as will be shown later in this chapter, competitive
elements were not absent from the American view of Détente

One other aspect of the Soviet concept of Détente, which also
received criticism in the West, should also be outlined here. In the
view of Moscow, Détente was divisible or compartmentalized.
Western governments have tended to argue that this was unacceptable. Real Détente, as they termed it, was possible only if the USSR
agreed to moderate its repressive domestic policies and ceased
adventurism in the Third World. It was hoped that this was to be
achieved through a policy of linkage. Kissinger was doubtful that
much could be achieved in the area of human rights, but he hoped to
restrain Soviet adventurism in foreign policy by offering certain
benefits, such as arms control and East–West trade. In this way, the
Soviet Union would be given a stake in the stability of the
international system, and a web of interdependence would evolve.

The Kissinger plan was fine in theory, but it had one serious
drawback – the complete rejection of the concept of linkage by the
Soviets. There were many reasons for this rejection. First, linkage
sounded patronizing. It implied that Moscow was the junior
partner, and that Washington had made some one-sided goodwill
gestures towards the Soviet Union. This was not how it was seen
inside the Kremlin. The Soviets argued that the Americans had been
forced to the negotiating table by the fear of the growing military
might of the USSR. The Soviet Union could no longer be ignored
by the United States in international affairs. Secondly, the benefits
of Détente were seen as mutual. The Americans needed arms
control as much as the Russians. The Soviets may have had
economic imperatives to cut back on the growth of defence expenditure, but Nixon too was coming under pressure from Congress
and public opinion because of the increasingly unpopular Vietnam
war. Trade was no different. After all, the United States was not
offering economic aid. Moscow was paying for imports with
hard-earned hard currency. The mutuality of East–West trade was
most clearly revealed by the American farmers, when they objected
to the grain embargo in the aftermath of the Afghanistan invasion.

The Soviet rejection of linkage did not only have negative aspects,
however. It was also relevant in understanding the asymmetries in

the superpowers' attitudes towards Détente. In the United States, the policy was oversold by the administration. Kissinger never believed that Détente would end superpower rivalry, but in order to gain domestic support this was implied. When the rivalry continued, the administration had simply provided the ammunition for its critics. Kissinger's concept of a web of interdependence proved too delicate a construct to survive for long. When one strand was broken, the web inevitably disintegrated altogether.

The Soviets' compartmentalized vision of Détente, on the other hand, proved to be a more hardy organism. Naturally, if gains were made across the board, that was only to be welcomed, but failure in one area did not necessarily lead to the abandonment of Détente in another. This attitude not only made it more likely that superpower Détente would be prolonged, it also created a firmer base for support at home. For, as the academician Georgi Arbatov, head of the influential US and Canada Institute, has expressed it: 'How can you put forward as a precondition of solving one difficult problem, the solutions of other problems, sometimes even more difficult? This is a sure way of pushing oneself into a dead end. So what linkage does is stimulate the interconnections to work for a deterioration of relations in all spheres, including the most important' (Arbatov, 1983, p. 77).

So far, it has been shown that there was a broad-based coalition in favour of Détente in the Soviet Union. This coalition was maintained by containing within it a competitive component. In the rest of this chapter we shall consider the extent to which the Soviet concept of Détente also had a co-operative element. Did the Soviet Union make unilateral gains? Did Moscow make concessions? How genuine was the Soviet commitment to Détente? Was there, as some Western analysts have suggested, a significant shift in policy, or even an abandonment of Détente from the mid-1970s – in practice if not in rhetoric? How can we explain the Soviet military build-up and the heightened Soviet activism in the Third World? To try to answer these questions four areas will be studied separately: Europe; East–West trade; arms control; Third World policy.

1   Europe

It could be effectively argued that Europe was the area of maximum success for Soviet Détente policy. The relations between the two blocs were improved and stabilized through the German treaties and the CSCE process. Indeed, the signing of the Helsinki Final Act in the summer of 1975 could be seen as the high point of European Détente. These agreements' main focus was to acknowledge officially what had been acknowledged unofficially long before – the division of Europe into two ideological and military blocs.

Nevertheless, even Détente in Europe, which successive General Secretaries have singled out as an area of progress, could not be described as a one-way street for the USSR. The Helsinki Final Act, from the perspective of the Soviet Union, may have recognized the division of Europe, but in the West it was remembered for its provisions on human rights. These provisions created difficulties as groups were set up in Eastern Europe to monitor their governments' compliance with the agreement. The follow-up conferences in Belgrade and Madrid were dominated by the human rights issue, and were, as a result, extremely acrimonious. Relations between the two blocs were also worsened by the decision on either side of the ideological divide to deploy a new generation of medium-range weapons. Shortly afterwards, the crises in Poland and Afghanistan brought relations in Europe to their lowest level since the beginning of the Détente process.

For the Soviets, however, the problems were not confined to those between the blocs. Eastern Europe remained an area of potential danger for the USSR. Brezhnev had hoped that Détente would aid alliance management, but legitimacy for Soviet hegemony over Eastern Europe remained elusive. This was most apparent in Poland, where a series of disturbances throughout the 1970s culminated in the birth of Solidarity in 1980.

Détente has done little to alleviate any of these problems. There are those in Eastern Europe who would say it has exacerbated them. Nevertheless, despite these doubts, leaders in the USSR and the Eastern bloc have remained, generally speaking, in favour of Détente. This was re-emphasized at the 27th Party Congress, when Gorbachev, in the one reference to Détente in his report, said he wanted relations with Europe to progress to a more lasting phase – to a phase he called 'mature détente' (*Pravda*, 26 February 1986).

2   East–West Trade

It was hoped that an increase in East–West trade, credit and technology transfer would give a timely boost to the ailing economies of Eastern Europe without incurring the political risks of reform. There was agreement in Moscow about this general policy line, but debate centred on a number of subsidiary issues. For example, how much trade with the West was optimal to aid the economy? And would East–West trade risk the political independence of the Soviet Union in the light of Kissinger's linkage policy?

Brezhnev was initially sceptical about the benefits of East–West trade, but by the time he unveiled his Peace Programme in 1971 he had been converted. By 1973, he had become one of its most fervent supporters, putting – or so it seemed – his personal prestige on the line.

Yet East–West trade was, at best, only a partial success. Trade increased with the West during the period – particularly with Western Europe – but it never provided the hoped-for boost to the economy, which continued to perform badly. A Soviet official has played down the importance of East–West trade in an interview with a Western journalist: 'Even at the height of détente,' he said, 'imports of technology and equipment added at most half a percent to our industrial growth' (*The Economist*, 16–23 March 1985, p. 22). The main reason for this poor showing was the inflexibility of the Soviet-type economy. It was unable to utilize imports efficiently and find hard currency markets for manufactured goods. As a result, all of Eastern Europe fell into debt in the late 1970s. Again, Poland was the worst case. By the time martial law was imposed in 1981, the country was virtually bankrupt. In the light of these problems, it was scarcely surprising that the debate on East–West trade was reopened in the 1980s. There is no sign, however, despite the disappointments, that Eastern Europe wanted to move in the direction of greater autarky.

In the case of the United States, the problems with trade started earlier and emerged in a rather different form. The US–Soviet trade agreement of 1972 had built up hopes of significant trade between the superpowers. But these hopes were stifled by two Amendments. The first, the Jackson–Vanik Amendment, sought to link the level of Jewish emigration to the granting of Most Favoured Nations (MFN) status to the Soviet Union – MFN status simply meant the lifting of import tariffs on Soviet goods. Despite the Soviet rejection of linkage, Moscow made some concessions on this issue, but they proved insufficient for Congress, which demanded a written pledge on future levels of emigration. Then came the Stevenson Amendment, which attempted to limit credit to the fairly low figure of $300 million over a four-year period. These two Amendments were something of a public humiliation for the Soviet Union, and for Brezhnev personally. When both Amendments were passed in the Senate, it was almost inevitable that the US–Soviet trade agreement would be abrogated. Abrogation was announced in Moscow on 10 January 1975.

It has been suggested that, because of this setback, Brezhnev was forced to abandon Détente and adopt a more adventurist policy in the Third World (see, for example, Gelman, 1984, pp. 58–9; Gelman, 1985, p. 58; Volten, 1982, pp. 129–32). There would have been some justification, if the Soviets had adopted such an attitude. After all, Kissinger saw trade as the key to his linkage strategy. With that gone, why should the Soviet Union act in a restrained manner? In fact, there is little evidence to suggest that this explains the increased Soviet activism in the Third World. Such a view would only make sense if the Soviets accepted linkage. But they did not.

Certainly, Brezhnev was under pressure in this period, especially at the Central Committee plenum of December 1974. But all evidence suggests that Brezhnev's Détente policy remained intact. Brezhnev rose in stature inside the Politburo in the mid-1970s, and continued to speak positively of Détente. Indeed, from about 1975, there were more frequent references to the process of Détente being irreversible. At the same time, Brezhnev redoubled his efforts to improve relations in Western Europe. For example, in the summer of 1975, after long-drawn-out negotiations on CSCE, the Soviets suddenly acquiesced on the inclusion of articles on human rights in the Helsinki Final Act. And, despite the recent furore over the Jackson–Vanik Amendment, the right of emigration was included in the agreement. Brezhnev did not even give up on East–West trade. It is interesting to observe that this campaign was a reasonable success, for trade with the West – even with the United States – continued to rise in the 1970s (see International Monetary Fund, 1977, p. 291; Dibb, 1986, p. 227).

3 Arms Control

The Soviets continued their military build-up throughout the 1970s. The military has always been very influential in Soviet politics and, as noted earlier, Détente was only acceptable after the attainment of rough parity with the United States. There was never any chance of Moscow willingly giving up this hard-won position. Perhaps, as a result, it was not surprising that the SALT process did no more than regulate the arms race – it did not halt it. The one attempt to cut existing levels, by the Carter administration in 1977, was rejected by the Soviets. The rejection was further evidence of the strength of the military in domestic Soviet politics. But that was not the only reason for the Soviets' negative reaction. Brezhnev said he was not in principle against deep cuts, but objected to the manner of Carter's proposal. After long negotiations, including an interim agreement in 1974, he wanted to see SALT II accepted and ratified before moving on to new proposals. The fact that Carter quickly withdrew his offer shows that Brezhnev's argument had some force (Garthoff, 1985, pp. 584–90, 801–15; Arbatov, 1983, pp. 72–3).

Nevertheless, Carter's proposals reflected Western disappointment with the arms-control process. This is not the place for a review of the pros and cons of SALT, but it is worth pointing out that, despite the rapid military build-up of the USSR, a rough parity continued to exist between the superpowers throughout the period. There is no evidence, as is sometimes suggested, that the Soviets took advantage of Détente to steal a significant advance on the United States (see Table 8.1).

It is left to the opponents of Détente to prove that an absence of arms-control agreements could have produced a better strategic position for the United States. Given the influence of the military in the Soviet Union, and the relative weakness of the executive and defence lobby in the USA in the wake of Vietnam and Watergate in the mid-1970s, this seems unlikely. Even SALT II does not appear so one-sided in hindsight. President Reagan described the unratified treaty as fatally flawed, yet he continued to abide by its restrictions – minimal though they were – until 1986.

It has also been argued that, as Brezhnev declined in health, the military gained in influence. The military was always a powerful factor, but there is little evidence that it was in the ascendancy in this

Table 8.1   The Soviet–American Strategic Balance

| | 1967[1] | | 1972[2] | | 1974[3] | | 1979[4] | |
	US	USSR	US	USSR	US	USSR	US	USSR
ICBMs	1054	500	1054	1527	1054	1400	1054	1400
SLBMs	576	100	656	459	656	655	656	923
Bombers	650	155	430	156	390	156	348	156
Missile and bomber warheads	–	–	5700	2500	7650	2500	9200	6000

Source: Holloway (1983), pp. 59–60.
[1] January 1967: first SALT proposal by the United States.
[2] May 1972: SALT Accords signed; balance on 30 June 1972.
[3] November 1974: Vladivostok Accord: balance on 30 June 1974.
[4] June 1979: SALT Treaty signed; balance on 30 September 1979.

period. Indeed, there are a number of facts that may point to the reverse being true.

First, there was some form of reassessment of military strategy around 1976, in which the Soviets appeared relatively satisfied, at last, with the nuclear and conventional balance. In the light of this review, all Soviet officials (military and party) made a firmer commitment to parity, to the 'unwinnability' of nuclear war and to arms control. This new campaign was opened by Brezhnev's speech at Tula in 1977, in which he explicitly repudiated the idea of superiority as a Soviet aim. This speech, in the judgement of the American political scientist, Raymond Garthoff, reflected 'a real desire by the Brezhnev leadership to level off Soviet defense programs and reduce the long-standing high level of Soviet defense expenditures and to stabilise strategic parity' (Garthoff, 1985, p. 586; for the Tula speech, see *Pravda*, 19 January 1977). At the 26th Party Congress in 1981, Brezhnev condemned the idea that nuclear war could be won: 'They [the Americans] want people to believe that nuclear war can be limited, they want to reconcile them with the idea that such a war is permissible. But that is sheer deception' (*Pravda*, 24 February 1981). This contrasts sharply with some earlier statements, particularly from the military. For example, the then defence minister, Grechko, contested the view that nuclear war was unwinnable: 'They hope in this way,' he said, 'to convince people of the durability of capitalism, a historically doomed social system' (Grechko, 1977, p. 172).

Secondly, there were a number of personnel changes at this time that may have favoured the arms controllers. The most notable involved the appointment of Ustinov to the Defence Ministry after the death of Grechko in April 1976. Ustinov was no dove, but the fact that he was the first civilian in the post since 1955 symbolized a change of emphasis in military matters. He seemed more willing than his predecessor to side with the party in debates against the defence establishment. For example, when Ogarkov, the then chief-of-staff, tried to re-open the debate on the winnability of nuclear war, Ustinov came out firmly against him – in company, it must be said, with the majority of the defence establishment. (For summaries of the Ustinov–Ogarkov debate, see Weickhardt, 1985a and 1985b.)

The arms control process may also have looked more attractive for economic reasons. The Soviet economy always had problems in developing new technologies, but this was exacerbated in the high technology revolution of the 1970s. It was not clear that the Soviet Union could always depend on matching NATO's modernization programme. The military balance in the late 1970s could have been viewed in Moscow as the most favourable possible in the real world, and arms control, notably SALT II, could help to preserve it. Arms control could have been even more urgent in the light of declining growth rates. It is worth noting, too, that the latest CIA statistics indicate a parallel decline in the growth of Soviet defence expenditure (see Table 8.2).

Table 8.2 Average Annual Growth Rates of GNP and Defence Expenditure in the USSR during five-year periods, in percentages (CIA estimates)

Period	GNP	Defence spending
1956–60	5.9	−2.1
1961–65	5.0	7.6
1966–70	5.2	4.5
1971–75	3.7	4.0
1976–80	2.7	2.0

Source: US Senate Committee on Foreign Relations (1986) pp. 22, 26.

All Western analysts rightly caution against reading too much into such statistics, but, taken in the round, there is little to suggest

an increase in the influence of the military during the 1970s. There is
no evidence that Moscow abandoned Détente for arms-control
reasons. A rise in the influence of the military could have explained
the heightened activism in the Third World, but, in fact, it is
necessary to look elsewhere for explanations.

4   The Third World

The Soviet military build-up and the violation of human rights were
important elements in undermining the support in the United States
for Détente. The main accusation against the Soviet Union,
however, concerned Soviet behaviour in the Third World after the
mid-1970s. Soviet adventurism in those areas was deemed by the
United States to be incompatible with Détente.

It is important to note, however, that at the time commonly
referred to as the high point of Détente (1971–73), the United States
was very active in the Third World – most notably in Vietnam,
Chile and the Middle East. In Moscow, in fact, the debate did not
centre on whether Soviet activism would antagonize the West, but
whether the Soviets were seeking concessions from Washington at
the expense of their Third World allies. For example, the superpower summit of May 1972 took place only two weeks after Nixon
had ordered the bombing of Hanoi and the mining of Haiphong
harbour. This was widely interpreted as a provocative act. Yet,
despite protests inside Moscow, led by Shelest, the summit went
ahead, and SALT I, the ABM Treaty and the Basic Principles
Agreement were all signed.

When the United States agreed to withdraw its troops from
Vietnam in the spring of 1973, it was a boost for Soviet diplomacy
and the supporters of Détente in Moscow. But any thought of the
Americans reducing their commitments in the Third World was
soon rebuffed when Allende was overthrown in Chile with the aid
of the CIA in September 1973. The coup caused a stir in the
international communist movement. But the Soviet government
responded with restraint. The Soviet press was slow to criticize the
United States and continued to press the case for a peaceful road to
socialism. At the 25th Party Congress in 1976 – a time when the
Soviet Union was said to have adopted a more adventurist line –
Brezhnev declared: 'The Chilean tragedy has by no means invali-

dated the communist thesis about the possibility of different ways of revolution, including the peaceful way, if the necessary conditions exist' (Communist Party of the Soviet Union, 1976, p. 35).

Nevertheless, Glassman, in his book, *Arms for the Arabs*, claims to have traced a connection between the Pinochet coup in Chile and a more opportunistic line for Moscow on the Middle East (Glassman, 1975, p. 123). Whatever the truth of this hypothesis, it is certainly not the case that the Soviet Union gained from the ensuing Arab–Israeli war of October 1973. It brought the superpowers closer to a direct confrontation than they had been since the Cuban missile crisis in 1962. This challenged the central tenets of the Détente relationship on both sides of the ideological divide. The war had other ramifications. Egypt was weaned away from the Soviet sphere by the United States, and relations between Cairo and Moscow continued to deteriorate until the Treaty of Friendship and Co-operation was abrogated in 1976.

Concern in Moscow over this major setback in an area of vital strategic importance has been well documented by Western analysts, yet the majority in the USSR seemed to keep faith with the policy of Détente. Arbatov summed this view up some ten years later, when he said: 'in the context of détente it was possible to localise this conflict (the October war) and even work out a basic framework for a comprehensive settlement in this area. I simply shudder at the thought of what might have happened if that war had occurred in a climate of tensions, such as exists now' (Arbatov, 1983, p. 195).

Thus, it becomes clear that at the height of Détente, Moscow made no gains in the Third World. The United States withdrew from Vietnam, opening up future opportunities for the USSR, but it was the United States that had been more active in the Third World. Washington, therefore, appeared to believe that a policy of super-power competition in the Third World was compatible with Détente. Why should not the Soviets believe the same? The main difference in attitudes seemed to lie, not in the respective concepts of Détente, but in the reaction to the other's activism. Moscow persisted with Détente, while the United States, on the other hand, became increasingly disillusioned and finally abandoned the last remnants of the policy after the Soviet invasion of Afghanistan.

This still does not confront the question of why the Soviets took a more activist line in the mid- to late 1970s. There appear to be two overriding factors – the opening up of opportunities and the growing ability of the USSR to exploit them.

A series of revolutions exploded in the Third World, beginning in 1974 with the overthrow of Haile Selassie in Ethiopia and the collapse of the Portuguese empire, which led to changes in many African states, including Angola. The following year, Vietnam, Laos and Cambodia were 'lost' to the West, and take-overs followed in Iran, Afghanistan, Nicaragua and Grenada in the late 1970s, and in Rhodesia in 1980. As can be seen from the above, the world was highly unstable in this period, but, although the instability opened up opportunities for the Soviets, they were not instigated by them.

Nevertheless, the Soviet Union was better placed than ever to take advantage of these opportunities. This was not an accident. The USSR had built up its conventional forces and transport facilities since at least the mid-1960s. It was, therefore, in a position to transport Cuban troops and military equipment to distant Angola in 1975 and to Ethiopia in 1977. This development greatly concerned the West, although the Soviet ability to assist distant allies remained inferior to that of the United States. Nevertheless, the willingness of Moscow to give military aid to the MPLA in the Angolan Civil War seemed to be the start of a relatively short but more activist period.

The Soviet behaviour did not connote an abandonment of Détente, for both superpowers had a competitive view of Détente. There was no need, therefore, to explain the rise in Soviet activism in terms of growing Soviet optimism about the changes in the correlation of forces or, as is also sometimes argued, in terms of disillusionment because of American actions over trade. Opportunities arose and, like the United States earlier, Moscow chose to exploit them.

Nevertheless, the United States was bound to see Soviet activism as a threat to its own interests. It is suggested here, however, that the threat was exaggerated, since the USA tended to characterize Soviet behaviour as an ideologically inspired spiral of activism. There may be some truth in this description, but it crucially fails to explain why Moscow intervened in some areas in the 1970s and not in others.

To explain this, it is necessary to consider more conventional aspects of superpower rivalry. For example: what are Soviet and Western interests in a particular area? On the basis of this calculation, what are the chances of a regional conflict blowing up into a superpower confrontation? What have been the Soviet commitments to the area over time – in economic, political and military terms? What are the advantages or disadvantages of instability in the region? What are the chances of the Soviet ally emerging victorious with Moscow's aid? And, finally, what are the economic costs of participation to the Soviet Union?

Thus, in Central and Latin America, despite considerable unrest, the Soviet Union maintained a low profile throughout the 1970s. With the exception of Cuba, its interests in the area were minimal. It was recognized as being in the American sphere and, while fostering unrest would disadvantage the United States, Moscow was not in a good geographical position to render effective aid. As a result, Moscow feared the economic costs if 'another Cuba' entered the socialist fold. Moscow has fairly consistently advocated the peaceful road to socialism in the region, despite the dismal record of this policy.

The Middle East, on the other hand, is an area of vital interest to Moscow. Unfortunately, it is also of vital interest to the West, for economic reasons and because of America's close links with Israel. There is a permanent danger, because of its importance to both East and West, that a regional crisis could soon bring direct superpower involvement. For this reason, the USSR, since its experience in 1973, has used its considerable influence with caution. It refused to back its allies, Syria and Iraq, when they attacked their respective enemies, the Lebanon and Iran. And, despite links with Libya, Moscow has generally kept Gadaffy at arm's length.

Africa is often cited as the continent where Moscow was most adventurist. Angola and Ethiopia are cases where the Americans publicized their concern about Soviet actions. In both cases the troops involved were not Soviet but Cuban, and in both cases the side Moscow supported was also backed by the Organization of African Unity. On Angola two further points should be made to put the Soviet actions into perspective. First, the United States was quite prepared to compete for influence in the country until the Clark Amendment prevented further aid. Only then did Kissinger begin to talk of such competition as being against the spirit of Détente. Secondly, the massive Soviet airlift and sealift of troops and equipment only took place after the South Africans had attacked Angola. The Soviet intervention could be justified, therefore, in terms of a defensive action. Likewise, in Ethiopia, troops were inserted to repel an attack from another Soviet ally, Somalia. There were grave fears at the time that Moscow would use the war to try to impose some kind of Marxist–Leninist federation on the Horn of Africa – an idea touted by the Soviets prior to the conflict. But this never happened. The Cuban and Ethiopian troops remained inside the border. This Soviet caution could have been presented as a victory for Détente and American diplomacy – particularly as Ethiopia had already slipped out of the American sphere, and Somalia soon abrogated its Friendship and Co-operation Treaty with Moscow. Instead, with a curious relish, the United States chose to depict the events in the Horn as a victory for Moscow and as a humiliating defeat for Washington. Brzezinski typified this approach when he said that SALT lay buried in the sands of the Ogaden – a desert of no economic or strategic interest to either East or West.

This still leaves the case of Afghanistan – the one area outside the Warsaw Pact where Soviet troops have intervened directly and in force. This action was clearly not only going to strain East–West relations but also to create fear and suspicion among other states in the region. Nevertheless, the American reaction was excessive. President Carter at one point described it as 'the greatest threat to peace since World War II' (quoted in Bradsher, 1985, p. 82). Yet the United States had no interest in the country and had tacitly accepted it as being in the Soviet sphere. On the other hand, it was in the USSR's southern backyard and clearly of vital strategic interest. Furthermore, its military and economic commitment to the Afghanistan regime had increased dramatically in the period since the April Revolution of 1978. The Soviets invaded as civil war threatened to consume the country.

This is not to justify Soviet actions in Afghanistan or elsewhere in the Third World. However, Afghanistan was a different case from either Angola or Ethiopia. To portray all these actions as part of a pattern – a spiral of activism – is a largely spurious construct. Opportunities arose and Moscow exploited them. With hindsight, however, the opportunities seem less important and the successes less dramatic. The Soviet allies in the Third World tend to be poor and unstable. For example, Angola and Ethiopia, embroiled in civil wars, no longer seem such strategic assets. Afghanistan now looks more like a danger contained than an opportunity exploited. Nevertheless, Afghanistan remains a propaganda coup for the opponents of Détente, for it gives more credence than deserved to those who perceived a spiral of Soviet activism in the Third World.

It gave more credence, too, to the charge that Soviet actions in the Third World brought about the demise of Détente. In fact, that was only a part of the story.

PART IV

The New Cold War

9 SDI and the New Cold War

STEVE SMITH

The US Strategic Defense Initiative (SDI) is, of course, only one aspect of the 'new Cold War' between the superpowers, but both in the public arena and in US–Soviet relations it has acquired a very high profile. Although it would be misleading to claim that SDI is the cause of the current downturn in US–Soviet relations, it is evidently the focus of much disagreement between the superpowers as well as a cause of considerable tension within the NATO alliance. This chapter aims to look at the history of SDI and to reflect on its development during its first three years, but in order not so much to produce yet another review of the technical problems facing SDI as to provide the basis for an examination of its consequences for US–Soviet relations. In short, how much has SDI contributed to the current state of superpower relations, and what role will SDI play in their future development?

First there is a need for a word of caution in any examination of SDI. There really is a serious problem in writing about SDI, because the use of the term implies the existence of something that has a clear and unambiguous identity. This is not the case with SDI. As anyone who has followed the debate since President Reagan's speech of 23 March 1983 will know, what SDI *is* keeps changing. The phrase 'Strategic Defense Initiative' refers to a research programme of enormous complexity and with numerous areas of technical development: at any one time, some of these areas are seen as more promising than others. More generally, there is still fundamental dispute as to the goal of SDI: is it to provide area defence or point defence, to replace or enhance deterrence? At the time of writing (August 1986) thinking about SDI in Washington contains many different strands of opinion, so that interviews with senior officials concerned with SDI often reveal rather different notions of what the programme is leading to, as well as fundamentally divergent opinions on whether or not it is negotiable.

The point, then, is simply that SDI covers so many technologies, and so many nuances of strategic thinking that we have to use the phrase very carefully: to give just the most obvious example, although in 1983 President Reagan spoke of SDI as providing a way of rendering nuclear weapons impotent and obsolete, this definition of SDI will find few adherents in Washington today. Having said this, though, however we define it, SDI looks like being the major area of disagreement between the superpowers for the years to come and, as such, constitutes a crucial element of the 'new Cold War'. Thus, if SDI really is non-negotiable, and is to be deployed, then this will have a considerable impact on US–Soviet strategic weapons developments, on arms control and on their political relations. Before assessing the likely impact of a continuation of SDI on US–Soviet relations it is necessary to trace the development of the programme, to assess the current technical debate about its feasibility, and then to look at the strategic consequences of the deployment of various versions of SDI.

The history of SDI conventionally begins on 23 March 1983, with President Reagan's speech to the American people, but this is itself a misleading starting date because both the US and the USSR have been engaged in research on the prospects for defence against ballistic missiles for more than twenty-five years.[1] The idea of defending against ballistic missiles is as old as the missiles themselves, although the scientific consensus, at least until recent years, has been that such a capability is beyond the bounds of technology. It was for this reason, rather than any concern for the destabilizing consequences of deployment that both the US and the USSR agreed to the ABM Treaty in 1972; a judgement supported by the USA's unilateral decision to dismantle its existing ABM site at Grand Forks, North Dakota, in 1976. Despite this, both superpowers spent large sums in research on ballistic missile defence (BMD), with the USSR upgrading its Galosh system around Moscow and the US spending approximately $200 million a year on research in the late 1970s and early 1980s (Schwartz, 1984, p. 344). Nevertheless, President Reagan's 23 March 1983 speech came as quite a surprise to the strategic studies community, because the consensus was still that BMD was not possible. What is clear about the genesis of the speech is that it was (and remains) very much President Reagan's initiative. As Ball (1985) and Barrett (1985) have shown, the President was influenced strongly by organizations such as the Heritage Foundation and Lt-General Daniel Graham's High Frontier project, as well as by individuals such as Edward Teller: each of these argued that US security should rest upon a US capability to defend itself against attack rather than depend on the threat of punishing the Soviet Union after any attack. Within the Department of Defense and the Joint Chiefs of Staff such proposals were seen as highly speculative, and there was not a large constituency of support for increasing BMD research.

This helps explain why the President's speech was very different in its gestation to normal presidential initiatives – it came from the top down. The normal procedure is that an initiative is worked through the departmental channels and then an agreed version is sent to the President for his approval. In this case, very few knew of the President's forthcoming initiative. Neither of the two officials most concerned with ballistic missile defence (John Gardner, Director of Defensive Systems at the DoD and Richard Cooper, Head of the Defense Advanced Research Projects Agency (DARPA)) was informed. Even George Keyworth, the President's science adviser, knew nothing of it until five days before the speech. Within the bureaucracy, the Joint Chiefs of Staff, when consulted on 11 February 1983, gave the proposal only lukewarm support, saying that they supported more research on strategic defence: they did not formally recommend that the President should go ahead with the proposal that became known as SDI (Ball, 1985, p. 39). As Barrett comments: 'Had Clark and McFarlane run the scheme through the orthodox interagency review process, immediate objections would have either slowed its progress or stopped the plan altogether' (Barrett, 1985, p. 16). This explains why the President announced the proposal before, rather than after, he asked for studies to evaluate its feasibility. For this reason, George Ball has called the speech 'one of the most irresponsible acts by any head of state in modern times' (Ball, 1985, p. 38).

After the speech the President called for two studies into BMD: the Defensive Technologies Study Team chaired by James Fletcher, and a study on the defence policy and strategic implications of BMD, comprising an interagency team chaired by Franklin Miller and a team of outside experts chaired by Fred Hoffman and known as the Future Security Strategy Group (FS^3). The Fletcher panel's findings, although classified, were summarized (US Department of Defense, 1984a); their main recommendation was for the development of a research programme to assess the technical feasibility of BMD. The aim of this should be to allow a decision to be made in the early 1990s on whether or not to proceed with the development of the systems. The FS[3] panel reported (US Department of Defense, 1984b) that it was essential that options for BMD be pursued and that, if deployed, BMD would enhance US security. As a result of these two reports, the President created the Strategic Defense Initiative Organization (SDIO) in January 1984, with Lt-General James Abrahamson as its head.

The creation of SDIO resulted in a massive increase in the requests for funding BMD research, with expenditure going up from about $462 million in financial year (FY) 1982 and $519 million in FY 1983 to $1400 million in FY 1985, $2759 million in FY 1986, and calls for sums of $4812 million and $5463 million for FY 1987 and FY 1988. Congress has, in fact, cut back on the sums requested, but, despite this, yearly expenditure on BMD has roughly increased ten-fold in the last five years.[2] The work of SDIO has been subdivided into five research areas: Surveillance, Acquisition, Tracking and Kill Assessment (SATKA); Directed Energy Weapons (DEW) Technologies; Kinetic Energy Weapons (KEW) Technologies; Systems Analysis and Battle Management (SA/BM); and Survivability, Lethality and Key Technologies (SLKT). Research is concentrated into the development of a technology base, with the majority of expenditure falling under this heading, and into major experiments designed to prove the feasibility of the critical components of SDI. The overall programme has three goals: the survivability of the defensive systems, their military effectiveness and their cost effectiveness. In the light of increased Congressional pressure on funding, the SDIO has progressively identified priorities. According to the SDIO's 1986 Report to Congress these are: to protect the technology base, to increase the emphasis on proof-of-feasibility experiments and to decrease the scope and number of capability demonstration projects (SDIO, 1986, pp. IV8–IV9). This has resulted in the pattern of actual and proposed expenditure (in $million) given in Table 9.1.

In addition to the research into specific technologies, the SDIO has also been involved in the crucial issue of the design of the overall SDI system. SDIO commissioned ten architecture studies and these Phase I studies were submitted in the late summer of 1985; subsequently, five of the teams working on these studies were selected to produce Phase II studies, which will be submitted near the end of

Table 9.1 SDIO Budget Trends FY 1985 – FY 1988

	FY 1985	*FY 1986*	*FY 1987*	*FY 1988*
SATKA	545.950	856.956	1262.413	1558.279
DEW	377.599	844.401	1614.955	1582.037
KEW	255.950	595.802	991.214	1217.226
SA/BM	100.280	227.339	462.206	563.998
SLKT	108.400	221.602	454.367	523.654
Management Costs	9.120	13.122	17.411	18.118
TOTAL	1397.299	2759.222	4802.566	5463.312

(*Source*: SDIO, 1986, p. VIII–6).

1986. Then one contract will be offered for a Phase III study that will design the complete SDI system within which the separate technologies will operate.

What is critical about the architecture studies is that they have already altered the conception of what SDI will involve: whereas the original thinking of the Fletcher panel and of outside analysts and critics was for a four-layer defensive system, intercepting Soviet missiles in their boost, post-boost, midcourse and terminal phases, the findings of the Phase I studies indicate that up to seven layers may be necessary, each with a leakage rate as high as 40 per cent. More saliently, the Phase I studies have indicated that there are serious problems with space-based components, resulting in SDIO now thinking of an architecture either with only a few space-based elements or with none at all (Pike, 1986, p. 4). The paradox is that this is directly in contrast to the popular notion of SDI, especially as denoted by the term 'Star Wars'. Accordingly, the amount of money devoted to space-based components has been drastically cut-back. For example, the space-based chemical laser project has had its funds cut by half in the FY 1986 budget, and its role has been redefined from boost-phase interception to midcourse discrimination. Similar fates have befallen the neutral particle beam and the X-ray laser (Waller *et al.*, 1986a, p. 44).

Nevertheless, SDIO has claimed some considerable technological breakthroughs in the first two years of its work (SDIO, 1985b; SDIO, 1986, pp. VII–A–1 to VII–G–5), a position supported by Secretary of Defense Caspar Weinberger and former Presidential Scientific Adviser George Keyworth (Waller *et al.*, 1986a, p. 13).

But, according to an unpublished report prepared for three US Senators, extensive interviewing with the key scientists reveals that there have not been major breakthroughs: 'There have not been amazing leaps in the technology development. Contrary to claims by Administration officials and SDI's top leadership, the program's scientists and military planners across the country have *not* concluded that SDI is militarily and economically feasible ... If anything, the dramatic progress SDI has achieved during the past two years has been in identifying the operational problems a strategic defense system would face' (Waller *et al.*, 1986a, pp. 22–23).

As is well known, SDI has engendered a massive literature arguing that the technological requirements are unattainable (see, for example, Tirman 1984; Carter, 1984; Office of Technology Assessment 1985; Bethe *et al.*, 1984; Drell, Farley and Holloway, 1984), but there have also been strong claims that these studies are unduly pessimistic (Jastrow, 1985; Payne, 1986). It is beyond the scope of this chapter to discuss this question in detail, and such a discussion would be tangential to the focus of this chapter. But, what we can say in summary is that the technical argument has gone through a number of phases. Shortly after President Reagan's speech, the reaction was very much on the lines that the hardware requirements were unattainable, a conclusion reached in the controversial study by Ashton Carter for the US Office of Technology Assessment (OTA) (Carter, 1984). SDIO's response was simply that the critics misunderstood the goal of SDIO, which was to see if the technologies offered the possibility of defence against ballistic missile attack.

The second wave of criticism followed the resignation of David Parnas from the SDIO's panel on Computing in Support of Battle Management, in June 1985. Parnas, a distinguished computer scientist, wrote in his resignation letter that 'the goals stated for the Strategic Defense System cannot be attained by the class of systems that you are considering' (Parnas, 1985, p. 1). In short, Parnas argued that the software requirements for the computing side of SDI were unattainable, and he supported his judgement with a series of eight brief research notes on the major software problems to be faced by SDI (see also Lin, 1985, and Jacky, 1985). The panel of which Parnas was a member duly reported to the SDIO in December 1985, and claimed that the software requirements were 'within the capabilities of ... technologies that could be developed within the next several years' (Eastport Study Group, 1985, p.v). However, they also claimed that the Phase I architecture studies had underestimated the software problems and the kind of architecture required to take account of these software problems would have to be rather different from those envisaged in the Phase I studies; specifically, this would have to be a less tightly co-ordinated architecture than envisaged in the Phase I studies, otherwise 'the United States could end up with a "cheaper" system that simply does not work' (Eastport Study Group, 1985, p. 27). For the SDIO's own panel on battle management, software problems were seen as the 'paramount' problem for SDI.

So, what is the current status of the SDI research programme? Although there have been major advances in technologies related to BMD, it is difficult to substantiate SDIO's claims that major breakthroughs have occurred; however, it is equally clear that the sceptics have underestimated the rate of progress. Nevertheless, an examination of the research record to date does indicate that the most likely deployment of any SDI components will not concentrate resources initially on boost-phase interception; for what research has shown is that any space-based components will be particularly vulnerable to Soviet counter-measures. The Office of Technology Assessment report on BMD, released in September 1985, concluded that one goal of SDI (and certainly of President Reagan) did appear to be dubious: 'Assured Survival of the US population appears impossible to achieve if the Soviets are determined to deny it to us.' (Office of Technology Assessment, 1985, p. 33).

The evidence indicates, therefore, that SDI will not be able to render nuclear weapons impotent and obsolete, the goal the President spoke of in his 1983 speech, and thus SDI looks as if it will be concerned instead to protect missile silos, thereby raising the uncertainty for the Soviets in any first strike. Even then, however, the OTA report concluded that it was not clear that this was the best way to ensure the survival of US ICBMs. Contrary, then, to the popular notions of SDI, all the indications are that point defence, rather than area defence, is the likely outcome. Additionally, as noted above, the current funding trends suggest that the weapons to be used will concentrate on mid-course rather than on boost phase interception and will be KEW rather than DEW systems.

The current debate about SDI, therefore, appears to be focusing on a choice between the relative advantages and disadvantages of boost-phase, space-based interception and mid-course, ground-based interception. The advantage of boost-phase defence is two-fold: the target is more easily identifiable in this phase of its trajectory because it is emitting a large infra-red heat signature, and it has not yet released its separate warheads (and any decoys and chaff). But interception in the boost phase is severely problematical, because it requires systems able to attack in a very short time-frame, currently 250–300 seconds. Such a mission requires systems to be placed either directly over the path of the missile (i.e. in space) or systems that can, via tremendous acceleration, get in line of sight of the target.

Each of these options has massive drawbacks. Whether a DEW is placed in orbit, or is based on the ground, and then uses (as in the excimer laser) battle mirrors to reflect the beam on to the target, there is a fundamental vulnerability of the space-based component. This is because the orbital requirements for the defence (i.e. pre-dictability of guaranteed coverage) give the attacker a clear indi-cation of the location of the space-based components, thereby making a pre-emptive attack on these components more easy. Any ground-based system designed for boost-phase interception not only has to accelerate much faster than the target, because of the curvature of the earth, but also has to be told exactly when to fire and at what co-ordinates. A generic problem for boost-phase interception is, therefore, that of communications, especially diffi-cult if the Soviets, as is surely likely, attempt to jam or confuse US communications. Thus the task of ensuring reliable communi-cations to space-based components and the task of communicating to ground-based components (which would have to be based on submarines) look particularly challenging. It is for precisely these reasons that SDI seems to be shifting to other phases for inter-ception.

The technology does exist for a terminal defence (such as is utilized in both the US and the Soviet ABM programmes) but terminal defence alone can not be expected to destroy more than a small fraction of incoming re-entry vehicles (RVs). This is because the terminal phase is very short (30 seconds to 1 minute) and, because it occurs in the atmosphere, it rules out many of the technologies envisaged for SDI (such as many DEW systems). Therefore, increased attention is being focused on mid-course interception, with the current favourite idea among SDI-watchers being ground-based non-nuclear kill (NNK) interceptors. The problem, of course, is that of discriminating the target during the mid-course, when the warheads, decoys and chaff are all travelling at the same speed and, because the warheads are not using any form of propulsion, are not readily indentifiable. Mid-course intercept-ion, therefore, requires massive battle management and software capabilities, in order to allow the US to track continuously the entire 'threat cloud' (which may contain more than 100,000 items, such as warheads, decoys and chaff), then to determine, by the use of DEW, which are warheads and then to co-ordinate the destruction of these by NNKs.

The technological history of SDI, then, is one that points to a rather different form of SDI being deployed than is referred to in the public debate. Naturally, SDIO will continue to research technolo-gies for interception in all phases of a ballistic missile's trajectory, and clearly the resultant architecture will attempt to include as many layers of attack as possible because of the synergistic nature of the systems. But what does appear to be evident is that such an SDI architecture will result in the defence not of population centres but of missile silos and of command, control and communications (C^3) facilities. It is crucial that this likely outcome be kept in mind when examining the impact of SDI on Soviet–US relations. This chapter will now turn to examine the strategic and political consequences of SDI before concluding by looking at the vexed question of SDI's negotiability.

The most obvious strategic consequence of SDI relates to the Soviet reaction to it. There are two aspects of this: first, what will they do to overcome it; secondly, will they attempt to build their own SDIski? Many of the critics of SDI have discussed in detail the counter-measures that the Soviets can undertake to overcome it (see especially, Carter, 1984, pp. 45–52; Tirman, 1984, pp. 115–28, 137–43; Office of Technology Assessment, 1985, pp. 170–7; Guert-ner and Snow, 1986, pp. 69–75). Basically, the Soviets have a wide range of options that can be divided into three main types, and these will only be mentioned in outline here:

(a) *Countermeasures to weapons.* These options include hardening the missile to make it more resilient to DEW attack in boost and post-boost phases and evading the weapons by reducing the boost phase (the Fletcher panel suggested that a fifty second boost phase might be achievable) or by developing manoeuvrable RVs for the terminal phase. Each of the developments under this heading would severely increase the size of any SDI system and would increase the problems of battle management and its associated software.

(b) *Countermeasures to sensors.* The Soviets could also make the target acquisition and discrimination process much more difficult by, for example, blinding the sensors, disrupting communications and deploying decoys. This would be particularly attractive were the United States to rely on mid-course interception, but would also apply to boost, post-boost and terminal defensive systems.

(c) *Countermeasures to the overall system's performance.* Precisely because of the interrelationship between the various layers of an SDI architecture, the Soviets could be expected to attempt to saturate each level so as to overwhelm its capabilities, thereby increasing the problems for the next layer. More saliently, the Soviets could rely on other ways of delivering nuclear weapons, such as cruise missiles, bombers or depressed-trajectory submarine-launched ballistic missiles. Furthermore they could attack SDI components directly by, for example, detonating a few nuclear weapons in order to degrade component performance, or by using DEW against them. They could also deploy salvage-fused space mines, i.e. weapons that explode if approached; deployment of these would be cost-effective and could be expected to accompany the deployment of SDI components. Of course, any one of these counter-measures may itself be overcome by counter-counter-measures, but the advantage seems to lie with the side attempting to evade the defence, particularly because the effect of a counter-measure to one part of the system may well be to increase the possibility of countering other parts of the system (Zimmerman, 1986). The unavoidable conclusion of a survey of possible Soviet counter-measures is that if they wish to overcome SDI then they will be able to do so. This does not undermine SDI if its goal is to reduce Soviet confidence in any first strike, but it does if its aim is to provide a leak-proof defensive shield.

The other aspect of the Soviet response is their own effort to develop an SDI. Although there is certainly evidence about their attempts in this regard (US Department of Defense, 1985; Stevens, 1984; Van Cleave, 1986; Payne, 1986, pp. 45–61), it is not certain that they would attempt to match the US step-for-step (Shenfield,

1985), since their efforts would most usefully be concentrated into developing counter-measures. Having said which, it seems clear that the Soviets would feel that they had to develop some form of SDIski, given the political ramifications of sole US possession of such a system. Although unofficial estimates place their capabilities in the relevant technologies at about 5–7 years behind the United States, their history of research into BMD indicates that they would go the SDIski route if they fail to limit deployment of the US programme.

The combination of Soviet counter-measures and development of their own SDI has a number of crucial consequences for the future strategic and political relationship between the superpowers. The most obvious of these is that both sides will become engaged in a considerable arms race, not so much out of antagonism but out of a desire to maintain military options. It should be remembered that even the supporters of SDI in the United States agree that SDI cannot work very effectively if the Soviets concentrate resources on overcoming it. As the OTA report of September 1985 stated in its conclusion (cited above), if the Soviets are determined to overcome SDI then it cannot assure the survival of the US population (Office of Technology Assessment, 1985, p. 33). The point is that, just as the Soviets can be expected to attempt to overcome SDI by developing counter-measures, so will the United States attempt to counter these; similarly, the development of a Soviet SDI will result in US military planners thinking of ways of overcoming it. Put simply, military advisers are concerned with being able to carry out their military mission and they will, in both superpowers, press for the systems and resources to be able to achieve this. Not only would both sides become involved in a series of counter-measures and counter-counter-measures, but there are two further strategic consequences that are worrying.

The first is that, although President Reagan sees SDI as a way of leading to massive reductions in offensive nuclear systems, it is *precisely* these systems that offer the best way of overcoming BMD: that is, one of the easiest ways of ensuring the destruction of targets, despite BMD, is to increase the number of launchers and warheads. Much has been made in the United States of the comparative costs of adding offensive and defensive systems, with the hope (certainly of Paul Nitze) that marginal costs will favour the defence, yet this fundamentally misrepresents the nature of military planning. For planners, the key consideration is achieving military missions, not the relative costs for one side of adding defensive lasers compared with the other side's costs in adding offensive systems. Thus, it seems unlikely that the Soviets would be willing to cut back on their offensive forces if SDI goes ahead; rather they can be expected to increase them. This, if combined with a Soviet SDI, will lead to an ever-spiralling arms race in space.

The second consequence is that the technologies envisaged for SDI do not simply threaten offensive systems: they are also well-suited for attacks on other space-based assets, crucially the reconnaissance and early-warning satellites of each side. In this anti-satellite (ASAT) role, these technologies present mammoth problems for the two sides, especially in the case of DEW, which travel at the speed of light. Unlike the current generation of ASAT systems, DEW technologies could threaten even those satellites in geo-synchronous orbits. Paradoxically, it is the US that has most to lose here, given its reliance on satellites for its C^3I and war-fighting capabilities (Carter, 1986; Smith, 1987).

The result, then, of a Soviet response to SDI by developing their own system and by attempting to overcome the US system will be an extension of the arms race in space. Although space is currently militarized to a high degree (see Jasani, 1984; Stares, 1985; Jasani, 1982), it is still an environment in which few space-based assets are vulnerable to attack. This would not be the case in a world in which the two sides develop BMD and ways around it. The most obvious effect of such a change would be severely to erode crisis stability: at present it is almost impossible to imagine either side resorting to the use of nuclear weapons in a crisis, but with an arms race in space the possibilities of mis-reading the other side's intentions would be considerable. For example, how would the United States react to a series of Soviet rocket launches that placed unidentified objects in close proximity to US early-warning satellites? This situation could look even more worrying were each side to deploy DEW in space, since these systems could just as easily attack satellites as missiles.

This problem is related to another aspect of the decline in crisis stability: this is that the existence on both sides of a leaky SDI could encourage thoughts of attacking first. This is not to suggest that either side would like to start a conflict, only to argue that military advisers may well feel that they have to inform political leaders that, *if* they 'know' that the other side is about to launch, then they would be 'better off' getting in first. This would be particularly so if either side felt its C^{3}I facilities to be vulnerable to a pre-emptive attack from DEW in space (see Blair, 1985; Ford, 1985; Bracken, 1983). Such a fear seems to be important in Soviet concerns about the US SDI programme; after all, as Caspar Weinberger commented in 1983: 'I can't imagine a more destabilizing factor for the world than if the Soviets should acquire a thoroughly reliable defense against these missiles before we do' (*Wall Street Journal*, 7 December 1983, p. 6). The worry, then, is that the effect of BMD may well be to make leaders believe that it is better to attack first in order to minimize the task of their own BMD and thereby reduce damage to their society; to reiterate, this does not mean that either side may want war, only that they feel that, if they *know* the other side is about to launch, then the advantages of striking first may far outweigh the option of trying to ride-out the attack.

Yet, of course, this is not the kind of world that President Reagan sees as being ushered in by SDI; indeed, in his 1983 speech he pointed out that, if SDI were accompanied by offensive systems, then it could 'be viewed as fostering an aggressive policy' (Reagan, 1985, p. 298). For President Reagan, the goal is to move away from a world based on offensive nuclear forces, where deterrence is ensured by mutual assured destruction (MAD), towards one based on defensive systems, with deterrence being assured by mutual assured survival (MAS). But it is necessary to point out that the goal of MAS is literally unattainable, not only because offensive systems are the most obvious way to swamp any BMD but also because there are other ways of delivering nuclear weapons.

However, even if this strategic transition were possible, how would we get from here to there? The worry is that, because each side would be developing BMD and counter-measures of different types and at different rates, it would be enormously difficult to manage this transition. The historical record of arms-control efforts dealing 'only' with offensive systems is not encouraging in this regard. More worrying, of course, is the thought that such a transition could not be managed at all; rather, each side would pursue both defensive and offensive technologies at the same time. Bearing in mind the possible military advantage in deploying counter-measures such as spacemines as and when BMD components were placed in space, this could be a very difficult period indeed of the nuclear age. The President has argued that the United

States would attempt to negotiate this transition, with reductions in offensive forces accompanying the deployment of defensive systems, but one is forced to point out that such a scenario is very unlikely to occur; this is simply because it requires the Soviets to give up systems that they have not yet been willing to negotiate away at the same time that the US is deploying a defensive system to destroy the remaining Soviet offensive forces.

SDI also promises to have major arms-control implications, specifically for the ABM Treaty. The United States has already announced its intention to abandon the numerical constraints placed upon its forces by the SALT II Treaty, although at the time of writing there is some hope that this might be reversed. What SDI does is to threaten the prospect of any strategic arms agreement in the remaining years of President Reagan's administration, at the same time as posing severe challenges to the ABM Treaty. The SDIO claims that it will undertake its research in compliance with the ABM Treaty (SDIO, 1986, pp. C–1 to C–15), but many independent observers claim that the USA will violate the Treaty within the next few years. The Reagan administration has argued that a wide interpretation of the Treaty is justified by the (unpublished) negotiating record, and that this interpretation allows SDI research and testing to go ahead, but certainly, according to one of the key US negotiators of the Treaty, this reading of the record is mistaken (Rhinelander, 1985). For the present, the United States says it will abide by the narrow interpretation that has been US policy since the signing of the Treaty, and that this will allow SDIO's work to continue for the foreseeable future. However, according to a detailed survey by Longstreth, Pike and Rhinelander (1985, p. 43), the US will, under this interpretation of the Treaty, violate it when it tests the Airborne Optical Adjunct in early 1989. The Reagan administration's position is that the Soviets have violated the Treaty themselves, particularly by the deployment of the large phased-array radar at Krasnoyarsk, but this assertion is questionable, since the Krasnoyarsk radar (although a possible technical breach) does not seem very suitable as the kind of radar useful for ABM battle management, and anyway is hardly a reason for US violation. Crucially, SDI's purpose is exactly that which the ABM Treaty sought to ban, and thus its continuance is fundamentally inconsistent with the Treaty. On virtually all interpretations, then, SDI looks as if it will lead to a breakdown in the

US–Soviet arms-control regime; the only possible exception would be if SDI were to become a bargaining chip, and we shall return to that question in the conclusion to this chapter.

Finally, on the strategic front, SDI threatens to cause serious problems for NATO, reflecting a continuing dilemma for the European–US relationship with regard to the Soviet Union. Although the SDIO is currently proposing a specific set of technologies for the defence of Europe, particularly the anti-tactical ballistic missile (ATBM), it is unlikely that Europe could be as well defended as was the USA by any SDI because of the much shorter flight-times involved. Such differences in the vulnerability of the European and North American legs of the Alliance could cause serious political problems within NATO, with governments worrying that this would encourage the USA to retreat into isolation, and peace groups fearing that the USA might be tempted to fight communism in Europe, being itself more secure from attack. More tangibly, there are the economic effects of the US SDI programme, and these threaten a brain-drain from Europe to the USA and a related economic boost for US high technology. But the really critical strategic concern relates to the role of nuclear weapons in the Alliance: on the one hand, any Soviet BMD would decrease the credibility of the French and British nuclear deterrents (recollect that the effect of the Soviet deployment of the Galosh ABM around Moscow was to make British governments from 1970 and 1979 spend £1 billion in modernizing the front end of Polaris in the Chevaline programme). On the other hand, any Soviet BMD would call into question the central military posture of NATO, which is the US guarantee to use nuclear weapons to prevent (or halt) a Soviet conventional attack on Europe. It was just such a worry that led to a Pershing II and Cruise deployment decision in 1979, a result of the effect of Soviet improvements in air defence on the then existing means of delivering US nuclear weapons from Europe, the F111. If improvements in Soviet air defence were sufficient to cause NATO to go through the tortuous and problematic decision to deploy Cruise and Pershing II, the effect of a Soviet BMD system would be far greater. In short, NATO faces a very serious strategic problem if SDI goes ahead, one that it will find difficult to manage because what is involved is a redefinition of NATO strategy. The utility of the existing strategy, flexible response, lies in its very ambiguity concerning the role of nuclear weapons. SDI will force this issue to be opened up, and it may not be easy to please everyone with any one solution.

In addition to these strategic consequences of SDI, there are a number of possible political ramifications that may affect US–Soviet and US–European relations for the remainder of this century. As was stated at the beginning of this chapter, SDI did not cause the current downturn in US–Soviet relations, but it does seem evident that if it really is non-negotiable then it will be a source of considerable friction between the superpowers. Indeed, we can go so far as to say that, unless it is limited by negotiation, then the outlook for US–Soviet relations looks very bleak; SDI, after all, symbolizes to the Soviets an attempt by the United States to attain a position of superiority over them, and this is inconsistent with conceptions of Détente. We shall return to the interrelationship between SDI and the general political climate between the super-powers in the conclusion, but what does seem clear is that both a unilateral US development of SDI or a concurrent US and Soviet development bodes ill for US–Soviet political relations. After all, if Caspar Weinberger can be so worried by the prospects of a Soviet BMD system, why should the Soviets not be equally concerned? And, as discussed above, if the result of SDI is that both sides develop defensive systems and counter-measures against the other side's defensive system, then this hardly looks likely to be compatible with a return to Détente.

But the political consequences extend much further. SDI will cause NATO a serious internal problem of how to manage its introduction, and this may well lead to serious reactions against the US linkage. SDI will also cause a potentially problematic psychological threat in that it will result in the European part of the Alliance being more vulnerable to Soviet pressure in any period of US–Soviet tension. The United States discussed a similar strategy of horizontal escalation in the late 1970s, the idea of which was to extend any US–Soviet conflict to Soviet allies (this usually meant putting pressure on Cuba). Put baldly, if the United States and the Soviet Union are in a conflict in another part of the world, the European members of NATO may feel especially vulnerable and may come under considerable pressure from the Soviets to influence their US ally. More worrying still is the prospect of a Soviet conventional response against the European part of NATO in any US–Soviet crisis. Finally, any decline in US–Soviet relations would be bound to have effects both on European and on Soviet–East European relations, and these could pose serious political problems within NATO.

However one looks at it, then, SDI looks as if it will be the focus of US–Soviet relations for the remainder of this century, unless it is the subject of a negotiated agreement. The final part of this chapter will discuss the likely nature of any US SDI deployment, the question of its future development and the effects of these on US–Soviet relations in the new Cold War.

What seems evident from the above survey is that SDI will not be as envisaged by President Reagan in his 1983 speech. We are not going to see nuclear weapons rendered impotent and obsolete, nor will we see MAD replaced by MAS. All the indications from budget trends suggest that SDI will be concerned with point rather than area defence, i.e. it will play a role of increasing the survival of US ICBM silos, thereby enhancing deterrence. Yet not only is it uncertain that this is the best way of ensuring their survival, the options being moving to mobile ICBMs such as Midgetman (and the original basing mode for the MX, which is now to be placed in silos) or hardening the silos further, but it is not obvious that their vulnerability is so severe as to justify the problems SDI will cause. After all, the Scowcroft Commission, set up by President Reagan to propose a solution to the problem of how to base the MX missile, reported in April 1983 that US ICBMs were not vulnerable enough to require either different basing modes or BMD (Scowcroft Commission, 1983, p. 17). Thus, silo vulnerability was not seen to be so serious as to require BMD one month after Reagan's speech and, given the dispersion of US forces on to the three legs of the triad, it seems that the problem is unlikely to become serious enough for BMD in the future. The point is that, even if ICBMs were vulnerable, there are many ways other than BMD to enhance their survivability, with one tempting prospect being trading SDI for limits on the Soviet heavy ICBMs (especially the SS18) that threaten them. But this would require giving up SDI deployment.

The whole situation has become rather curious in recent months with Richard Perle claiming in October 1985 that the Soviet SS25 (a single warhead mobile ICBM, similar to the US Midgetman) was destabilizing: a logic diametrically opposed to that of the Scowcroft Commission's report, which proposed just such a development on both sides as the most stabilizing way forward! So the kind of SDI that the United States is likely to deploy first looks very much like a solution to a non-existent problem. Naturally, US leaders argue that area defence is still the goal, but even President Reagan has recently shown signs of arguing that SDI's primary role will be to enhance, not replace, deterrence.

The realization that SDI will, at best, be concerned with protecting ICBM silos and C^3I facilities does call into question the advisability of the programme. Not only must we ask if such a solution is worth the costs SDI will impose on the US economy, but it is also questionable whether it can actually serve as a solution at all. As was discussed previously, if it looks as if SDI will be unable to result in a significant boost-phase interception rate, then the Soviet Union's prospects of overwhelming it look rather good.

All of this has to be seen in the light of the strategic and political implications of deploying SDI. It is for exactly this reason that there has been renewed speculation that President Reagan may be willing to negotiate limits on SDI in return for an arms-control deal that imposes severe cuts on Soviet ICBMs. By the early summer of 1986 there had been many suggestions in the US press that such a deal was possible, and the Soviet arms-control offer of June 1986 proposed just such a deal (Gordon, 1986, pp. 1–2). Essentially, the Soviets offered to cut back strategic arsenals to 8000 warheads, with a maximum of 4800 on ICBMs, in return for a US undertaking not to withdraw from the ABM Treaty for fifteen to twenty years. But this was conditional on the USA's accepting a strict interpretation of the ABM Treaty, and this would severely limit SDI research, prohibiting any testing of components in space.

In his response to this offer, President Reagan proposed that the United States would continue to adhere to the ABM Treaty for another five to seven years, but that after this either side could deploy defensive systems. In the interim, SDI research could continue under the US interpretation of the ABM Treaty. Although this led to a number of reports in the US press that a grand compromise was at hand (see, for example, Cannon and Pincus, 1986; Gelb, 1986), it is evident that the two sides are still far apart. The US offer is really only a way of allowing SDI research to continue, while the Soviet offer is aimed at preventing just that by a strict interpretation of the Treaty. On the basis of the Reagan administration's record on arms control generally, and on SDI specifically, it appears difficult to accept that President Reagan is willing to accept any meaningful limitations on the programme. Such a position will also massively affect both the prospects for an offensive arms agreement, since the two are firmly linked in Soviet eyes, and negotiations on limits on nuclear testing, the continuation of which is required for the testing of key components of SDI, such as the X-ray laser.

The prospects, then, for a negotiated limitation on SDI do not look promising. But SDI may be limited in other ways: the most immediate relates to Congressional attempts to cut back on SDI expenditure. Congress has already cut the funding requests for SDI in FY 1985 and FY 1986 and, in the case of FY 1987, is proposing a ceiling of around $3.5 billion as opposed to the request for $5.4 billion (a rise of 77 per cent over the FY 1986 figure). In May 1986, forty-six Senators wrote to the chair of the Senate Armed Services Committee to call for an increase for FY 1987 of no more than 3 per cent. They argued that SDI had received excessive funding, and that the programme was proceeding too fast and without a clear set of goals (Wilson, 1986). In the longer term, SDI will naturally be affected by the outcome of the 1988 Presidential election, but the fear is that by then the programme will have gained such bureaucratic momentum as to be effectively unstoppable. The Soviet leadership, from its offers at Geneva and its attempts to stop SDI, does not seem content to wait until 1988; in this regard it looks as if the next two years may be the crucial ones for the future of SDI.

In conclusion, then, SDI looks as if it will be a critical barometer of US–Soviet relations for the next few years. Of course, SDI will add to the problems confronting the resolution of the two sides' political relationships, with good relations difficult to achieve if SDI continues on its present course. The spill-over effects of SDI on strategic arms control, on the ABM Treaty and on nuclear testing merely add to the problems in the way of a return to Détente. Together, the current strategic and arms-control postures of the Reagan administration fuel Soviet fears of US aggressive intentions, politically if not militarily. In the longer term, the strategic implications of a US deployment of SDI will further strain the US–Soviet political relationship, as well as causing severe problems for the NATO alliance and for the two independent European nuclear powers.

In sum, the continuation of SDI, which looks increasingly like a way of enhancing deterrence rather than replacing it, seems more

consistent with a continuation of a second Cold War than it does
with a return to Détente. The Reagan administration's views on the
advantages of a defence-dominated world are likely to prove
illusory, given the natural reaction of the military on both sides to
respond to BMD by attempting to overcome it; we cannot look
forward to a world where nuclear weapons are obsolete, only to
one, if SDI continues, in which the superpowers are engaged in a
more complex and destabilizing arms race than hitherto. Regarding
the future of US–Soviet political and strategic relations, the most
worrying period will be the transition phase, as new defensive
systems begin to be deployed. Will the Soviets allow this
deployment to occur unchallenged?

But if SDI in these various ways will contribute to the continuation of the second Cold War, the future course of SDI, like its
history, is more an expression of the dominant approach in the
Reagan administration to how to structure US–Soviet relations than
it is a source of the problems they now face; SDI is a symptom of this
approach rather than its cause. The crucial point is that the Reagan
administration is generally distrustful of arms control as a way of
dealing with the Soviets, a view that permeates most of the key
senior office-holders in the National Security Council, the Department of Defense and even the Arms Control and Disarmament
Agency in the Department of State. There is a powerful consistency
between US policies on arms control and on strategic and defensive
weapons modernization, and it is in the build-up of strategic and
defensive forces that the administration sees the best hope of
enhancing US security. Put bluntly, key officials such as President
Reagan, Caspar Weinberger, Fred Ikle, Richard Perle and Kenneth
Adelman do not believe in arms control and certainly do not trust
the Soviets to keep to any agreements made. The paradox is that
arms control itself would be unnecessary if the US leadership felt it
could trust the Soviets. But, rather than go down the arms-control
road to enhancing security, the Reagan administration prefers
instead to rely on a unilateral search for security, without recognizing, or acknowledging, that security in the nuclear age is
indivisible and is incapable of being achieved unilaterally. The
current debate about the future of SDI indicates this only too clearly:
it is a system that cannot be expected to be effective without the very
arms-control agreements that it is designed to replace.

For these reasons, SDI looks like a search for a technological fix, a technological end-run, to what is irredeemably a political problem. US–Soviet relations since 1945 have always been fraught with problems, and these cannot be overcome by an appeal to exotic technological solutions. The US–Soviet relationship involves two superpowers with different interests and different historical and ideological dynamics; these differences cannot be resolved by technology. SDI also increasingly resembles what has been called 'fallacy of the last move' thinking, in which current Soviet offensive capabilities are compared with future US defensive capabilities; for this reason, there is little prospect of President Reagan's vision being realized. Yet, while pursuing this vision, SDI will have seriously destabilizing consequences for the very political relationship that it seeks to transcend. And, as a way of enhancing deterrence, it does not appear to compare favourably with other contenders; most saliently, if the United States fears a Soviet first strike in a time of crisis, then it should be concerned both to reduce the possibility that the Soviets might impute to the USA an intention to strike first and to deploy strategic systems that are themselves stabilizing. The fact that SDI is being pursued at the same time as the United States is building up its ICBM silo-based force (and is even considering MIRVing the Midgetman, in direct contradiction to the Scowcroft Commission's recommendations) makes it difficult to accept that fears about stability or Soviet pre-emption are really behind these programmes.

The future of SDI will determine whether these fears are misplaced. There is a possibility that President Reagan may go for the 'grand compromise' and negotiate limitations on SDI in return for large cut-backs in Soviet ICBM forces; there is a chance that Congress will cut into the research programme, or that the winner of the 1988 presidential election will cancel it. But the prospects for such outcomes do not look promising. Although President Reagan may well want to sign an arms-control agreement with the Soviets, his views of what can continue in the way of SDI research and what the ABM Treaty permits are very different to those of the Soviet leadership.

The most likely outcome, then, is the continuation of SDI, and this will have enormous consequences on the strategic relationship between the superpowers. This continuation seems inconsistent with a return to Détente. The problems caused by SDI can only be removed by a change in the fundamental approach of the United

States towards the Soviet Union, and it seems unlikely that the Reagan administration is willing to change what is such a central strand of its philosophy. So, although SDI will have considerable effects on the future of US–Soviet relations, its impact must be seen within the general approach of the Reagan administration to dealing with the Soviet Union. The ultimate paradox is that by the time SDI gets deployed there will have been such a lengthy period of mistrust between the superpowers that, apart from each side's attempts to overwhelm BMD and the effect of this on crisis stability, the United States may be better defended but less secure.

Chapter 9: Notes

1 For overviews of the history of SDI and its predecessors see Carter and Schwartz, 1984; Chalfont, 1985; Drell, Farley and Holloway, 1984; Tirman, 1984; Payne, 1986; Office of Technology Assessment, 1985; Jasani, 1984; Guertner and Snow, 1986; Zuckerman, 1986. Soviet research is discussed in Van Cleave, 1986; US Department of Defense, 1985; Pike, 1985.
2 Detailed reviews of the financial aspects of SDI as well as the work in the specific programme areas discussed below can be found in the yearly report by SDIO to the Congress (see SDIO, 1985a, 1986). These are evaluated in considerable depth in an unpublished paper by John Pike, 1986, and in an unpublished report to three senators (see Waller *et al.*, 1986a, a shortened version of which is published as Waller *et al.*, 1986b).

10 Defence Policy Options for Britain in the New Cold War

DAVID ROBERTSON

It is convenient that a commonly used starting date for the new Cold War is 1979. This was the year when the Thatcher government first took office and started an unprecedented increase in peace-time defence expenditure in Britain. In some ways the years 1979–86 might have been expected to open a new era in British defence planning. In fact they signalled a time when the appalling constraints that will face the Ministry of Defence (MoD) for the rest of this century first became apparent. Between 1979 and 1986 defence expenditure rose by at least 20 per cent, but, by the spring of 1986, it was announced that Britain was not only abandoning the NATO commitment to an annual increase of 3 per cent, but that during the years 1987–89 there would be a 6 per cent cut in defence expenditure (MoD, 1986b). This financial background is examined in more detail later. One simple guide to the implications may help. The 3 per cent per year growth in real expenditure was 1 per cent *less* than the minimum at which General Rogers, NATO's Supreme Allied Commander Europe (SACEUR), argued that the Warsaw Pact's conventional superiority could be countered. Quite simply, then, Britain (seen as a member of NATO) is not going to have the finances to mount its part in a credible conventional defence of Europe. (Nor is any other European country – Britain was probably the only European member of the Alliance to live up to the 3 per cent guide between 1977 and 1986 (House of Commons, 1985).)

Five major functions are recognized for the UK military, and these have been more or less consensual in Britain for more than twenty years:

1 A minimum deterrence nuclear strategic force.

David Robertson

2 A major land and air contribution to NATO's central front.
3 A major anti-submarine warfare (ASW) contribution in the
   English Channel, Eastern Atlantic and North Sea.
4 A minor capacity for non-NATO military intervention 'out of
   area'.
5 The defence of the United Kingdom's land and air space.

These simple statements cover a good deal of complexity and are
not necessarily comprehensive. One currently pressing example is
the UK's NATO commitment to rapid reinforcement of Norway in
the event of war. Is this simply an extension of the central front
commitment, or a separate task that Britain might decide to
renounce? Nor do the functions necessarily imply discrete tasks for
the armed services. Obviously the defence of the UK itself would
require a good deal of the same naval and air force activity that falls
under the NATO ASW role. Indeed, the defence of the UK is a
prime NATO obligation, because of the country's role as a
reinforcement depot and staging point for the US troops tasked for
the central front.

There are two general reasons why this policy may be changed in
the next few years; why, indeed, it may have to change. The first is a
question of resource capacity, the second refers to a change in the
nature of the threat Britain faces. This second theme has two
elements – the subjective threat assessment that British defence
planners make (that is, the extent to which they continue to see the
USSR as dangerous) and the continuation of the view that Britain's
security is tied to US interests and leadership. Quite apart from this
subjective estimate is the objective question of Soviet relative
military capacity and the changes in this either through arms control
or arms race.

I have already touched on the first dimension – the UK probably
cannot afford to continue carrying out all five functions. The
financial constraints are such that even the most pro-defence Conservative government will not be able to ignore them. Britain now
not only of all NATO countries spends the highest proportion of its
GNP on defence, save for Mr Reagan's America – it spends the
second highest sum of money *in absolute terms* (MoD, 1986a).
Something has to be given up.

As far as the subjective threat estimate goes, it is crucial to realize
that the defence policy consensus in the UK is breaking up, with the

capture of the Labour party (and probably the Liberals) by the nuclear disarmament movement. In fact the lack of consensus is greater than this. The Labour party's defence policy as adopted by the 1984 party conference calls, though in muted terms, for a very different idea of what NATO's general defence policy ought to be, in conventional as well as nuclear terms. A newer version of the policy, put before the NEC in July 1986, goes even further on the conventional front. Furthermore, the specific version of nuclear disarmament now adopted involves expelling US nuclear bases. This risks so offending the biggest NATO ally that the Labour party's earnest insistence on their (non-nuclear) solidarity with NATO is largely meaningless. Particularly important here, is that Labour has finally grasped that an anti-nuclear country has no business anyway in an alliance whose declared policy probably involves the first use of nuclear weapons within ten days of a war starting. Exactly how much of this policy would be implemented were Labour to win the next election, and what their electoral chances are is not germane – what is beyond doubt is that the nuclear, and therefore effectively the *whole* of the British defence consensus is in danger of being shattered.

Finally, defence policy may have to change because of a change in the nature of the military threat Britain and its allies face, or at least because the British perception of this threat might change. Here we have to consider two distinct types of alteration in the threat, either of which could quite plausibly be forecast. The Soviet threat to Europe may well become very much more severe, or at least change its precise nature as a result of a largely conventional arms build-up by the Warsaw Pact, arising from technological developments in conventional weaponry. Alternatively, the threat might be reduced as a result of arms-control negotiations. This chapter first discusses each of these possible sources of enforced policy change. Finally, it treats the awkward question of what a major defence review should aim at. Because the financial problem is the unavoidable one, and because it underlies all other speculation, I start with a discussion of defence economics.

Defence Costs and Budgetary Constraint

Only one other NATO member, the United States, carries out all five of the NATO tasks outlined earlier. America is vastly wealthier than the UK, and its defence expenditure is roughly ten times more. The significant fact is that this huge expenditure only buys the United States armed forces around six times greater. No other European country tries to do as many different things as the UK, though Germany and France do certain things rather more than does Britain; the French nuclear deterrent is larger than Britain's, the German army is several times bigger than Britain's. Only France of Britain's European allies maintains an 'out-of-area' capacity. Both Germany and France, and indeed all other European members of NATO, rely for their manpower on conscription, which Britain gave up in 1962; so the United States is, yet again, the only other country in NATO to practise as expensive a defence policy as the UK.

The inevitability of Britain reducing its commitments in some area or other was first accepted, ironically, by the Conservative government in 1981, when the then Secretary for Defence, John Nott, published the most serious defence review since the sixties, *The Way Forward* (MoD, 1981). At the time this was published the UK was committed to the NATO 3 per cent annual increase in the defence budget for some years to come, and the plans were to buy only the C4 or Trident 1 missile system to replace the Polaris force, at about half the cost of the Trident D5 that is now planned. Even under these more favourable conditions, Nott was convinced that the full range of existing defence commitments, and the existing force structure, could not be afforded at any politically realistic expenditure level. His defence review identified a specific part of the force structure to cut, though it is less clear that the cut involved a defence function that was suitable for de-emphasis. Nott wanted to cut the surface fleet of destroyers, frigates and aircraft carriers by about one-third. He also hoped to replace existing large and manpower-intensive ships with cheaper designs calling for smaller crews. No real monetary target was ever put on these proposals, which were not implemented in any case, because in 1982 the Falklands conflict intervened and won the navy a moratorium on its sentence. We can make a very rough estimate of the savings, given that the Nott review was generally held to involve a cut of one-third in the surface navy. In the budget for 1986–87, £953 million is allowed for surface units of the fleet, including staffing and all other costs (MoD, 1986a). A one-third cut would thus trim less than £320 million, or 1.7 per cent of the total defence budget. Furthermore, it should be noted that the 1986–87 budget is highly suspect because of a refusal in the last two years by the government actually to order the laying down of the three new frigates per year required to keep the fleet at the pre-Nott level. (As a check on this very rough estimate, it is reassuring that the same calculation, based on the 1982 defence budget, produces an identical cut as a percentage of the overall budget.) This cut was never imposed, yet in 1986–87 it is publicly admitted that expenditure plans by the three armed services exceed the budgetary total by a round £1 billion – the *entire* navy is only planned to cost £2.6 billion for the year. The sheer extent of the shortfall caused by the 1986–87 budget became apparent in weeks when the Secretary of Defence started a campaign in Cabinet for an immediate increase of £500 million (*The Times*, 17 July 1986, p. 1).

The House of Commons Select Committee on Defence (which is dominated by defence-minded Conservative MPs) has repeatedly called attention to the logically inescapable fact of underfunding in a budget that has never been subject to a functional review pronounced as inevitable five years ago (House of Commons, 1986).[1] It has also stated on record that it does not believe the government can safely manage the various acquisition plans it appears to have on the projected non-growth budget figures for the next few years. These include not only Trident, of which perhaps £10 billion will be expended between 1985 and 1995, but the new European Fighter Aircraft (EFA). No plausible figures have been given for this project. The Defence Committee lists the EFA as costing '£3000+', with an in-service date of 1995 (House of Commons, 1985, annex A). The Tornado refit for the RAF will have cost at least £17 billion at 1985 prices. Cost growth in the next generation of high-technology weapons systems is accepted as huge, and it is not thinkable that EFA can realistically be costed at less than Trident. Thus, just two projects will account for an average of 12 per cent of the total defence budget and about 25 per cent of the equipment budget in the decade ahead. The more mundane business of updating things such as battlefield communications, identification friend-or-foe radar, artillery rounds, or even equipping further armoured regiments with new tanks and buying all three services a badly needed new generation of helicopters, have to come out of the rest. To give another comparison – 12 per cent of the current equipment budget would be £1.1 billion – the *total* equipment budget for all land forces

Table 10.1 Estimated Functional Costs of the UK Defence Budget in 1986–87 (£millions, 1986 prices)

German Commitment	NATO ASW	UK Defence	Out of Area	Nuclear Force	Total
8018	3117	5243	1259	862	18500
43%	17%	28%	7%	5%	100%

The details of these calculations are too lengthy to be reported here. They can be found in Laird and Robertson (1987).

is to be only £1.7 billion – and this at a period when few major re-equipment plans are in process.

Defence budgeting is nearly always discussed in these terms of separate service costs and particular procurement plans. This is largely because MoD declines to give proper functional costing – we are not told how much it costs, for example, to maintain our army and tactical airforce role in Germany.[2] Yet any discussion of future policy requires us to think in these terms: defence policy is not made, or certainly should not be made, in terms of acquisitions policy, but in terms of task needs and therefore task costs. It is possible to calculate very rough figures for these functional costs, and Table 10.1 reproduces one set of estimates in terms of the 1986–87 budget.[3]

Although the figures in Table 10.1 can be no more than illustrative, they at least allow us an idea of the order of magnitude involved in the different functions. They are based on current costs, so that the nuclear strike-force is much cheaper than it will be in the big spending years on Trident. However, it probably represents the order of magnitude after 1995 when Trident procurement will be finished. Thus Table 10.1 is more suitable for long-term analysis of defence function costings. The obvious point from the table, and MoD does not deny this, is that it is the German commitment, and not the Naval ASW role, that is the major expense. I return to this point at length later.

Nuclear Weapons and Defence 'Dissensus'

In only one reading of Table 10.1 will there not be a serious underfunding of the defence programme – that is if Britain abolishes all its nuclear weapons. This has led many to argue for nuclear disarmament on essentially financial grounds. However, there are two reasons why defence financing is not the primary consideration. The first is that the costs of the nuclear force are easy to misinterpret. The second is that the implications of abandoning the nuclear strategic force are so enormous that such a policy, however desirable, requires far more than a financial justification.

It is true that Trident will put a huge strain on the defence budget until 1995; it may even be true that abandoning the existing force would wipe out the likely deficit in the next year or so.[4] Both of these facts need to be put into context. The Navy's ballistic missile submarines have the peculiar character of being not just one weapons system but an entire defence role. In France, for example, an argument could be made against a new SLBM design on the grounds that France's nuclear role is a multi-system one, and thus it is possible to say that financial constraints are relevant to how the role should be implemented – there would remain both the airborne and ICBM legs of the nuclear triad. In Britain, we could have argued, ten years ago, that the Tornado programme for the RAF, which cost at least 50 per cent more than Trident, was too expensive and should be altered. But this would not imply abandoning any RAF role. If Tornado were absolutely essential for, say, its ground attack role in Germany, then it could only have been chosen as the programme to drop after an exhaustive analysis of the money saved by abandoning some other role, and then a comparison of the relative defence utilities. The bald statement that Trident is too expensive is, in itself, meaningless.

No party does in fact make this argument officially, although it is often what parliamentary and media debate come down to. There are two strands to the anti-Trident debate, one of which does attempt to argue simply that Trident, as a particular weapons system with which to carry out the nuclear strategic role, is more expensive and sophisticated than is needed.[5] A lot can and has been said on this issue. For convenience here, we can simply assume that some cheaper alternative can be found. In the short run this will still impose a major strain on the defence budget, *because any large new weapons acquisition will do so for ever more.* Furthermore, a cheaper system will not be cheaper than Trident (or than Polaris currently is) by 1995, when the acquisition stage is over. Thus, finding an alternative system to Trident does not get the nuclear strategic force off the hook – it still remains the case that the nuclear strategic force, as one of the five functions that Britain cannot continue to afford, must be subjected to a general defence cost-effectiveness analysis.

But we are not in this section primarily concerned with a decision to drop Britain's nuclear strike force that might arise from a cost-effectiveness analysis *within* the current defence policy consensus. That is the business of the final section. Here, we are concerned with the fact that one of the ways in which the nuclear strike force might be abandoned would in itself be a breach with that consensus so fundamental that it would have knock-on effects across the range of our defence functions. If the British Labour Party comes to office in the next election, and carries out both the letter and the spirit of its defence policy, it will do the following, in order of immediacy.[6]

- It will immediately decommission the Polaris fleet.
- It will cancel the Trident programme.
- It will order the removal of all US nuclear facilities from Britain.
- It will abandon Britain's independent theatre/tactical nuclear capacity.
- It will begin to work inside NATO for a 'No First Use' declaration and policy.
- It will start an internal diplomatic campaign inside NATO for a complete abandonment of the flexible response doctrine, since it is based on nuclear weapons.

It must be admitted that the party is almost entirely silent on what it would do were the political moves in the last two points to come to nothing. It would certainly be the view of some members of the party leadership that a Britain that had adopted out of principle a non-nuclear defence could not indefinitely remain a member of an alliance whose doctrine might require a first use of tactical nuclear weapons within days of a war starting. Others, though not authoritative sources of Labour Party thinking on defence, take the logic of this policy further (Alternative Defence Commission, 1983). The general thrust is that NATO should take all possible steps to allay Soviet fears of aggression by rendering itself literally incapable of an aggressive war. Thus, for example, tanks should be de-emphasized in favour of anti-tank defences; dual capable combat aircraft should be made only conventionally capable and preferably should have short ranges, and so on. This line of thinking is sometimes summed up by saying that NATO must have a policy of 'genuinely defensive deterrence'.

At the same time that they enunciate this policy, Labour leaders stress their total commitment to NATO, and insist that they will at least maintain, and possibly increase, Britain's conventional capability. It might well be asked why they should bother so doing. The policy in fact implies that their threat assessment of the Warsaw Pact, and their sense of the political relations inside NATO, must be radically different from the consensus of the last thirty years. How do they define the role of NATO, and the alliance itself, that they think it desirable to adopt this policy and yet desirable to remain loyal to an alliance when this policy is fundamentally contradictory to views of the rest of the alliance? This is not to criticize the Labour Party policy, but to insist that it implies a major new *political* thrust to British defence policy, possibly more original than its exponents themselves realize.

To start with, expelling US bases from the UK either implies a curious blindness to how the Americans will react, or an indifference. Either way, such a policy signals a refusal to continue with the tradition of an American-led, if not dominated, alliance. This might be less surprising were it Labour Party policy, as it is that of the centre parties, to press for the development of a stronger European third force in world defence politics. But this is also denied, on the grounds that a stress on Western European collaboration further deepens the East–West divide and acts against Détente (Alternative Defence Commission, 1983). One crucial point seldom commented on is that the expulsion of the Cruise missile bases from Britain would not simply involve revoking an agreement with the United States. Cruise missiles are in Britain as part of a general NATO theatre nuclear modernization programme, to which nearly all other European countries have contributed. To remove the British bases is to attack the governments of Italy, West Germany and the Netherlands, all of whom, with great political difficulty, have agreed to similar emplacements.

Secondly, it must be accepted that abolishing Britain's nuclear force is, among other things, a huge act of faith. It involves rejecting the whole idea that the Soviet Union might ever engage in nuclear blackmail, especially as it can hardly be part of Labour policy to rely on the US nuclear umbrella. This is a separate point from the question of de-nuclearizing the whole alliance's strategy because it refers to the independent aspect of Britain's nuclear strike force.

Abolishing any reliance on nuclear weapons in NATO, which is the long-term aim, should also not be seen as a rather orthodox hope. It is indeed the aim of almost all strategists to 'raise the nuclear threshold' by improving conventional capacity – that, after all, is official US policy. But such policies are predicated on the ultimate back-up of nuclear weapons, if only of America's central strategic capacity. No voice from within the defence consensus, not even the McNamara 'Gang of Four', has ever gone beyond a 'no first use' position. Even those, in other countries and other parts of the political spectrum, who believe that it is possible to re-write 'flexible response' to minimize the nuclear bottom line have to rely on new theories of how to remedy conventional weakness. It is crucial to realize that the Labour Party explicitly rejects most of the panaceas, whether they be a faith in technology via 'Emerging Technology' smart weapons or a faith in new tactics as with 'Airland Battle' or 'Follow-on-Forces-Attack'. Nearly all the suggestions for conventional reform on which other optimists rely are disowned as potentially aggressive.

We have to see Labour Party policy as portending a much more serious shift in British defence thinking than merely a different choice of weapons system to engage the enemy. What it actually indicates is much more basic – it is a change in the 'threat assessment' on which defence policy is based. Simply put, the Labour Party does not believe that the Warsaw Pact is a threat to world peace, and does not believe that there is need for any very great degree of deterrence at all. While they may not go the whole way to a 'moral equivalence' position, they certainly see the US–USSR interaction, rather than the endogenous aims of the USSR, as the main threat. The consequences of this shift in threat assessment, the first serious re-thinking of assumptions about Britain's own security since the late 1940s, could be a total restructuring of defence policy. The obvious re-structuring would be an enormous shrinkage in defence capacity as perceived needs declined. The party is already committed to dropping what small 'out of theatre' capacity the UK retains, on the grounds that our world role is no longer consistent with the ability to intervene anywhere outside Europe. It has always noted, and objected to, the fact that Britain's contribution to NATO is excessive by the standards of our neighbours.

Should this policy be to any great degree implemented, the least that can happen is that Britain will not only drop its nuclear weapons but become an increasingly isolated member of NATO, making an increasingly small and technologically traditional conventional contribution. It will be under great temptation, if it cannot persuade others to adopt the British threat assessment, to move towards a form of isolationism. This will be reinforced, in all probability, by the fact, argued above, that the budgetary strain will not be significantly lessened by removing the nuclear costs. The great attraction of the Labour analysis is that it is indeed a new theoretical position; others may well follow policies with much the same end-point because of financial squeeze without taking any real political decision. This we turn to in the final section.

It may be objected that too much emphasis is being placed on something that may well not come about, just one opposition party's ideal policy. This is to miss the enormously important political point. At least one major party of state, and possibly also the Liberal Party, has in fact publicly argued for a view of Britain's defence policy quite distinct from the current reality of NATO. Even if these parties do not win office or do not fully implement these policies, there is no doubt that they are popular among at least a large minority of the population.[7] It seems impossible to deny that the threat perception, and the perception of where Britain's interests lie, that have underlain defence policy for nearly forty years are not simply under attack, but have ceased to be consensual. We can no longer expect the British electorate to continue in the long run to suffer economic and social sacrifices in their name.

THE POTENTIAL IMPACT OF ARMS CONTROL

The only way in which there can be an *objective* change in Britain's security situation is by a change in the physical aspect of the potential threat from the Warsaw Pact. This can come from a new arms race, to our disadvantage, or from arms control, which may be either for or against our interests.

Although we can hardly predict the future of international arms control, it is relatively easy to see what sorts of moves the super-powers might make that could have an appreciable impact on

Britain's 'objective' security situation. As far as nuclear arms control goes, there is probably very little that could make much difference. As the Thatcher government has pointed out repeatedly, the super-power arsenals are so great that even 'deep cuts' would have no obvious implication for Britain's nuclear strike force.[8] On the assumption, surely reasonable, that neither the USA nor the USSR actually reduces their stocks below a generous assured destruction level, Britain will remain an easy target for utter annihilation. Nor will any upgrade via Trident make Britain capable of launching a serious first strike. The more urgent question is whether or not a Soviet response to America's SDI programme could render the new Trident fleet ineffective. If Britain's nuclear targeting doctrine goes unchanged, so that the destruction of Moscow is the paramount goal, this is just about possible (Freedman, 1985, pp. 81–99). However, no credible version of strategic defence can be expected to protect the bulk of the Soviet urban population outside Moscow, however effective the point-defence of missile silos becomes. If Britain, like France, is content to threaten major urban destruction outside the Moscow region, the Trident force should continue to be a credible deterrent well into the next century.

It might be thought that theatre arms-control negotiations, by which the Warsaw Pact would remove the SS20 missiles and NATO its GLCM and Pershing II batteries, would constitute an environmental change to which British defence policy would have to adapt. There is no room in this chapter to argue this point at length. It can be said, though, that many analysts have serious doubts about whether *either* side's theatre nuclear modernization programmes responded to any real military need. Given the relative conventional balances, the use of theatre nuclear weapons would almost inevitably be at NATO's initiative, and adequate capacity will remain to take this absurdly risky step whether or not the theatre forces up for negotiations are present. The Soviet capacity to reply in kind will also remain. In any case, Britain's own theatre capacity, mainly the Tornado force using gravity bombs, is rela-tively unimportant.

This all suggests that it is conventional arms control that is important to the UK. There can be no doubt that it would be of enormous advantage to the UK to have some development allowing a reduction in the continental commitment. Unfortunately, con-ventional arms control has made even less progress than nuclear arms control. The Mutual and Balanced Force Reduction talks, for example, are coming to an end after thirteen years with absolutely nothing achieved. Nor is it likely that the Soviet Union will ever find it in their interest to make such cuts as would sensibly allow for a reduction in the 55,000 men committed by the UK to the German front line. Some analysts hope instead for progress in the 'confidence building' approach to arms control. The argument is that serious agreements to give advance warning of exercises and troop movements might so reduce the risk of surprise attack that forward deployment of NATO troops would be less necessary. In the British case this might, in a very optimistic scenario, allow enough mobilization time so that a greater proportion of our contribution to Germany could be made up of reserves. Although this is not impossible, it is not clear that the savings would be very great, especially as the tactical air component of our continental commitment, arguably the most important, would remain a front-line regular force activity.

In fact it is in the conventional arena that the worst news probably lies for the UK. Appeals for greater conventional defence, in order to reduce the nuclear risk, have been common in NATO almost as long as it has existed, and particularly since the Kennedy–McNamara years. In the last few years, this demand has taken a new form with the enthusiasm in America for a technological solution to force imbalances. The technology in question, usually referred to as 'emerging technology', relies on very sophisticated sensing, tracking, target identification and 'smart' multiple warhead missiles.[9] A typical example is the idea that advances in remote sensing, allied to smart munitions, can give us a system by which a small number of missiles armed only with conventional warheads could find and destroy a Soviet tank unit two or three hundred kilometres into Warsaw Pact territory. In other words, extremely high levels of conventional technology could carry out the nuclear functions of flexible response.

How well grounded this faith is we cannot be sure – few of the weapons in question have even been tested yet, hence the 'emerging' label. We can be sure of two things: any such reliance on high technology force multipliers will be very expensive indeed, and that there is no reason at all to assume that the Soviet Union will not follow suit. NATO is at least as vulnerable, for example, to sophisticated attacks on air bases, and the fixed forward defence strategy to which it is wedded makes its tank units equally open to remotely sensed destruction by smart conventional weapons.

In summary, there is no obvious reason to expect the conventional warfare context to become less threatening or expensive, and some reason to expect that maintaining even the current relative capacity of the British Army of the Rhine and RAF Germany will escalate in cost.

WHAT ARE THE OPTIONS?

I have argued three things so far.

- Britain can no longer afford its defence policy.
- This policy no longer has much political legitimacy.
- The external context can only become less favourable.

Somehow or other the UK will have to redefine its defence interests, and re-structure its defence capacity, within the next decade. This conclusion does not, however, imply any particular answer. Even on nuclear weapons, for example, it does not follow that current debate is particularly well tuned. It may be that many of those who currently vote for parties committed to the abandonment of nuclear weapons, *within an otherwise unchanged defence policy*, would not do so given alternative scenarios. So if it became clear that we could not retain unchanged the NATO alliance with Britain as a unilateralist nation, one popular answer might be to be nuclear and not in NATO. There is, after all, no good reason to suppose French public opinion is unique (Laird, 1984).

The key question for UK defence policy must be about the nature and degree of commitment to the NATO alliance. With very few exceptions it is assumed that the defence of Germany, which is the bottom-line of NATO strategy, is integral to Britain's own security – certainly each annual defence statement reiterates this view. In the earlier days of NATO there was no possible argument. At that stage, perceptions were coloured by early Cold War events and interpretations, the chief of which was that the Soviet Union actively sought to expand westwards. As the Eastern and Western blocs have solidified, as the nuclear parity has removed all possibility of a rational war of conquest, it has become less possible to believe this. Most analysts in NATO itself now regard a central-front war as a consequence rather than a cause of superpower conflict, with the initial clash seen as most likely to occur elsewhere, probably in the Mediterranean, The Gulf, or the Indian Ocean. It is not that a war on the central front is unthinkable, but that if it came it would be of a different nature, an accident, and not part of a deliberate Soviet conquest of Western Europe. At the same time as this sense that the central front is not a likely flash-point grows, NATO is being pushed in different directions by the American leadership. Two examples of this are the new American strategy of 'horizontal escalation', and the demand for a greater 'out-of-theatre' commitment by European NATO members to support US perceptions of the alliance's vital interests elsewhere in the world. In other words, just as the threat of war in Europe declines, the Alliance sees the danger of that war being unnecessarily escalated by the locking-in of the Alliance to a more general US–Soviet conflict.

For Britain, the demands of alliance are very great, and it is no longer obvious that they are fully consonant with home defence. It may just be possible to maintain Britain's core alliance commitments, the naval role and the continental land and air roles, and a minimum UK air and territorial defence, if all else goes. Certainly the UK's independent capacity for out-of-theatre intervention must go – any policy agreed both by the Conservative government in the 1981 defence review and the Labour Party cannot for long be held off. The nuclear role is more complex. If de-nuclearization comes about as the Labour Party plans it, the major step towards redefining our NATO commitment will have been taken. But there is a major reason why the Labour Party version of unilateral disarmament may be the only version. One undeniable strength of their argument is that Britain is bound to be a more enticing nuclear target while it has nuclear weapons on its soil. How on earth can we expect the British public to be prepared to be a nuclear target because another state has major nuclear facilities in the country when the UK itself has given them up? Only if there were continued acceptance of the 1950s doctrine under which the United States would take a nuclear attack on Britain to be the same as one on the continental USA would this begin to make sense. But no one seriously believes in the US nuclear umbrella any more, at least as far as the US central strategic forces go, and 'no one' includes most decision-makers in Washington.

For heuristic purposes we can portray future defence options as falling into a two-dimensional space, where the dimensions are to some extent independent of each other. The first dimension measures the extent to which Britain is prepared to commit its ever scarcer resources to NATO's central front. The second reflects the decision on retaining an independent strategic nuclear force. We can take the latter as consisting just of two options – a British nuclear force or not – though there are other intermediary possibilities such as the European nuclear deterrent beloved of parts of the SDP. The dimension measuring NATO commitment is infinitely divisible in theory, but three major sectors can be identified. At one end is a continuation, at least on paper, of the full current integration. At the other, seldom mentioned in public, would be a deliberate iso-lationism, if not neutrality (Chichester and Wilkinson, 1982). The more real-world version of this would be a stance somewhat like that of France, where decisions about how, when and if to join the battle along with the rest of NATO are reserved until the crisis, and with British forces no longer integrated into the NATO military structure. In between, there are any number of points. What they all have in common is a major cut in peace-time forward deployment of land and air assets to Germany. Table 10.2 represents these general options. Very rough costings have been added, based on the same data from which Table 10.1 was calculated; these are for purely illustrative purposes.

The logic of Table 10.2 is that defence of the UK mainland clearly has to be a priority. It is hard, however, to distinguish between defending Britain and carrying out some of the NATO tasks, especially the naval functions of ASW work in the Channel and the North Sea, and coastal defence. What is clearly identifiable is the cost of the continental commitment. MoD's own figures, given recently to put Trident into perspective, suggest that over the period of Trident acquisition the air and land commitment to Germany will run to about 55 per cent of the total defence budget. My figures in Table 10.1 support this as an order of magnitude. A real and permanent saving could be made by effectively giving up the historic commitment to 55,000 men to defend the 65-mile zone of the intra-German border currently allotted to the British 1 Corps and RAF Germany. Nor are these forces that have any alternative role to play in defending the UK or, even if Britain retains sea-lift capacity, in some unimaginable defence of vital British interests elsewhere in the world. In fact, the history of UK defence policy for twenty years has been one of slowly chipping away at this commit-

Table 10.2   Future Policy Dimensions

	Nuclear	*Non-nuclear*
Isolationism	Gaullist position	Neutralist territorial defence.
	(£10500m)	(£8800m)
Reduced integration	Major reduction of forward deployed land and air assets	Major cuts in armoured and tactical air assets. Abandonment of out-of-area intervention capacity.
	(£14500m)	(£12800m)
Full integration	Economically impossible.	Politically impossible.

These figures assume: (1) The first column involves retaining out-of-area capacity in keeping with a more Conservative policy – without this the figures would be around £1300m less. (2) The cost of a reduced European contribution has been calculated, arbitrarily, as £4000m, compared with the current figure of £8018m. Clearly it could be a lot less.

ment by, for example, keeping up to a whole division of the BAOR in the United Kingdom, or redesigning command structures to reduce the number of unit headquarters needed in Germany.

What is likely to make the options in the central row of the table so attractive is that the conventional forces in Germany are not only the most expensive, but are also the ones where the recurrent and replacement costs are likely to increase most. A much higher proportion of the costs at the moment are on personnel than for other defence functions, but also the potential high technology arms race in this area is liable continually to escalate the procurement costs.

An actual formal abandonment of a commitment to NATO is highly unlikely. Again it may be easier to cut the BAOR/RAF Germany role without giving up completely the image of good NATO citizenship, because Britain contributes so much more than other European nations to the maritime tasks. As these are in part things we would have to do anyway, policy-makers are unlikely to miss the opportunity to maximize good will and Britain's security at the same time. Naturally, there are endless variants of these central row policies. The tactical air role is unlikely to be reduced immediately, if only because the Tornados will have been bought by then in any case. Nor will the armoured divisions immediately be brought home, because in the short run it would cost as much or more to rehouse them in the UK. Rather, I am suggesting that a process of inexorable cost attrition will be allowed to reduce the viability of the continental commitment.

There is, in fact, no alternative. And it will certainly be better intentionally to run down one function than to limp on doing everything badly. The nuclear question then becomes important in a novel way. Abolishing Britain's nuclear weapons will not, in the long run, remove the need to pull out of Germany. But the more philosophical–ideological nature of Britain's defence posture will largely be determined by whether it retains a nuclear strike force or not. If Britain abandons nuclear weapons it will become a sort of Sweden in NATO – if it keeps them it will be a sort of France in NATO. Either role is tenable, honourable, affordable. Either will probably destroy NATO's solidity.

Chapter 10: Notes

1 See House of Commons, 1986. This was a response to the 1986–87 defence estimates, and echoed a detailed and pessimistic analysis of the future budget contained in the 3rd report for 1985–86 (House of Commons, 1985). There is a considerable amount of economic analysis by defence analysts backing the central idea that the budget was underfunded even with the 1981 review (D. Greenwood, 1983).

2 In the debate on the 1986–87 defence estimates, 27 June 1986, the Minister for the Armed Services claimed that 55 per cent of the total defence budget for 1985–95 would be spent on the army and RAF commitment to Germany. No details were given of how these figures were arrived at.

3 This table is the result of a complicated and highly inferential calculation. The essential steps are: (1) using the 'functional analysis of the Defence Budget' in volume 2 of the annual statement on the defence estimates, calculate an average cost for each of the 60 line items over the period 1979–86; (2) distribute each line item proportionately over the five defence functions, making a priori assumptions of the share of each line item where, as usual, there is no official information. Although these assumptions are inevitably inaccurate, it is highly unlikely that the relative share of defence expenditure going on the different functions would vary significantly with different assumptions.

4 It is interesting that the Labour Party defence policy statement, presented

to the NEC in July 1986, is reported to make estimates of the costs of the Polaris force and the 'out-of-theatre' capacity very close to mine, though it is not known on what basis these calculations are made (*The Guardian*, 22 July 1986, p. 4).

5 The Social Democratic Party's official policy as of July 1986 was to replace Polaris, when this became necessary, with some system cheaper and less powerful than Trident. What system is not decided, though both an all-British, or Franco-British submarine-launched ballistic missile system, or Cruise missiles carried on submarines, have been suggested. There is no evidence whatsoever that the research by MoD or the Cabinet committee investigations between 1979 and 1981 found a viable system that was any cheaper than Trident 1. Probably most analysts now accept that there is no real alternative to Trident.

6 The current official policy is enshrined in an NEC report accepted by the party conference in 1984, *Defence and Security for Britain* (The Labour Party, 1984), but it is likely to be replaced by a new document at the party conference in autumn 1986. No major changes are contained in the new document except for some assessment of likely expenditure on NATO.

7 Public opinion poll data fluctuates wildly in this area. A rough generalization would be that there is a hard core of unilateralist sentiment of about 30 per cent of the electorate. As much as 60 per cent may be opposed to positioning US Cruise missiles in the UK. One perhaps extreme poll result was obtained by Gallup for CND in December 1985. This reported 75 per cent rejecting first use of nuclear weapons, and 60 per cent agreeing that Britain should leave NATO if it did not renounce first use as a strategy. Even among Conservative voters the figures were, respectively, 70 per cent and 51 per cent (*The Guardian*, 16 December 1985, p. 2).

8 The government's position has always been that Britain's nuclear arsenal is so minimal that it makes no sense to allow Polaris to be counted into arms control talks, even when the USSR offers concessions on SS-20 deployment. It should be noted, though, that there is internal dissention on this issue, which surfaced at the party conference in 1985. The Secretary of Defence, taking this position, clashed with the Foreign Secretary, who was prepared to admit that, *after* deep cuts had been achieved, the British force might then be considered (*The Times*, 11 October 1985, p. 3).

9 An extremely useful discussion of 'emerging technology', with challenging cost estimates, is to be found in Canby, 1986.

11 Eastern Europe and the New Cold War

JACQUES RUPNIK

Reflecting on the Yalta legacy forty years on, Z. Brzezinski recalled that: 'Until Yalta, the key issue perplexing the wartime alliance was Poland, the key to control of Eastern Europe. Thereafter the issue has increasingly been Germany, the key to control over Western Europe' (Brzezinski, 1984, p. 280). In some ways the Polish and the German questions still represent the connection in Soviet policies towards the two halves of Europe and thus also Moscow's permanent dilemma in Eastern Europe is seen as both a buffer zone and a foreign policy instrument vis-à-vis Western Europe. Hence the recurring debates concerning the trade-offs between control and influence, between the internal security of the Soviet bloc and the opportunities of fostering external change.

In short, Eastern Europe reveals the constraints imposed on Moscow's policy towards the West by the very nature of Soviet-type regimes.[1] These dilemmas seemed easier to handle in Stalin's days: absolute priority was given to the internal cohesion of the Soviet bloc, even at the cost of reducing contacts between the two halves of Europe to the absolute minimum. In contrast, the so-called 'new Cold War' of the 1980s came after more than a decade of East–West Détente with all that it entailed in terms of political ties and economic interdependence, thus making the Soviet use of the East European card vis-à-vis Western Europe both more effective and more difficult to handle. Perhaps more important, and again in marked contrast to the early 1950s, the regime crisis in Poland had to be reconciled with the broader East–West security confrontation over the deployment of intermediate nuclear weapons (INF) in Europe. In short, Soviet hopes of using the East European card in dividing the NATO alliance on the INF issue precluded de facto any attempts to 'seal off' Eastern Europe in the aftermath of the Polish crisis. In the balance between influence and control, Poland thus represents the continued priority of internal control combined with Soviet efforts to limit Western influence in Eastern Europe, while the German question (in the context of the Euromissiles conflict) shows the changing foreign policy opportunities in Western Europe. In this respect the new Cold War of the 1980s differed from the 'original' version of the late 1940s and early 1950s. In contrast to the global character of the East–West conflict after the Second World War, the 'remake' of the 1980s was more like an exercise in limited Cold War or in the 'dividability' of Détente. The East European factor accounts, at least in part, for the difference.

Yalta Revisited: The Polish Question Old and New

If the Solidarity movement was in some respects the by-product of the looser state control over society associated with the Détente of the 1970s, the military coup of December 1981 marked the end of an era and revived old debates about the impossibility of the reform of communist systems in Eastern Europe associated in the minds of most East Europeans with the Yalta legacy. Indeed the Polish clamp-down brought out into the open an East–West controversy concerning the myth and realities of Yalta. President Mitterand of France drew the lesson from Poland that there was a need to 'pull out' of the Yalta system: the imposition of illegitimate regimes in Eastern Europe is, in the long-run, destabilizing for the whole of Europe. Chancellor Schmidt, anxious to preserve improving relations with his East German counterpart, argued, on the contrary, that the Polish crisis showed that we had to learn to live with Yalta. Two opposite conclusions but a common assumption that Yalta indeed represents the partition of Europe. Referring to the same issue at a White House commemoration of the fortieth anniversary of the Warsaw uprising, quashed by the Nazis as the Red Army watched from the other side of the Vistula, Ronald Reagan called for 'full compliance' with the Yalta agreement: 'We see that agreement as a pledge by the three great powers to restore full independence and to allow free democratic elections in all countries liberated from the Nazis after the Second World War. There is no reason to absolve the Soviet Union or ourselves from this commitment'.[2]

There was, of course, some irony in Reagan's defence of Roosevelt, who has, since the late 1940s, been accused by conservative Republicans of 'selling out' Eastern Europe at Yalta. But another contrast is perhaps more revealing: while most Europeans (East and West) tend to consider Yalta, in the aftermath of the Polish crisis, as the prime cause of the partition of Europe and thus of the Cold War, both Washington and Moscow (admittedly for opposite reasons) have rejected this argument and called for a better observance of the Yalta Agreement.

The official Soviet and East European argument during the Polish crisis identified political change in Poland with a 'cold war' challenge to Soviet influence in Eastern Europe as accorded by Yalta and Helsinki. Vadim Zagladin, the deputy head of the Soviet Central Committee's international department, put it as follows:

> the Helsinki charter and the entire detente process are based on the recognition of the changes that took place in Europe following World War II ... The strengthening of socialism in Poland contributes to the strengthening of detente ... The attempts by certain Western sectors to support and encourage the antisocialist forces in Poland are now evident, and their objective is also clear: to shift Poland's position within Europe, to remove it from the alliance of socialist countries. (*La Republica*, 11 December 1980)

Still, the Soviet decision against direct military intervention owed as much to the fear of resistance and the possible spillover effect of an armed conflict in the centre of Europe as to the concern to preserve the chances of a limited Détente with Western Europe on INF. But the propaganda argument about Western interference remained, especially in General Jaruzelski's discourse in the aftermath of his military coup:

> Poland is being regarded as a tool, as a lever for putting pressure on the Soviet Union, on the Socialist community ... It has been allotted the role of a detonator under the edifice of peace which is founded on agreements signed in Yalta and Potsdam which cannot be separated from each other ... (Van Oudenaren, 1984, p. 53)

A pamphlet, published jointly by the Polish and Soviet Embassies in Paris, sums up the position as follows: 'The cause of evil in the post-war world does not lie in Yalta but rather in departures from it' (Bureau Soviétique d'Information et Service de Presse de l'Ambassade de Pologne, 1985, p. 16).

This post-Solidarity controversy shows that Yalta is unfinished business in that the periodic crises in Eastern Europe reveal that the Soviet control over the societies concerned remains a major source of instability, and thus of East–West tension, in either the late 1940s or in the early 1980s. But the contradictory interpretations of Yalta stem perhaps from the ambiguities of what actually happened at the Crimean conference in 1945. The Declaration on Liberated Europe adopted there called indeed for 'free and unfettered' elections in Eastern Europe (Laloy, 1982). Hence the argument that any Soviet violation of the agreement was bound to provoke a Western reaction, one which in the event led to the Cold War and to the formation of two hostile blocs in Europe. Hence also the idea that democratic and non-violent reform is compatible with the letter of the Yalta declaration as well as with its Helsinki successor.

The problem with this kind of reading of what happened at Yalta is that it omits the concrete content that was given to the lofty democratic principles in specific negotiations over Poland. Roosevelt not only accepted, but even proposed, that the communist-controlled Lublin committee provide the basis for a future government of national unity. This meant a *de facto* repudiation of the claims of the legitimate Polish government based in London and which, with the Polish Home Army, represented the cause for which the Western powers initially went to war. From this point of view, as Adam Ulam has argued, the Yalta declaration appears as an exercise in Western self-deception: How can you turn a country to a foreign power and yet demand that it be done through free elections and in accordance with high principles of morality and democracy? (Ulam, 1973). In other words, it was clear from the outset that, for Stalin, security concerns were not confined to territorial matters or to spheres of influence in the traditional sense, but to direct political control. Military presence led to ideological absorption. The Baltic model of 1940 was extended after 1945 to East–Central Europe. As Stalin explained at the time to Milovan Djilas: 'This war is not as in the past; whoever occupies a territory also imposes his own system as far as his army can reach' (Djilas, 1962, p. 114).

There are a number of reasons why the Western powers were reluctant to admit (to themselves) that for Stalin security concerns were likely to lead to sovietization: the belief, widely shared in the West during the war, that the wartime experience would lead the Soviet Union to tone down its revolutionary, ideologically motivated ambitions and to revert to a more traditionally Russian imperial posture; there was also, on the part of the United States, the 'Pacific first' policy, which made East–Central Europe a secondary matter, and the electoral concern to 'bring the boys back home' as soon as Germany would be defeated. Last, but not least, there were simply military considerations, such as the delay in the opening of the second front, which in the end allowed the Red Army to 'get there first' (though this is not true for Prague or Vienna). All these reasons, including a fair mixture of cynicism and ignorance in Western attitudes towards the East–Central European predicament, can be explained (though they are sometimes more difficult to account for in terms of ethics or long-term strategy). The problem starts when, after the initial postwar euphoria had passed, the West could not help confronting the discrepancy between the Yalta-type public diplomacy and the realities of East–Central European politics.

There are several ways to deal with the relationship between the local Cold War that started in Eastern Europe virtually the very day the war ended and the Cold War between East and West that is usually dated from 1947 (the date of both the Marshall Plan in Western Europe and Cominform in Eastern Europe).

Charles Bohlen and later Averell Harriman (1975) pointed out that it was out of the question, in 1944–45, simply to ignore democratic principles with regard to Eastern Europe (even though they could not be upheld in practice given Soviet military superiority in the area) because, for Western public opinion, they remained identified with the war effort and with Poland in particular. In other words, public opinion made it impossible simply to 'give away' Eastern Europe but also, on the contrary, impossible to adopt immediately a firm anti-Soviet stand given the public's rather favourable disposition towards the Soviet Union and Stalin (who, of course, did not face such dilemmas). This duality corresponds to the basic ambiguity of Western policy towards Eastern and Central Europe: verbal refusal to accept the region's political incorporation into the Soviet orbit without having the means or the determination to oppose it. This, it has been argued (Lynn Davis, 1974), is among the prime causes of what became known as the Cold War.

The ultimate lesson in political 'realism' – if that is the way to qualify Western passivity in the face of Soviet control of Eastern Europe – was, of course, Kennan's. The acceptance of the unavoidable, he argued, would have prevented a drastic deterioration in Soviet–American relations and could have helped make Soviet domination of Eastern Europe less brutal. It would not have avoided the formation of the two blocs, but it could have fostered a better relationship between them. In other words, the question is to what extent the Cold War was associated with the actual formation of the two blocs or rather with the reluctance to accept them as stable and lasting components of the postwar international system.

Several months before the communist takeover in Czechoslovakia, Kennan further elaborated this idea:

> The halt in the communist advance in Western Europe has necessitated a consolidation of communist power throughout Eastern Europe. It will be necessary for them, in particular, to clamp down completely on Czechoslovakia. As long as Communist political power was advancing in Europe, it was advantageous to the Russians to allow the Czechs the outer appearances of freedom. In this way Czechoslovakia was able to serve as a bait for nations farther West. Now that there is a danger of the political movement proceeding in the other direction, the Russians can no longer afford this luxury. Czechoslovakia could too easily become a means of entry of really democratic forces into Eastern Europe in general.
>
> The sweeping away of democratic institutions in Czechoslovakia will add a formidable new element to the underground anti-communist political forces in the Soviet satellite area. For this reason the Russians proceed to this step reluctantly. It is a purely defensive move . . . It is unlikely that approximately one hundred million Russians will succeed in holding down permanently, in addition to their own minorities, some ninety million Europeans with a higher cultural level and a long experience in resistance to foreign rule. One of the most dangerous moments to world stability will come when, some day, Russian rule begins to crumble in the Eastern European area. (in Etzold and Gaddis, 1978, p. 93)

Kennan's analysis foreshadows some of the main issues in more recent debates about the rise and fall of Détente, in the light of the Polish crisis of 1980–81. As such, it suggests several remarks. First, the margin of manoeuvre tolerated by Moscow in Eastern Europe remains directly related to its foreign policy objectives vis-à-vis

Western Europe. When the internal dynamics threaten to get out of hand, or the overall context of East–West relations becomes unfavourable to such foreign policy goals, tight controls are promptly imposed. Secondly, such a move was interpreted by Kennan (even before it had actually happened) as 'defensive'. Similar arguments were heard again thirty years later, after the Soviet invasion of Afghanistan. The Western view is that a system that identifies security with control renders the distinction between 'offensive' and 'defensive' moves virtually irrelevant. Thirdly, what might be presented as stabilizing in the short term remains inherently destabilizing in the long run: not just for the East European area as such but to the whole East–West balance in Europe. The recurrent Polish crises show precisely how precarious and how potentially unstable the Yalta system has become. Finally, there is a striking contrast, and yet a basic similarity, in the fate of Poland and Czechoslovakia, which illustrates the duality of Western and Soviet policies. The contrast might indeed be traced back to 1938, when the West abandoned Czechoslovakia at Munich only to go to war over Poland a year later. During the war, the Polish government in London remained resolutely anti-Soviet, whereas its Czech counterpart, with Munich on its mind, tried to be rather accommodating towards Stalin (see Mastny, 1979). Both earned, for opposite reasons, the displeasure of the West. After the war Poland was sovietized promptly while Czechoslovakia toyed for nearly three years with a closely watched experiment in self-limiting democracy. The Polish case came to be regarded in the West as the touchstone of Soviet behaviour and, as such, became the cause of the Cold War. The communist coup in Czechoslovakia was rather the consequence of a slow but steady slide into an East–West Cold War. The Poles saw themselves as the victims of Yalta, whereas the Czechs pretended to thrive on it and tried to build bridges between East and West. Two approaches, two itineraries, but in the end the result was all too similar.

   The contrasting implications of the Prague Spring of 1968 and of the 1980–81 Solidarity movement in Poland are no less revealing. Although very different in some respects, both experiments could be described as reform movements attempting to deal with the internally destabilizing nature of the Soviet constraint while carefully avoiding the internationalization of the crisis. While the August 1968 invasion of Czechoslovakia was perceived in the West as merely an *incident de parcours* and became a launching pad for the Détente of the 1970s, the military coup in Poland marked the collapse of Détente and became associated with the 'new Cold War' of the 1980s. The international context accounts at least in part for this contrast. In 1968, the Americans were bogged-down in Vietnam and were unlikely to jeopardize the prospects of the SALT negotiations in the name of an unlikely defence of 'socialism with a human face' in Prague. The Polish crisis came after the invasion of Afghanistan had broken the back of Détente, so there seemed little to be lost for the West (except for the Germans) in making an issue (including economic sanctions) out of the Polish crisis. But whether helping to bring about Détente or the 'new Cold War', the 1968 and the 1981 crises in Eastern Europe have revealed that, in contrast to the situation immediately after the Second World War, the area, although important, is no longer paramount in the shaping of East–West relations.

Eastern Europe and the Divisibility of Détente 'in the Shadow of Missiles'

In the origins of the Cold War, Eastern Europe (especially Poland) had been the stake, the bone of contention. In the new Cold War of the 1980s, centred on the issue of INF deployment, Western Europe was the stake, with Eastern Europe involved as a rather reluctant pawn in the Soviet strategy towards the West. But whereas in Stalin's days the East European factor was relatively easy for Moscow to maintain or control, the 1980s revealed significant differences between Moscow and some of its East European allies regarding the linkage between missile deployment and the legacy of Détente with Western Europe.

The German Question

The creation of the GDR represents for the Russians perhaps their main gain of the last war, namely the neutralization of German power. According to Jim Brown's fitting definition, it is both the creation and the protectorate of the Soviet Union. Yet it is accorded almost universal toleration for what it avoids rather than for what it

represents or has achieved. It is an artificial national entity performing an international service, 'essentially negative but deemed highly
necessary' (Brown, 1984, p. 8). It is precisely this function of the
GDR that also makes Soviet control over Poland and Czechoslovakia so important for Moscow as the pivot of its strategic
influence in Central Europe. When in the late 1960s Moscow gave
the green light to Willi Brandt's Ostpolitik, the then East German
leader, Walter Ulbricht, voiced his opposition and formulated the
policy of *Abgrenzung* (demarcation) as a precondition for any
rapprochement between the two German states. Ironically, more
than a decade later it was Moscow who tried to impose a form of
Abgrenzung on its East German ally, considered as too involved in
inter-German Détente at a time of a major East–West conflict over
missile deployment in Europe.

The German question was at the heart of the East–West controversy over the deployment of medium-range missiles in Europe.
Prior to the deployment, Moscow had tolerated, at times even
encouraged, a specifically East German voice on European security
issues with regards to inter-German relations. Andropov's
replacement of the Soviet Ambassador in East Berlin, Abrassimov,
was meant precisely to give greater scope to the East German leader,
E. Honecker, in this respect. Honecker used the opportunity to
encourage a new East German quest for a historical identity. Almost
overnight, Luther and Frederick II, Clausewitz and even Bismarck
were rehabilitated as 'positive' figures of German–Prussian history.
The East German Protestant Church was allowed to develop ties
with its West German counterpart and even to provide tacit support
for an independent 'green' peace movement. All this in the hope that
East Germany at both official and unofficial levels would encourage
West German opposition (both in government policy and in the
peace movement) to the deployment of the Cruise and Pershing
missiles.

However, once the deployment had started at the end of 1983,
Moscow's use of the East German card was reversed. And this was
at a time when simmering disagreements about the handling of
East–West relations were brought into the open between Moscow
and some of its allies. While Moscow was reverting to the thesis that
inter-German Détente could not flourish 'in the shadow of other
missiles', the East German leader stated that the Warsaw Pact's
'countermeasures', namely the deployment of SS21, SS22 and SS23

missiles in the GDR and in Czechoslovakia 'evoked no joy' in his country (*Neues Deutschland*, 26–27 November 1983). He then argued for a policy of 'damage limitation' (*Schadenbegrenzung*) in the face of a developing East–West arms race. While Soviet Foreign Minister Andrei Gromyko demanded the cancellation of US missile deployment in Europe as a precondition for the resumption of disarmament negotiations, Honecker spoke of a 'community of responsibility' of the two German states in making sure that 'reason and realism prevail, so that co-operation instead of confrontation will come to the fore' and thus that the process of Détente and disarmament could be revived (*Neues Deutschland*, 23 February 1984).

These differences of emphasis turned into overt polemics in the summer of 1984. Moscow embarked on a campaign against West Germany revanchism, which was obviously also meant as a warning to East Berlin. A *Pravda* article entitled 'In the shadow of American missiles' (27 July 1984) claimed that inter-German relations could not avoid the logic of East–West conflict brought about by 'aggressive' NATO policies. In the end, Honecker cancelled his visit to West Germany, but without altering his foreign policy discourse or his policy of developing inter-German ties (economic, travel, etc.).

East Berlin and Budapest vs Moscow and Prague

The controversy between Moscow and East Berlin concerning the implications of Euromissiles raised more general questions about East European autonomy in their policies towards Western Europe. And it is precisely on this issue that the Hungarian leadership decided to challenge some long-established tenets of the Soviet bloc's foreign policy discipline. An authoritative article by Matyas Szüros, the International Secretary of the Central Committee in Hungary, argued in favour of a re-definition of 'proletarian internationalism', the code word for alignment with the Soviet Union; this meant not to overestimate the 'general laws of socialism' but also that, except in extraordinary circumstances, the policies of a socialist state ought to be guided by national interest. Secondly, Szüros put forward the thesis that small European nations, on both sides of the East–West divide, have a part to play in preserving Détente despite superpower confrontation (Szüros, 1984).

Such views were promptly rebuffed by the Czechoslovak Party leadership, which obviously voiced not just its own but also Moscow's concerns. Arguing that no particular interests can have priority over those of the socialist community as a whole, an article in *Rudé Právo* (30 March 1984) rejected any idea of an independent role for small states as mediators between great powers. This received prompt authoritative backing from the Deputy Chief of the Soviet Central Committee department dealing with the East European parties, O. B. Rakhmanin, who (under the pseudonym of O. V. Borisov) argued that imperialist counter-revolution rather than Détente was the order of the day and that to see the role of small states outside the general laws of class-struggle smacked of nationalism and opportunism (Wise, 1984).

Instead of backing down, the Hungarian leadership decided to spell out even more explicitly its concept of a central European Détente insulated from the superpower Cold War:

In the future Europe will certainly remain the initiator and propagator of détente . . . Those small and medium-sized European states that belong to either alliance can have a positive effect upon the international atmosphere through dialogue and through constructive relations, through which more possibilities could arise for the improvement of relations between the Soviet Union and the United States. This could have a decisive influence upon the process of détente. It is a fact that several capitalist countries, based on historical ties or current conditions, demonstrate interests of varying intensity in socialist countries. Austria, Finland, or the FRG, for example, have developed more active relations with our country than with other socialist countries. These are not special privileges, since precisely this type of attention is also received, for example, by Bulgaria from its Balkan neighbors Greece and Turkey, or by Cuba from Spain, and by GDR from the FRG. This also applies in reverse. It is not only our conviction but also our concrete experience that one can use these specific opportunities for the good of common goals while concurrently pursuing national interests. (Szüros, quoted in Asmus, 1985, p. 755).

Although the Prague regime's posturing as the whipping boy of the socialist camp was not altogether surprising, the emergence of an East German–Hungarian joint challenge to Moscow's views on

East–West relations was unprecedented. The trend was made all the more explicit when Moscow's *New Times* reprinted in April 1984 Prague's attack on Hungarian foreign policy, while the East German party paper *Neues Deutschland* reprinted the Hungarian position. This practice was resumed at the end of July 1984 at the time of *Pravda*'s attack on inter-German Détente and has continued to the present.

To this new breach in Soviet bloc unity we should add the Romanian factor. If Hungarian support for Honecker's policies was explicit, Romania's was implicit. In line with Ceausescu's image as a maverick in the Warsaw pact, Romania played its own card in the Euromissiles controversy. Having gone as far as to support President Reagan's 'zero option' in 1982, Ceausescu continued in his foreign policy pronouncements to put on the same level Soviet and American missiles (SS20s vs Cruise and Pershing II) throughout most of 1983. The following year, however, witnessed an interesting change in the Romanian argument. While on a visit in Bonn – maintained despite the cancellations by Honecker and Bulgaria's Zhivkov – Ceausescu defended the Soviet view that the SS22 missiles then deployed in East Germany and Czechoslovakia were actually 'countermeasures' to the NATO missiles deployed in Western Europe. This rapprochement with Moscow was clearly related to Romania's economic difficulties at home, and to financial constraints abroad. Still, it did not prevent Ceausescu from not joining the Soviet-led boycott of the Olympic games in Los Angeles and from making a vehemently nationalist defence of foreign policy autonomy on the 40th anniversary of Romania's liberation (see Pick, 1984). Honecker was the only East European leader present probably thinking that, whatever the limits of Ceausescu's declining international aura, he might still prove to be a useful ally vis-à-vis Moscow.

How are we to account for this challenge to Moscow on East–West relations carried out simultaneously by several states of the Warsaw Pact? East Germany and Hungary (as well as Romania) are the only non-Slavic nations in the Soviet bloc; their nationalisms have historically been anti-Russian. The ruling elites tend to use traditional components of the dominant political culture in the society as a substitute form of legitimacy at a time of the complete discrediting of the official Marxist ideology throughout Eastern Europe. It could also be argued that, given the failure of the Polish experiment, Hungary and East Germany were the prime beneficiaries of Détente and thus most reluctant to toe the Soviet line in the early 1980s. As the two economically most prosperous and consumer-oriented countries in Eastern Europe, they were highly dependent on East–West trade. It has sometimes been argued that the Hungarian reforms were made possible only by foreign policy conformism, while Romania's foreign policy deviance was tolerable to Moscow only because of its highly authoritarian internal regime. Recent developments suggest that internal stability (whether achieved through prudent reformism Hungarian-style or 'enlightened authoritarianism' East German-style) is the main precondition for greater foreign policy self-assertion in East–Central Europe.

There is another explanation, however, one not incompatible with the previous one, but one that relates it to the uncertainties and ambiguities of Soviet policies towards Western Europe. In the aftermath of the Polish coup, Moscow was left with only East Germany and Hungary as plausible partners in attempts to wean some West Europeans, namely the West Germans, to a separate European Détente confined to security matters. Having failed in this attempt, Moscow tried to 'punish' the West Europeans by withdrawing East European co-operation. These policy shifts (towards limited Détente under Andropov or towards the new Cold War under Chernenko) were poorly implemented in Eastern Europe owing to the uncertainties related to the series of successions in Moscow. Hence Ross Johnson's plausible hypothesis that 'the East Europeans gambled that through a combination of lobbying, Soviet indecision and anticipated future Soviet shift back to a softer line vis-à-vis Western Europe, they could promote their own interests while avoiding a frontal clash with Moscow. That veteran communist leaders Kadar and Honecker pursued such a high-risk strategy is testimony to the strength of the motives that impelled the East European states, INF notwithstanding, to pursue expanded relations with Western Europe throughout 1984' (Ross Johnson, 1984, p. x).

This strategy seems to have been vindicated after Gorbachev's coming to power. To be sure, the first authoritative article in *Pravda* (21 June 1985) on the topic of Eastern Europe after Gorbachev's succession to power warned against the dangers of 'revisionism', 'nationalist tendencies', including 'Russophobia and anti-Sovietism'.

But, by the autumn of 1985, marked by Gorbachev's visit to Paris on the eve of the Geneva summit, the Soviet leadership seemed keen again to cultivate Western European opposition to SDI. Ideological discourse and (often strained) relations with Western communist parties were replaced by a rhetoric of peace aimed at the Western European left, in general, and the socialist parties, in particular. It is in this context that a truce seems to have been reached with the Hungarians and the East Germans, both of whom have shown skill in cultivating ties with West Germany's government and opposition. In other words, besides the obvious economic advantages of East Europe's close ties with the West in terms of lowering the Soviet cost of East European stability, Budapest and East Berlin (and to a lesser extent this applies to Romania) might still prove to be politically useful in Soviet–West European relations, after Reagan and Kohl.

Thus, East European attempts to preserve a degree of foreign policy autonomy in the context of East–West tensions in the 1980s illustrate the dual nature of all such efforts: a genuine search on the part of the ruling elites to increase their margin of manoeuvre, and thus a degree of substitute legitimacy; an important component of Soviet decoupling strategies vis-à-vis the Atlantic Alliance. When Moscow suddenly drops its long-standing opposition to Balkan co-operation (Tito's creation) and Bulgaria becomes a warm supporter of a de-nuclearized zone in the Balkans, we must take into account Zhivkov's own desire to receive international recognition (and to avoid the deployment of Soviet missiles) and Moscow's prime aim in this matter – to detach Greece from NATO. If such a goal were indeed reached in the long run, the limited autonomy granted to Zhivkov's Bulgaria would seem a small price to pay. A similar argument could, of course, be made concerning Scandinavian or Central European disarmament plans. As in the days of the Rapacki plan, for a 'neutralized' Central Europe, the name of the game is, as Pierre Hassner put it, 'who is Finlandizing whom?'.

Several conclusions can be drawn from the old and the more recent East European part in East–West relations, whether we call this the 'new Cold War' or 'divisible Détente'. The first is that however effective an asset of Soviet policy this region could prove to be, Moscow will always choose to curb its initiative and restore imperial control as soon as it is convinced that the centrifugal trends in the Warsaw Pact are developing faster than the expected erosion

of Western Europe's Atlantic ties. The ideological cohesion of the
Soviet bloc is no longer what it used to be, indeed Moscow has
given up trying to win the hearts and minds of the East Europeans,
but when faced with the choice between influence and security
Moscow will always choose the latter (see Rupnik, 1985).

The second conclusion is that Soviet foreign policy manipulation
of Eastern Europe as a proxy proved by no means easy to handle.
The Soviet Union thought of East German or Hungarian autonomy
in foreign policy as a means to encourage neutralist tendencies in
West Germany. It soon discovered that the German question has a
momentum of its own and that guided autonomy can soon lead to
centrifugal tendencies.

Finally, the dominant trend of the past decade in Eastern Europe
has been a longing for 'Europeanization', the assertion of a (still
mutilated) European identity in the face of what is perceived by the
population and the independent intellectual elites as a military and
ideological partition of the continent by two superpowers, who are
perceived as not belonging to Europe. Hence, there is also a degree
of convergence with those in Western Europe who are prepared to
confront the contradictory nature of a system of nuclear balance,
one which has ensured forty years of peace but, at the same time,
denied the other half of Europe its basic democratic and national
aspirations. Despite the Brezhnev and the Sonnenfeld 'doctrines',
considering that East–West Détente ought to encourage the development of 'organic ties' between Moscow and the Western peri-
phery of its Empire, it might be argued that the Helsinki process had
the opposite effect in creating a framework favourable to the spread
of Western influence and of a relatively greater autonomy of the
society vis-à-vis the state. The Polish case showed the limits of this
process, but the rediscovery of a European identity continued in
various forms despite the 'new Cold War' of the 1980s. This trend is
strongest today in Central Europe, in the lands of the former
Austrian Empire. It is expressed both at the state level with close
economic, cultural and political ties being established between the
two Germanies as well as Hungary, Austria and the Slovene and
Croatian Republic of Yugoslavia. While Czechoslovakia is missing
on the state level it is all the more involved in the unofficial
rediscovery of a Central European cultural identity. Milan Kundera
(1984) best expressed this nostalgia for a lost Europe in his famous
essays on 'The tragedy of Central Europe', a tragedy in which small

nations belonging culturally to the West were 'kidnapped' by the East. Forty years ago Stalin thought of Eastern Europe as a buffer zone meant to insulate the Soviet Union from Western influence; it turned out to have the opposite effect. Control over states, however authoritarian, does not guarantee the allegiance of the societies. In terms of culture and society, the real 'iron curtain' lies today between the Soviet Union and its East–Central European neighbours.

Chapter 11: Notes

1 These dilemmas are best formulated by Pierre Hassner (1984)
2 Quoted in the *International Herald Tribune*, 20 August 1984. However, the revelation of the Polish government spokesman, J. Urban, in June 1986, showing that the United States knew of the military coup plans at least six weeks in advance and decided not to warn Solidarity, casts some doubt over such statements. Indeed, it suggests that some elements in the US administration believed that the Solidarity experiment was doomed anyway, and that it was merely likely to encourage West European illusions about the benefits of Détente with Eastern Europe.

PART V

Conclusion

12 *On Ending the Cold War*

WAYLAND KENNET

The future of the Cold War is in the hands of the countries that are fighting it. Who are they? First and foremost, obviously, the United States and the Soviet Union. But in addition there are the member states of NATO and the Warsaw Pact, and behind them the special friends of the two superpowers: Israel, South Korea, etc., for the United States, and Cuba, Vietnam, etc., for the Soviet Union. The multiplicity of warriors, enjoying a wide variety of sovereignty and independence, complicates the field whose future we have to consider.

This complexity was born with the Cold War itself. Many in the West agree that the main responsibility for starting it lay, way back in the 1940s, with a series of actions taken by Stalin's Soviet Union: its interventionist policy in Persia, the *coup d'état* in Prague, the Berlin blockade. These actions, and its insistence in 1945 on staying put wherever it met the Allied armies, give or take minor administrative adjustments and Berlin, gave Europe a new political shape that has lasted ever since.

The Soviet conviction that the defence of its political system justified curtailing the sovereignty of its neighbours was too much against Kant's categorical imperative to permit Western inaction. What was so special about the Soviet Union that it could not be expected to live with continuous governments of another colour? The rest of us have to. What if all the boys behaved like that? Where would it stop? If the Soviet Union needed a buffer of communist states, why should those buffer states not require a further ring of buffers of their own and so on until only New Zealand was left to be buffed against? The new nightmare was born, or the old one reborn, and Stalin had fathered NATO.

Though British and United States policies about a postwar world had woven in and out of each other through agreement, disagreement and misunderstanding since the United States entered the Second World War in 1941 (and there is no disentangling them), the initiative in standing up to the Soviet challenges of 1945–49 was undoubtedly more Britain's than the United States's. Stalin's actions reminded Europe of his own prewar annexation of the Baltic States, and of Hitler's step-by-step expansion across neighbouring territories. Britain reached for the alliance that had only so recently been put away and, this time, the United States responded immediately. American troops would not have been in Western Europe for the last forty years if Britain had not invited them.

But origins usually go back farther than we think. We in the West still do not know for sure what Stalin, his generals and his party thought when they saw the successful development of nuclear weapons in the West being kept from them by their allies all those years. The more they knew about it, through their spies, the more they must have felt deceived. Origins determine natures and structures, and the Cold War is a structure of mistrust, ossified.

At the time of its origin, the Cold War appeared to almost everybody in the West to be just and necessary. We believed we had not wronged Stalin; he, on the other hand, had refrained from disarming and had threatened and advanced in a way we had not expected, because we were so far from wanting to do anything like that ourselves. NATO was thus founded with a clear sense of moral justification. But with maturity comes complexity and, in the life of an alliance as in the life of an individual, luggage grows and grows. NATO's luggage and the Warsaw Pact's are the greatest arsenals ever seen on earth. It will be the point of much which follows in this chapter that the titanic armaments of the modern United States and Soviet Union are themselves shaping policy: they are infecting it with their own rigidity and might, and constricting its growth and movement by the length of time it takes to design, develop, test, procure and deploy them. For the moment it is enough to note that this was not so in the beginning; they were not there.

Something can be learnt about the nature of the Cold War from its very name. The words carry with them the kind of semi-despair that naturally occupies the space between hot war and peace. The Cold War and NATO, our tool for fighting it, are and always have been for Europeans a pitiful distortion of the Europe that we can so easily imagine, which seemed to come so tantalizingly near our grasp in 1945. It was and is sad and stupid that we had not been able to earn peace by our war, but it was and is better to have a Cold War than another hot one of any kind, let alone the kind we are now capable of.

The peoples of Western Europe do not accept the Cold War as normal, still less as beneficial, and two generations now in their muffled and decent way have lived in the vain hope that it might somehow pass from them. This is so in our free and undivided countries, more so in divided Germany, and most so in the unfree countries of Eastern Europe. In this, we Europeans differ from our two superpowers.

The North Atlantic Treaty of 4 April 1949 has two main provisions. Article I says the signatories will try to resolve their disputes (and this clearly means disputes not only among themselves, but with all countries) peacefully, and in accordance with the purposes of the United Nations. It is first and foremost, then, a treaty for peaceful negotiation in solidarity.

Article 5 says that an attack on any signatory, provided it happens in Europe or North America, shall be considered an attack on all, and that signatories will assist the victim by 'such action as they deem necessary, including the use of armed force', and shall report it to the United Nations Security Council. It then lays down in more detail the geographical area within which it applies, which in time created the familiar distinction between 'in area' and 'out of area.' In the second place, then, it is a treaty for common defence in a limited area, which is the way we all principally think of it.

The Treaty gave rise to an Organization, and this has come over the years to assume two functions that have been reasonably derived from the Treaty. One is the common or harmonized procurement of armaments and adoption of strategies and tactical doctrines for actually fighting the war it exists to prevent. The other is harmonizing national policies for negotiation with the Warsaw Pact countries on military and military-related matters. Of these matters, arms control is the more politically important, and the control of what are called 'strategic' exports the more economically important. Attempts to load more functions on to NATO, often in the cultural field, have not generally been successful.

Beyond the Treaty NATO can in the nature of things have little to say, however much the United States puts pressure on the Europeans to turn NATO into a *de facto* world policeman, and recently even into a *de jure* one by amending the Treaty. The USA's worries about Nicaragua or Libya cannot be a NATO matter, nor can British worries about the Falklands, nor French ones about Chad. NATO thus has a two-way thrust. It somewhat tends to perpetuate the Cold War, because it is a military organization; conversely, it somewhat limits the spread of the Cold War because it is itself geographically limited in its application and operation.

NATO is sharply different from its opposite number, the Warsaw Pact Organization, in being voluntary. One country, Spain, has recently held a referendum on whether to remain in NATO, and has decided to do so. (We are hardly likely to see that happen in Eastern Europe.) Uninterrupted majorities in the free parliaments of the NATO countries have kept them in the Treaty for thirty-five years, though with differing commitments. In Eastern Europe it is the uninterrupted presence or propinquity of Soviet troops that have not only kept the countries in the Warsaw Pact but have also precluded the development of the free institutions that might take them out.

The military structure set up under the Warsaw Pact formally reflects this reality: the Ministers of Defence of the signatory countries are relegated to the status of deputies to the Commander-in-Chief of the armed forces to which their several countries contribute, and the Commander-in-Chief is always a Russian. In NATO, although the Supreme Allied Commander in Europe is always an American, it is the other way round; he takes his orders from a committee of national Ministers of Defence.

These are striking differences. But in the obligations it lays on its signatories, the Warsaw Pact itself is strikingly similar to the North Atlantic Treaty. Like that Treaty, it starts by reaffirming the United Nations Charter, by providing for each signatory to render assistance in accordance with Article 5 of the Charter to any signatory that has been attacked, and like that Treaty it has a geographical limitation: to trigger the Warsaw Pact the attack has to be 'in Europe'. So Afghanistan, for instance, or Mongolia cannot be a Warsaw Pact question.

The two great military institutions of postwar fears and mistrusts have come increasingly to dominate our political life in Europe. They do so on three levels: moral, economic and political. For thirty years now, young people have been growing up into the knowledge that the destruction of our species and indeed of many others is not only imaginable but practicable. They look with incredulity and horror at the two international military institutions that are devoted to keeping this possibility alive. Within each, they see a superpower carrying out its self-appointed task, each guarding against the possibility that the other might become capable of destroying half of mankind before it is itself in a position to destroy the other half.

The early knowledge of these things must tend to destroy there and then the person's inward vision of public morality, and hence the social cohesion that comes from the resemblance and intermingling of all the separate personal visions. Those who have lived long with the great threat know it is all only for deterrence. But children have a direct and unreflecting experience of being deterred long before they know what deterrence is. A child is deterred by a frown or a raised hand. Growing up brings knowledge of more severe penalties, of the death penalty itself. It brings knowledge in time of the structure of mutual deterrence, which may be maintained even among nations. The knowledge that 'deterrence' may be exerted on a nation by posing the risk not of defeating that nation in war, but of destroying mankind altogether, infects retrospectively the whole ladder that began with the frown in infancy. This is not to suggest that a 'deterred' child is demoralized by the thought that, if he refuses to refrain from what he is doing, his parents may in the end destroy mankind. It is to suggest that the young adult may feel the whole fabric of moral education is vitiated by the fact that it is now the destruction of mankind at the end of the ladder that began with that frown. From this can follow a belief that moral education is or was absurd as a whole. There is a generation difference here. Those over fifty felt in their childhood that the worst that could befall them was to have their own heads cut off. Those younger felt it was the death of mankind. We have not heard the last of this.

The economic effect is easier to express. The best things in life (love, blue sky, conversation) are free, but the second best (health care, travel, opera) are very expensive indeed. There is capital-producing labour (making the scythe), there is necessity-producing labour (reaping the corn), there is pleasure-producing labour (playing the violin), there is harmless drudgery (playing the violin badly), there is wasted labour (digging holes and filling them up again), and there is the arms industry. Labour produces the arms industry, which in its turn produces neither capital nor necessities nor pleasure. Its products are very expensive to store and maintain, and to the extent that they serve their purpose they are destructive of capital, of necessities, of pleasure and of life itself. Of no other industry can this be said. The arsenals of the nuclear powers, paradoxically maintained in a world that becomes in every other way more unified, merely increase the numerical values that can be attached to these equations, and thus their horrific effect.

The possible futures of this obscure and nauseous process are made harder to perceive and to plan by the very militarization of perception and planning. As more money is spent on arms, as the arms get more potent and most of all, as more and more of the rare people capable of complicated perception and planning are involved in the design, production and handling of arms, so do perception and planning in general, within the industrial North, take a more and more military coloration. We pay our military planners for worst-case analysis. A military planner should (*must*, sometimes, if he is to be any good) have the following thought: 'Because my country's adversary could be stronger than he looks, and could be lying despite all appearances, and could be implacably hostile although I can neither detect signs of it nor imagine reasons for it, therefore I must act as if he were all these things. Only thus can I give my own people the margin of safety that I have been entrusted by its rulers to provide.' Throughout most of history this strand of military planning has been kept in healthy check either by kings who were wise enough or by elected civilians who embody the common sense of the people at large. It is one of the main faults of militarized governments that they cannot provide this check.

In the Soviet Union, worst-case analysis has extended its sway over general political decision-making by an intensification of the Russian tradition of the military wise-father. Kutuzov, as Tolstoy saw him, carried the Tsar in his hand. The motionless and mountainous old generals of this century up there on the dais with their medals clanking in the cold wind, of whom Ustinov was the most recent example, are built into the power structure very near indeed to the top. The American way is the opposite: it is the excessive tolerance of ingenious and blinkered youth. A combination of too much money at the disposal of a pampered and corrupt arms industry, and the habit of appointing fund-raisers to head universities instead of teachers or scholars, has produced a race of civilian whizzkids who, already influential as advisers in the Kennedy age, are now appointed to high executive posts where they are more than a match for elderly presidential cronies from the corporation or the law firm. Thus it is that the Soviet Union and the United States treat each other as intelligent and energetic bundles of malign intent, which they are not.

The West European tradition and the West European will are different. Parties within our democracies polarize on the Moscow–Washington axis, just as Third World governments do. But the great central mass of European opinion, after two world wars with their saturation bombing and occupation, looks glumly at the two superpowers and wishes they would behave differently. In so far as one of them is mainly in Europe and has suffered saturation bombing and occupation like the rest of us, and in so far as the other is democratic with a great liberal tradition like most of the rest of us, we are puzzled and inhibited. Our tradition is denied, and our will for the future is continually thwarted by our sense of inconsistency in high places. We need changes in Moscow and Washington: we do not wish to be their apple of discord.

There is hope: it depends on achieving the right combination in each alliance of diversity and freedom with a reasonably disciplined approach to East–West dealings. We have the diversity on our side all right; NATO has never been above including the odd military dictatorship, which we fear less than we fear Russia, as with Portugal and Greece under earlier dispensations. Military rule in Turkey is a regularly recurring phenomenon, like the seasons, and while we are right to tolerate it we are wrong to give such short shrift to the consequent unease in Greece. (The biggest out-of-area operation ever undertaken by a European member of NATO has been the invasion and occupation for twelve years of part of neutral Cyprus by a Turkish army of twenty thousand men.) And since the election of President Reagan, hardly a month has gone by without a severe challenge to the unity of NATO in the form of United States actions that are not in our European interests, about which we were not consulted, and the relevance of which to the interests of the United States itself often escapes us, though we would not presume to think that our opinion about that was to be preferred to American opinions.

On the other side, the repeated revolts of the East German, Polish, Hungarian and Czechoslovak peoples have registered diversity so strongly as to have become events of domestic political importance to us also. Rumania conducts an independent foreign policy. Hungarian economic reforms are regarded with 'respect' by Mr Gorbachev. And, all the time, the very Marxism that seems enough in US Republican minds to prove a charge of terrorist intentions is recognized throughout the rest of the world as a poetical construct of economic theory and political myth, the study of which greatly improves the ability to understand reality, but which was false in its economic postulates when it was first published, and has since been shown to be incapable of practical application. Those in Eastern Europe who are supposed to be supported in their every feeling and intention by their reverence for the great gospel are in fact not so, as anyone knows who has been there, even if their thought-processes and language are indelibly tinged by it.

The embarrassment of all this for us fat little piggies-in-the-middle is the extreme willingness of the superpowers to take us under their wings, to show leadership, and to assume roles in which they represent us in dealing with the other superpower and even elsewhere in the world. We feel we cannot speak up too openly about this because we need our friendly neighbourhood super-power's protection; we need it because the two are so hostile to each other. We are in effect arranged in their monstrous confrontation like so many iron filings. The 'grand concern' of Western Europe is not the Marxism that we invented a century and a quarter ago and have lived with ever since without excessive terror; it is the military confrontation that the United States conducts in the name of not being overrun by it, and that the Soviet Union conducts in the name of not seeing it overrun. Nor are we too much terrified by the colour of the governments that may appear after natural revolutions in little tropical countries, and still less by the historical or theoretical beliefs of the trade union negotiator next door. We are made more afraid and more angry by the waste of the wealth our ingenuity has piled up and is still piling up, which ought to be going to relieve suffering and prevent death in the poor South.

There is in the world a hideous economic contrast. More than half the people in the world are poor, a third are malnourished, at some moments a quarter are starving. To right this requires much thought, and that is beginning. We do not lack a possible analogy to help us forward. When the industrial revolutions began in our individual countries, more than half of each of our own nations was living in grave poverty. Capitalism as an economic force did not redeem them. 'Communism' was not then available or, in the later industrial revolutions when it was available, was not tried. What did redeem the poor was their own accession to political power. Some, in southern Europe, redressed the balance by a series of bloody revolutions. Others, in Northern Europe, did so by forcing their way without bloodshed into legislative assemblies that had been set up earlier without bloodshed to regulate the affairs of the rich, but proved capable of regulating the affairs of rich versus poor without bloodshed also.

Let us consider the analogy between national histories in the nineteenth century and world history in the late twentieth. Surely we must wish world history to follow, for instance, the excited but bloodless British calendar 1688, 1832, 1870, and not the bloody continental one 1789, 1848, 1870. Can we sensibly consider the people of the Third World as analogous to the industrial working classes of the nineteenth century, the Third World bargaining with its sole desired assets, which are raw materials and later pollutability, as its predecessor proletariats bargained with theirs, which were labour and later skills? If so, should we enquire whether the United Nations can be turned into a sort of legislature through which Third World accession to a share of power can be mediated? It was certainly set up for another purpose: that of endorsing and enforcing the intended concordant will of the five strongest powers on earth, the members of the Security Council. Here also there is an obvious analogy with the growth of national democracies. But that will never become concordant, and the very device that was intended to ensure a practical harmony among the five as they faced the lesser states, the veto, has become the means of perpetuating the discord among the former. Any plan to adapt the United Nations should probably include a reform of the voting system; equal weight for China and for the Seychelles cannot bring forth the changes we need. Models of possible weighting systems abound. The bundle of conundrums is itself familiar in various national experiences.

An alternative, or perhaps conjunctive, way to adapt the United Nations might be found in the method of work used during its ten-year existence by the United Nations Conference on the Law of the Sea. This is a way of working towards a consensus without voting, known as the 'single negotiating text', which constitutes a sort of legislation by diminishing objection. It is described, and its potential for more general application in world affairs is beautifully thought out, in an article by Philip Allott (Allot, 1985).

This must be an agenda for two or more generations. Perhaps the part of the agenda that falls to the generation that writes this book cannot realistically be more than to understand the need of some change of this sort, and to propagate it. The main obstacle to our understanding of this need is the existence of the Cold War itself as a self-defining, self-perpetuating, anachronistic and other-excluding political process. Throughout this book, we have been considering Détente as if it were a dependent subsidiary of the Cold War, an episode in the Cold War – perhaps a recurring episode, certainly a benign one, but an episode none the less. It is defined by that which it is a lessening of, or a hole in.

'Détente' may in practice have much in common with its personal version, relaxation. With this, the common experience is that a determination to relax is unlikely to succeed in achieving relaxation, and that doing something else or thinking about something else usually succeeds better. Equally, to end the Cold War it will not be enough to seek to relax it from time to time; we have to transcend the thermometer and concentrate on making it obsolete at any temperature.

Four ways of ending the Cold War and beginning to address the needs of a world of injustice have been advanced. One is to have a hot war and get it over with, doing what we can to keep it limited, in the belief that one side or the other can win without destroying humanity. That suggestion is not only ignorant, but wilfully ignorant of facts available to all, and thus evil.

The second is to 'spend the other side into the ground' and obtain a military superiority such as to enable one's own side to impose its will on the other and exert a general mastery of the world. This notion is ignorant too, although it need perhaps not be wilfully ignorant. We have before us examples of people in high places in the United States today (and in the Soviet Union yesterday) who believe this is possible and desirable, simply because they lack knowledge of the world and lack political and emotional imagination.

A third way is that the armed states, and especially the nuclear weapons states, should on a pre-arranged vesting day convey control of their arsenals to a reorganized United Nations, which would then, somehow, overnight miraculously achieve what the devoted labours of the best of a generation failed to achieve between 1945 and 1953, i.e. devote those arsenals to enforcing the concordant will of the majority of mankind upon whatever discordant minority might from time to time arise. Far from being evil this solution is virtuous in the extreme but, like living in a garden with no clothes on and observing the instructions, it has been tried already.

The fourth way, though it may well if tried prove as prelapsarian as the last, is to continue the human experiment among sovereign nations that, however, behave much better and are much more lightly armed than is the case now. To put it like that is easy, and not very convincing. Is it possible to describe 'better behaviour' and 'lightly armed' more precisely?

Better behaviour must start from the acceptance that sovereignty is equal for all sovereign states, and that no sovereign state has a right to greater security than any other, except when that right is conferred by sheer population difference. (It will be impossible under any circumstances for the Seychelles to enjoy the same degree of security as China.) If sovereignty is equal for all, then all conflicts of interest among sovereign states are of equal gravity. Thence it follows that the Cold War between the United States and the Soviet Union is no more important to the world at large than that between, say, Greece and Turkey. In the realm of abstract morality, that is already the case. Our need now is to carry it over into the realm of common understanding and daily practice.

Naturally it would be easier to reach general acceptance of the reality of political sovereignty if that sovereignty could be exercised in conformity with what already exists in international law, and if international law could be developed to take account of the many things (e.g. international terrorism) of which it does not yet take account, and if the various courts and tribunals that now exist to administer it could be greatly strengthened. All these things, and especially the last, would require a dramatic change of course from both of the superpowers, far more dramatic than that required from any of the rest of us.

If 'better behaviour' depends on more variety and independence being permitted to all nations, including the members of the military alliances, 'lightly armed' would call for an unprecedented work of policy alignment not only within the alliances but between them, and among all countries of actual or potential military might: China, Japan, India, Pakistan, Syria, Israel, even (God help us) South Africa.

The United States and the Soviet Union are today badly out of kilter. This was also true in early 1977, when President Carter, having made disarmament a major plank in his election campaign, sought to move into action. In March, he sent Cyrus Vance, his Secretary of State, to Moscow with proposals for going far beyond the SALT II negotiations he had inherited into 'deep cuts' in nuclear weaponry, '. . . to 10, 20, even 50 per cent'. The proposal was rudely and immediately rejected by the Soviet Foreign Minister, Andrei Gromyko, and in fact Carter was left unsupported even by the Arms Control Community in Washington. The Soviet Government, convinced that the 'correlation of forces' had permanently shifted in its favour, was looking forward to total victory.

In the first half of 1986 the new Soviet General Secretary has not so much released an arms-control bombshell as pattern-bombed the whole field, starting with his three-stage framework in January, going on with his addition to Marxist–Leninist doctrine at the 27th Congress of the CPSU in February (Gorbachev, 1986, p. 11), accompanying it with suggestions for a new international security regime including everything from Third World debt to the environment, and using the sympathetic phrase 'a reasonable sufficiency' to describe the quantity of weapons that states should not need to exceed. Later in the year, he made proposals to accommodate Mr Reagan's desire for SDI research (to be coupled with an extension of the ABM Treaty), proposals for internationally verified conventional and short-range nuclear disarmament in Europe up to the Urals, for a complete test ban, for a complete ban on the possession of chemical weapons, in fact for virtually the whole range of arms-control measures that have hitherto been advanced singly and without co-ordination.

This time it is the administration in Washington, or a sufficient part of it, that has been bewitched by a vision of victory, expressed in a 'National Strategy' to incorporate the SDI with its instant threat to Soviet ICBMs, a 'New Maritime Strategy' that promises a form of 'forward deterrence' (so forward as to have all Soviet sea-based nuclear weapons ready-targeted) and an 'Air–Land Battle' concept that targets Warsaw Pact Forces, and probably nuclear power stations and much else, deep inside East Germany, Poland and Soviet Russia.

The likelihood of an unimpeded, technology-based United States 'victory' has become smaller than ever in the wake of the Shuttle, Titan and Delta disasters, of budgetary problems, and of congressional doubt. But, in the Pentagon, longing continues unabated to secure something of the dream before a new president blows it away. Europe watches aghast. The Perle–Weinberger–Reagan period in Washington has been a very bad one for disarmament. But disarmament has so far eluded even the best efforts of the most sincere governments. Of course, any package of arms reductions between East and West that looks like being adopted is pitifully vulnerable to the military–industrial–bureaucratic complex in the United States, and to the military one in the Soviet Union. But such packages have never yet been very serious, because they have covered too few types of weapons and too few countries. Even when the current dream of 'victory' has swept out of Washington as it swept in, disarmament between the East and West will not be obtained in dribs, drabs and 'building blocks', but only in a more comprehensive deal than has yet been attempted.

It is impossible to reduce one type of weaponry without exposing any inequality that exists in the remaining types. It is impossible, for instance, to reduce nuclear weapons between the two great blocs without bringing into view and increasing the importance of the imbalance that now exists in both conventional and chemical weapons. And you cannot reduce the military might of the two top countries very far without exposing and increasing the importance of the military might of countries three, four and five down the line. This is so in the 'central' arms race and the confrontation in Europe, and it is also so in the various 'regional' arms races and confront-ations around the globe.

Fruitful disarmament proposals must therefore take into account all types of weapons and all relevant countries. This fact means that proposing governments must put very much more intellectual effort into perceiving what is needed and planning their proposals than they have yet dreamed of. That means substantial staff of high intellectual ability, slotted high into the government structure. Earlier this century governments did indeed attempt to produce comprehensive disarmament plans; Britain and France in 1954, and the United States and Soviet Union themselves in 1960–62 did so. Because they were not quite comprehensive enough, and perhaps because mankind was not yet familiar enough either with the power of the military–industrial vested interests, or with the hideous economic contrast between the North and the South of the world, they failed. No comprehensive proposals was advanced by any country thereafter until 1986, when Gorbachev's Soviet Union made the proposals just listed.

The negotiating forums are not too numerous and contain the wrong sets of countries. Disarmament everywhere depends on a start being made by the superpowers, since their nuclear threat bounces round the world giving rise to a series of direct and indirect reactions that strongly nourish the natural political tensions in each region. No nuclear weapon was ever developed except for fear, justified or unjustified, of another nuclear weapon. But the three-in-one forum for nuclear disarmament at Geneva contains only the superpowers, not the other three nuclear powers, and not those others again on whose territories the superpowers' nuclear weapons are also deployed. The main forum for conventional disarmament in Europe, the MBFR in Vienna, does not include Hungary. And so on.

These partialities will have to be rounded up to comprehensiveness. The presence in the forums of all the relevant countries would have a particularly good effect on relations within NATO, because it would allow Britain and France to take direct responsibility for their own nuclear disarmament policies instead of passively relying on information and advice from the United States and, in the case of Britain at present, passively endorsing all the US proposals.

Such moves as this could unlock the possibility of a more lightly armed world. But where should we imagine the process would stop? It has been said that in certain circumstances, namely the circumstances of advanced disarmament, a boy scout with a notched staff is a threat to international order. There is a whole literature on the possible stages of a disarmament process: the minimum transitional deterrent, international verification of remainders, the reduction to levels necessary only for the preservation of internal order, and so on. But one consideration alone should be sufficient to persuade us to start on the process: disarmament would buy time. It is true that nuclear weapons have been invented and cannot be uninvented. But that does not mean they cannot be physically dismantled. At present, a mistaken political signal, a false reckoning, a mad dictator, could start our last war within a few minutes. In future, if SDI goes forward, a computer malfunction could start it off within a few seconds. Disarmament down to a stable and verified low level would mean that this could not happen. Mass weapons of mass destruction would take months to rebuild, and those months could be used to reduce mistaken political signals, false reckonings, even mad dictators, to manageable problems. Even if the whole system did break down into renewed mistrust and fear, mankind would still be better off than we are now by the months it would take to get back to high armament levels like the present. Disarmament does not propose Utopia; it proposes a breathing-space.

If these things or something like them prove possible, those now young do perhaps stand a good chance of seeing an end to the Cold War. If they do not, then it will presumably continue, as it does now, to license all the other cold wars around the world which, with ours, now cost eight hundred billion dollars a year. And while we in the North are distracted with fear and suspicion, the vast majority of mankind will be acceding to a share of world power, a great share. Whether this is done in bloodshed and chaos, or by the adaptation of existing institutions to mediate the change is a question that will be settled probably in the next ten years.

References

Acheson, D. (1970), *Present at the Creation: My Years at the State Department* (London: Hamish Hamilton).

Allott, P. (1985), 'Making the New International Law: Law of the Sea as Law of the Future', *International Journal*, vol. 40, Summer, pp. 442–60.

Alternative Defence Commission (1983), *Defence Without the Bomb* (London: Taylor and Francis).

American Historical Review (1981), vol. 86, no. 2, pp. 353–67.

Anderson, T. H. (1981), *The United States, Great Britain, and the Cold War, 1944–1947* (Columbia, Mo.: University of Missouri Press).

Anstey, C. (1984), 'The projection of British Socialism: Foreign Office publicity and American opinion, 1945–50', *Journal of Contemporary History*, vol. 19, pp. 417–51.

Arbatov, G. (1973), *The War of Ideas in Contemporary International Relations* (Moscow: Progress).

Arbatov, G. (1983), *Cold War or Detente?* (London: Zed Books).

Arendt, H. (1973), *On Revolution* (Harmondsworth: Penguin).

Asmus, R. D. (1985), 'The dialectics of détente and discord: the Moscow–East Berlin–Bonn Triangle', *Orbis*, vol. 28, no. 4, pp. 745–74.

Avon, The Earl of (1960), *The Memoirs of Sir Anthony Eden: Full Circle* (London: Cassell).

Ball, G. (1985), 'The war for Star Wars', *New York Review of Books*, 11 April, pp. 38–44.

Barclay, R. (1975), *Ernest Bevin and the Foreign Office 1932–69* (London: privately printed).

Barker, E. (1971), *Britain in a Divided Europe 1945–70* (London: Weidenfeld and Nicolson).

Barker, E. (1983), *The British Between the Superpowers 1945–1950* (London: Macmillan).

Barrett, L. (1985), 'How Reagan became a believer', *Time Magazine*, 11 March 1985, p. 16.

Baylis, J. (ed.) (1983), *Alternative Approaches to British Defence Policy* (London: Macmillan).

Bell, C. (1962), *Negotiation from Strength* (London: Chatto and Windus).

Bell, M. (1985), 'Die Blockade Berlins – Konfrontation der Alliierten in Deutschland', in J. Foschepoth (ed.), *Kalter Krieg und Deutsche Frage* (Gottingen/Zurich: Vandenhoeck & Ruprecht), pp. 217–39.

Beloff, M. (1961), *New Dimensions in Foreign Policy: A Study in British Administrative Experience 1947–59* (London: Allen and Unwin).

Berkhofer, R. (1969), *A Behavioral Approach to Historical Analysis* (New York: Free Press).

Bernal, J. D. *et al.* (1947), *The Communist Answer to the Challenge of Our Times: A Report of the Lectures by J. D. Bernal et al.* (London: Thames Publications).

Bethe, H., Garwin, R., Gottfried, K. and Kendall, H. (1984), 'Space-based ballistic missile defense', *Scientific American*, vol. 251, no. 4, pp. 37–47.

Bethell, N. (1984), *The Great Betrayal* (London: Hodder and Stoughton).

Blair, B. (1985), *Strategic Command and Control: Redefining the Nuclear Threat* (Washington, DC: Brookings).

Boardman, R. (1976), *Britain and the People's Republic of China 1949–74* (London: Macmillan).

Bohlen, C. (1973), *Witness to History 1929–69* (New York: Norton).

Bowker, M. and Williams, P. (1987), *Superpower Détente: A Reappraisal* (London: Sage, for the Royal Institute of International Affairs).

Bracken, P. (1983), *The Command and Control of Nuclear Forces* (New Haven, Conn.: Yale University Press).

Bradsher, H. S. (1985), *Afghanistan and the Soviet Union* (Durham, NC: Duke University Press).

Brzezinski, Z. (1983), *Power and Principle* (New York: Farrar, Straus and Giroux).

Brzezinski, Z. (1984), 'The future of Yalta', *Foreign Affairs*, vol. 63, no. 2, pp. 279–302.

Brown, J. F. (1984), *Continuity and Change of Soviet Interests and Dilemmas in Eastern Europe* (Paris: The Atlantic Institute).

Bullock, A. (1983), *Ernest Bevin: Foreign Secretary* (London: Heinemann).

Bullock, A. (1985), *Ernest Bevin* (Oxford: Oxford University Press).

Bureau Soviétique d'Information et Service de Presse de l'Ambassade de Pologne (1985), *Yalta, la base de la paix en Europe* (Paris: Soviet and Polish Embassy Press Pamphlet).

Caldwell, D. (1982), *American–Soviet Relations from 1947 to the Nixon–Kissinger Grand Design* (London: Greenwood).

Calleo, D. (1970), *The Atlantic Fantasy: The US, NATO, and Europe* (Baltimore, Md: Johns Hopkins University Press).

Campbell, D. (1984), *The Unsinkable Aircraft Carrier* (London: Michael Joseph).

Canby, S. L. (1986), 'The Conventional Defence of Europe', in L. B. Wallin, op. cit.

Cannon, L. and Pincus, W. (1986), 'Reagan sees his chance on arms control', *International Herald Tribune*, 4 August, pp. 1, 6.

Carlton, D. (1981), *Anthony Eden: A Biography* (London: Allen Lane).

Carr, E. H. (1961), *What is History?* (New York: Vintage Books).

Carter, A. (1984), *Directed Energy Missile Defense in Space* (Washington, DC: US Government Printing Office, for the Office of Technology Assessment).

Carter, A. (1986), 'Satellites and anti-satellites: the limits of the possible', *International Security*, vol. 10, no. 4, pp. 46–98.

Carter, A. and Schwartz, D. (eds) (1984), *Ballistic Missile Defense* (Washington, DC: Brookings).

Chalfont, A. (1985), *Star Wars: Suicide or Survival?* (London: Weidenfeld and Nicolson).

Charlton, M. (1983), *The Price of Victory* (London: British Broadcasting Corporation).

Chichester, M. and Wilkinson, J. (1982), *The Uncertain Ally: British Defence Policy 1960–1990* (Aldershot: Gower).

Churchill, W. S. (1950), *The Hinge of Fate* (Boston: Houghton Mifflin).

Clarke, R. (1982), *Anglo-American Collaboration in War and Peace 1942–1949* (Oxford : Clarendon Press).

Colville, J. (1976), *Footprints in Time* (London: Collins).

Colville, J. (1981), *The Churchillians* (London: Weidenfeld and Nicolson).

Colville, J. (1985a), *The Fringes of Power: Downing Street Diaries 1939–1955* (London: Hodder and Stoughton).

Colville, J. (1985b), 'How the West lost the peace in 1945', *Commentary* vol. 80, no. 3, pp. 40–7.

Combs, J. A. (1984), 'Cold War historiography: an alternative to John Gaddis's post-revisionism', Society for Historians of American Foreign Relations *Newsletter*, vol. 15, no. 2, pp. 9–19.

Communist Party of the Soviet Union (1976), *Documents and Resolutions, 25th Congress of the Communist Party of the Soviet Union* (Moscow: Novosti Press).

Communist Party of the Soviet Union (1981), *Documents and Resolutions, 26th Congress of the Communist Party of the Soviet Union* 23 February – 3 March (Moscow: Novosti Press).

Conquest, R. (1970), *The Nation Killers: The Soviet Deportation of Nationalities* (Glasgow: Macmillan).

Cox, A. M. (1976), *The Dynamics of Détente* (New York: Norton).

Current Digest of the Soviet Press (1971), vol. 23, no. 12, 20 April.

Dalton, H. (1962), *High Tide and After: Memoirs 1945–1960* (London: Muller).

Davis, L. E. (1974), *The Cold War Begins: Soviet–American Conflict over Eastern Europe* (Princeton, NJ: Princeton University Press).

De Santis, H. (1980), *The Diplomacy of Silence: The American Foreign Service, the Soviet Union, and the Cold War 1933–1947* (Chicago: University of Chicago Press).

De Tocqueville, A. ([1835] 1945), *Democracy in America* (New York: Vintage Books), Vol. 1.

Dibb, P. (1986), *The Soviet Union: The Incomplete Superpower* (London: International Institute for Strategic Studies/Macmillan).

Diplomatic History (1981), vol. 5, no. 4, pp. 353–82.

Djilas, M. (1962), *Conversations with Stalin* (New York: Harcourt Brace Jovanovich).

Drell, S., Farley, P. and Holloway, D. (1984), *The Reagan Strategic Defense Initiative: A Technical, Political and Arms Control Assessment* (Stanford, Calif.: Center for International Security and Arms Control, Stanford University).

Eason, W. (1973), 'Demography', in E. Micliewicz (ed.), *Handbook of Soviet Social Science Data* (New York: Free Press).

Eastport Study Group (1985), 'A Report to the Director, Strategic Defense Initiative Organization', unpublished paper.

Eisenhower, D. D. (1961), *The Public Papers of the Presidents of the United States: Dwight D. Eisenhower 1960–1961* (Washington, DC: US Government Printing Office), pp. 1035–40.

Ellwood, D. (1985), 'From "re-education" to the selling of the Marshall Plan in Italy', in N. Pronay and K. Wilson (eds), *The Political Re-education of Germany and Her Allies After World War II* (London: Croom Helm), pp. 219–39.

Epstein, L. D. (1954), *Britain – Uneasy Ally* (Chicago: University of Chicago Press).

Etzold, T. E. and Gaddis, J. L. (eds) (1978), *Containment: Documents on American Policy and Strategy* (New York: Columbia University Press).

Farrar, P. (1983), 'Britain's proposal for a buffer zone South of the Yalu in November 1950: was it a neglected opportunity to end the fighting in Korea?' *Journal of Contemporary History*, vol. 18, pp. 327–51.

Fieldhouse, D. K. (1984), 'The Labour Governments and the Empire-Commonwealth 1945–51', in R. Ovendale (ed.), *The Foreign Policy of the British Labour Governments 1945–51* (Leicester: Leicester University Press), pp. 83–120.

Ford, D. (1985), *The Button* (New York: Simon and Schuster).

Ford, G. (1979), *A Time to Heal* (London: W. H. Allen).

Foreign Office Papers, political series (FO 371), Public Record Office, Kew, Surrey, England.

Franck, T. M. and Weisband, E. (1971), *Word Politics: Verbal Strategy among the Superpowers* (New York: Oxford University Press).

Frankel, J. (1975), *British Foreign Policy 1945–73* (London: Oxford University Press).

Frankland, N. (ed.) (1958), *Documents on International Affairs 1955* (London: Royal Institute of International Affairs/Oxford University Press).

Freedman, L. (1985), 'British nuclear targeting', *Defence Analysis*, vol. 2, June 1985, pp. 81–99.

Freymond, J. (1964), *Western Europe since the War* (London: Pall Mall).

Gaddis, J. L. (1982), *Strategies of Containment* (New York: Oxford University Press).

Gaddis, J. L. (1983), 'The emerging post revisionist synthesis of the origins of the Cold War', *Diplomatic History*, vol. 7, no. 3, pp. 171–90.

Gaddis, J. L. (1986), 'The long peace: elements of stability in the postwar international system', *International Security*, vol. 10, no. 4, pp. 99–142.

Gardner, R. N. (1956), *Sterling–Dollar Diplomacy: Anglo-American Reconstruction of Multilateral Trade* (Oxford: Clarendon Press).

Garthoff, R. (1985), *Détente and Confrontation* (Washington, DC: Brookings).

Gelb, L. (1986), '"Horse trading" for a Summit', *International Herald Tribune*, 1 August, pp. 1–2.

Gelman, H. (1984), *The Brezhnev Politburo and the Decline of Détente* (Ithaca, NY: Cornell University Press).

Gelman, H. (1985), 'Rise and fall of Détente', *Problems of Communism*, vol. 34, no. 2, pp. 51–72.

Glassman, J. D. (1975), *Arms for the Arabs* (Baltimore, Md.: Johns Hopkins University Press).

Goff, R., Major, J. and Warner, G. (eds) (1964), *Documents on International Affairs 1960* (London: Royal Institute of International Affairs/Oxford University Press).

Gorbachev, M. (1986), 'Political Report of the CPSU Central Committee to the 27th Congress of the CPSU', *Current Digest of the Soviet Press*, vol. 38, no. 8, pp. 4–40.

Gordon, M. (1986), 'Soviet arms plan poses hard problems for US', *International Herald Tribune*, 4 July, pp. 1–2.

Gore-Booth, P. (1974), *With Great Truth and Respect* (London: Constable).

Grechko, A. A. (1977), *The Armed Forces of the Soviet Union* (Moscow: Progress).

Greenwood, D. (1983), 'Economic constraints and political preferences', in J. Baylis (ed.), op. cit., pp. 31–61.

Greenwood, S. (1983), 'Return to Dunkirk: the origins of the Anglo-French Treaty of March 1947', *Journal of Strategic Studies*, vol. 6, no. 4, pp. 49–65.

Guertner, G. and Snow, D. (1986), *The Last Frontier* (Lexington, Mass.: Lexington).

Halle, L. (1967), *The Cold War as History* (New York: Harper and Row).

Halliday, F. (1983), *The Making of the Second Cold War* (London: Verso).

Halliday, J. (ed.) (1986), *The Artful Albanian: The Memoirs of Enver Hoxha* (London: Chatto and Windus).

Harriman, A. W. (1975), *Special Envoy to Churchill and Stalin 1941–1946* (New York: Random House).

Hartz, L. (1955), *The Liberal Tradition in America* (New York: Harcourt Brace and World).

Hassner, P. (1984), 'Soviet policy in Western Europe: the East European factor', in S. Terry (ed.) *Soviet Policy in Eastern Europe* (New Haven, Conn.: Yale University Press), pp. 285–314.

Henderson, N. (1982), *The Birth of NATO* (London: Weidenfeld and Nicolson).

Herken, G. (1980), *The Winning Weapon: The Atomic Bomb in the Cold War* (New York: Knopf).

Herz, M. F. (1966), *Beginnings of the Cold War* (New York: McGraw-Hill).

Hirschman, A. (1970), *Exit, Voice, and Loyalty* (Cambridge, Mass.: Harvard University Press).

Hoffmann, S. (1983), *Dead Ends* (Cambridge, Mass.: Ballinger).

Hogan, M. J. (1984), 'Revival and reform: America's twentieth century search for a new economic order abroad', *Diplomatic History*, vol. 8, no. 4, pp. 287–310.

Holloway, D. (1983), *The Soviet Union and the Arms Race* (New Haven, Conn.: Yale University Press).

House of Commons, (1985), *Third Report from the Defence Committee, Session 1985/6*, paragraphs 41–58 (London: HMSO).

House of Commons, (1986), *The Sixth Report from the Defence Committee, Session 1986/7* (London: HMSO).

Huisken, R. (1981), *The Origin of the Strategic Cruise Missile* (New York: Praeger).

Hyman, H. (1953), 'The value systems of different classes: a social psychological contribution to the analysis of stratification', in R. Bendix and S. M. Lipset (eds), *Class, Status and Power* (Glencoe, Ill.: Free Press), pp. 426–42.

International Monetary Fund (1977), *IMF Direction of Trade Annual 1970–1976* (Washington, DC: IMF).

Ireland, T. P. (1981), *Creating the Entangling Alliance: The Origins of NATO* (London: Aldwych Press).

Jacky, J. (1985), 'The "Star Wars" defense won't compute', *Atlantic*, June, pp. 18–30.

Jacobson, H. K. and Stein, E. (1966), *Diplomats, Scientists and Politicians: The United States and the Test Ban Negotiations* (Ann Arbor, Mich.: University of Michigan Press).

Jacobson, J. (1983), 'Is there a new international history of the 1920s?', *American Historical Review*, vol. 88, no. 3, pp. 617–45.

Jasani, B. (ed.) (1982), *Outer Space: A New Dimension of the Arms Race* (London: Taylor and Francis).

Jasani, B. (ed.) (1984), *Space Weapons: The Arms Control Dilemma* (London: Taylor and Francis).

Jastrow, R. (1985), *How to Make Nuclear Weapons Obsolete* (Boston: Little, Brown).

Kassof, A. (ed.) (1968), *Prospects for Soviet Society* (New York: Praeger).

Kaufman, A. (1968), 'The Cold War in Retrospect', in I. Howe (ed.), *A Dissenter's Guide to Foreign Policy* (Garden City, NY: Anchor Books), pp. 65–94.

Kennan, G. (1968), *Memoirs 1925–1950* (London: Hutchinson).

Kennedy, P. (1981), *The Realities behind Diplomacy: Background Influences on British External Policy 1865–1980* (London: Fontana).

King, G. (ed.) (1963), *Documents on International Affairs 1959* (London: Royal Institute of International Affairs/Oxford University Press).

Kissinger, H. (1982), *Years of Upheaval* (Boston: Little, Brown).

Kolko, G. (1970), *The Politics of War: The World and United States Foreign Policy 1943–1945* (New York: Vintage Books).

Korbel, J. (1972), *Détente in Europe* (Princeton, NJ: Princeton University Press).

Kramish, A. (1960), *Atomic Energy in the Soviet Union* (London: Oxford University Press).

Krauthammer, C. (1985), 'The multilateral fallacy', *The New Republic*, vol. 193, no. 24, pp. 17–20.

Kundera, M. (1984), 'The tragedy of Central Europe', *New York Review of Books*, 26 April, pp. 33–8.

Kuniholm. B. R. (1980), *The Origins of the Cold War in the Near East: Great Power Conflict and Diplomacy in Iran, Turkey and Greece* (Princeton, NJ: Princeton University Press).

Kuniholm, B. R. (1984), 'Comments', *American Historical Review*, vol. 89, no. 2, pp. 385–90.

Labour Party (1984), *Defence and Security for Britain* (London: The Labour Party).

Lafeber, W. (1981), 'Comment', *Diplomatic History*, vol. 5, no. 4, pp. 362–4.

Laird, R. F. (1984), *France, the Soviet Union and the Nuclear Weapons Issue* (London: Westview Press).

Laird, R. F. and Robertson, D. (forthcoming, 1987), *Strains Within NATO* (Brighton: Wheatsheaf).

Laloy, J. (1982), 'La légende de Yalta', *Projet*, no. 163, pp. 279–86.

Leifer, M. (1972), *Constraints and Adjustments in British Foreign Policy* (London: Allen and Unwin).

Lin, H. (1985), 'The development of software for ballistic-missile defense', *Scientific American*, vol. 253, no. 6, pp. 32–9.

Lipset, S. M. and Bendix, R. (1959), *Social Mobility in Industrial Society* (Berkeley, Calif.: University of California Press).

Longstreth, T., Pike, J. and Rhinelander, J. (1985), *The Impact of US and Soviet Ballistic Missile Defense Programs on the ABM Treaty* (Washington, DC: National Campaign to Save the ABM Treaty).

McCagg, W. O., jun. (1978), *Stalin Embattled 1943–1948* (Detroit, Mich.: Wayne State University Press).

McCormick, T. J. (1982), 'Drift or mastery? A corporatist synthesis for American diplomatic history', *Reviews in American History*, vol. 10, December, pp. 318–30.

McGeehan, R. (1971), *The German Rearmament Question: American Diplomacy and European Defense after World War II* (Urbana, Ill.: University of Illinois Press).

Macmillan, H. (1969), *Tides of Fortune 1945–55* (London: Macmillan).

Macmillan, H. (1971), *Riding the Storm 1956–59* (London: Macmillan).

Macmillan, H. (1972), *Pointing the Way 1959–61* (London: Macmillan).

Maier, C. S. (1970), 'Revisionism and the interpretation of Cold War origins', *Perspectives in American History*, vol. 4, pp. 313–47.

Maier, C. S. (1980), 'Marking time: the historiography of international relations', in M. Kammen (ed.) (1980), *The Past Before Us: Contemporary Historical Writing in the United States* (Ithaca, NY: Cornell University Press), pp. 355–77.

Maier, C. S. (1981), 'The two postwar eras and the conditions for stability in twentieth century Western Europe', *American Historical Review*, vol. 86, no. 2, pp. 327–52.

Manderson-Jones, R. B. (1972), *The Special Relationship: Anglo-American Relations and Western European Unity 1947–56* (London: Weidenfeld and Nicolson).

Marder, M. (1981), 'In wrestling the Russian bear, basic rules are in dispute', *Washington Post*, 1 January.

Mastny, V. (1979), *Russia's Road to the Cold War: Diplomacy, Warfare and the Politics of Communism 1941–1945* (New York: Columbia University Press).

May, E. R. (1967), 'American imperialism: a reinterpretation', *Perspectives in American History*, vol. 1, pp. 123–283.

May, E. R. (1984), 'Writing contemporary international history', *Diplomatic History*, vol. 8, no. 2, pp. 103–13.

Mellor, F. (ed.) (1972), *Casualties and Medical Statistics* (London: HMSO).

Milward, A. S. (1984), *The Reconstruction of Western Europe 1945–51* (London: Methuen).

Ministry of Defence (1981), *The United Kingdom Defence Programmes: The Way Forward*, Cmnd 8288 (London: HMSO).

Ministry of Defence (1986a), *Statement on the Defence Estimates 1986*, vol. 1, Cmnd 9763–I (London: HMSO).

Ministry of Defence (1986b), *Statement on the Defence Estimates 1986*, vol. 2, Cmnd 9763–II (London: HMSO).

Moreton, E. and Segal, G. (eds) (1984), *Soviet Strategy toward Western Europe* (London: Allen and Unwin).

Morgan, K. (1984), *Labour in Power 1945–51* (Oxford: Clarendon Press).

Morgan, R. (1974), *The Unsettled Peace: A Study of the Cold War in Europe* (London: British Broadcasting Corporation).

Nash, R. H. (ed.) (1969), *Ideas of History*, Vol. 2, (New York: Dutton).

Northedge, F. S. (1970), 'Britain as a second-rank power', *International Affairs*, January, pp. 37–47.

Northedge, F. S. (1974), *Descent from Power: British Foreign Policy 1945–73* (London: Allen and Unwin).

Northedge, F. S. (1980), 'The co-ordination of interests in British foreign policy'. Paper given at the annual conference of the British International Studies Association, December.

Northedge, F. S. and Wells, A. (1982), *Britain and Soviet Communism* (London: Macmillan).

Nunnerly, D. (1972), *President Kennedy and Britain* (London: Bodley Head).

Office of Technology Assessment (1985), *Ballistic Missile Defense Technologies* (Washington, DC: US Government Printing Office).

Orwell, S. and Angus, I. (eds) (1970), *George Orwell: The Collected Essays, Journalism and Letters* (Harmondsworth: Penguin).

Ovendale, R. (1985), *The English-Speaking Alliance: Britain, the United States, the Dominions and the Cold War 1945–51* (London: Allen and Unwin).

Parnas, D. (1985), Letter of Resignation to James Offut, Assistant Director, BM/C3, Strategic Defense Initiative Organization; unpublished letter dated 28 June.

Paterson, T. G. (1979), *On Every Front: The Making of the Cold War* (New York: Norton).

Payne, K. (1986), *Strategic Defense: 'Star Wars' in Perspective* (Lanham, Md.: Hamilton Press).

Pick, H. (1984), 'Maverick Romania taunts Russia with nationalistic parade', *The Guardian*, 24 August.

Pike, J. (1985), 'Assessing the Soviet ABM Programme', in E. P. Thompson (ed.), *Star Wars* (Harmondsworth: Penguin), pp. 50–67.

Pike, J. (1986), 'The Emperor's newest clothing – changes to the SDI as a result of Phase I Architecture Studies'; unpublished paper dated 16 February.

Porter, B. (1982), 'Washington, Moscow, and Third World conflict in the 1980s', in S. Huntington (ed.), *The Strategic Imperative* (Cambridge, Mass.: Ballinger), pp. 253–300.

Prins, G. *et al.* (1983), *Defended to Death: A Study of the Nuclear Arms Race from the Cambridge University Disarmament Seminar* (Harmondsworth: Penguin).

Reagan, R. (1984), in *Realism, Strength, Negotiation: Key Foreign Policy Statements of the Reagan Administration* (Washington, DC: US Department of State), pp. 2–6.

Reagan, R. (1985), 'Excerpts from President Reagan's March 23 1983 speech on defense spending and defensive technology', in Office of Technology Assessment, *Ballistic Missile Defense Technologies* (Washington, DC: US Government Printing Office), pp. 297–8.

Reston, J. (1976), 'Negotiating with the Russians', in N. A. Graebner (ed.), *The Cold War: A Conflict of Ideology and Power* (Lexington, Mass.: Heath), pp. 18–33.

Rhinelander, J. (1985), 'Reagan's "exotic" interpretation of the ABM Treaty', *Arms Control Today*, vol. 15, no. 8, pp. 3–6.

Riste, O. (ed.) (1985), *Western Security, The Formative Years: European and Atlantic Defence* (Oslo: Norwegian University Press).

Roberts, H. L. and Wilson, R. A. (1953), *Britain and the United States: Problems in Cooperation* (London: Royal Institute of International Affairs).

Rose, C. R. (1959), 'The relation of socialist principles to British foreign policy, 1945–51', D. Phil. thesis, University of Oxford.

Ross Johnson, A. (1986), *The Impact of Eastern Europe on Soviet Policy towards Western Europe* (Santa Monica, Calif.: RAND).

Rothwell, V. (1982), *Britain and the Cold War 1941–1947* (London: Cape).

Rothwell, V. (1986), 'The future of Germany and Anglo-Soviet relations in World War II', *Crossroads* (Jerusalem), forthcoming.

Rupnik, J. (1985), 'L'État de l'Empire', *Rapport Annuel Mondial sur le Système Économique et les Stratégies 1985/6* (Paris: IFRI), pp. 44–61.

Sampson, A. (1967), *Macmillan: A Study in Ambiguity* (Harmondsworth: Penguin).

Schwartz. D. (1984), 'Past and present: the historical legacy', in A. Carter and D. Schwartz (eds), op. cit., pp. 330–49.

Scowcroft Commission (1983), *Report of the President's Commission on Strategic Forces*, unpublished report dated April 1983.

Seaborg, G. T. (1981), *Kennedy, Khrushchev and the Test Ban* (Berkeley, Calif.: University of California Press).

Seldon, A. (1981), *Churchill's Indian Summer: The Conservative Government 1951–55* (London: Hodder and Stoughton).

Seton-Watson, H. (1977), 'Thirty years after', in M. McCauley (ed.), *Communist Power in Europe 1944–1949* (London: Macmillan), pp. 220–30.

Shenfield, S. (1985), 'Soviets may not imitate Star Wars', *Bulletin of the Atomic Scientists*, vol. 41, no. 6, pp. 38–9.

Shlaim, A. (1978), *Britain and the Origins of European Unity 1940–1951* (Reading: University of Reading).

Shulman, M. D. (1963), *Stalin's Foreign Policy Reappraised* (Cambridge, Mass.: Harvard University Press).

Smith, G. (1980), *Doubletalk* (New York: Doubleday).

Smith, S. (1987), 'US Defensive Capabilities and Space', in S. Kirby and G. Robson (eds), *The Militarization of Space* (Brighton: Wheatsheaf).

Spanier, J. (1971), *American Foreign Policy Since World War II*, 4th edn (New York: Praeger).

Spiers, E. (1981), 'The British nuclear deterrent: problems and possibilities', in D. Dilks (ed.), *Retreat from Power: Studies in Britain's Foreign Policy of the Twentieth Century*, Vol. 2 (London: Macmillan), pp. 152–69.

Spriano, P. (1985), *Stalin and the European Communists* (London: Verso).

Stares, P. (1985), *Space Weapons and US Strategy: Origins and Developments* (London: Croom Helm).

Steel, R. (1964), *The End of Alliance: America and the Future of Europe* (London: Deutsch).

Stern, P. (1979), *Water's Edge* (London: Greenwood Press).

Stevens, S. (1984), 'The Soviet BMD Program', in A. Carter and D. Schwartz (eds), op. cit., pp. 182–220.

Stevenson, R. W. (1985), *The Rise and Fall of Détente* (London: Macmillan).

Stoessinger, J. G. (1976), *Henry Kissinger: The Anguish of Power* (New York: Norton).

Strang, Lord (1961), *Britain in World Affairs* (Westport, Conn.: Greenwood Press).

Strategic Defense Initiative Organization (1985a), *Report to Congress on the Strategic Defense Initiative* (Washington, DC: US Department of Defense).

Strategic Defense Initiative Organization (1985b), *SDI – A Technical Progress Report*, submitted to the Secretary of Defense (Washington, DC: US Department of Defense).

Strategic Defense Initiative Organization (1986), *Report to Congress on the Strategic Defense Initiative* (Washington, DC: US Department of Defense).

Szüros, M. (1984), 'The reciprocal effect of national and international interests in the development of socialism in Hungary', *Tarsadelmi Szemle*, no. 1, January, pp. 13–21.

Tirman, J. (ed.) (1984), *The Fallacy of Star Wars* (New York: Vintage Books).

Tolstoy, N. (1981), *Stalin's Secret War* (London: Cape).

Truman, H. S. (1951, 1952), Private Papers, Declassified Documents on Microfiche (Washington, DC: Library of Congress).

Truman, H. S. (1963), *Public Papers of the Presidents of the United States: Harry S. Truman, 1947* (Washington, DC: US Government Printing Office), pp. 176–80.

Tyroler, C. II (ed.) (1984), *Alerting America: The Papers of the Committee on the Present Danger* (McLean, Va: Pergamon-Brasseys).

Ulam, A. (1973), *The Rivals* (New York: Viking).

United States Bureau of the Census (1960), *Historical Statistics of the United States, Colonial Times to the Present* (Washington, DC: US Government Printing Office).

United States Department of Defense (1984a), *The Strategic Defense Initiative: Defensive Technologies Study* (Washington, DC: US Department of Defense).

United States Department of Defense (1984b), *Defense Against Ballistic Missiles: An Assessment of Technologies and Policy Implications* (Washington, DC: US Department of Defense).

United States Department of Defense (1985), *Soviet Strategic Defense Programs* (Washington, DC: US Department of Defense).

United States Department of State (1967), *Foreign Relations of the United States, 1945*, Vol. 5 (Washington, DC: US Government Printing Office).

United States Senate Committee on Foreign Relations (1986), *Soviet Imperatives for the 1990s: Hearing before the Subcommittee on European Affairs of the Committee on Foreign Relations*, 1st Session, 12 September, Part 1 (Washington, DC: US Government Printing Office).

Urban, G. R. (ed.) (1982), *Stalinism: Its Impact on Russia and the World* (London: Temple Smith).

Van Cleave, W. (1986), *Fortress USSR* (Stanford, Calif.: Hoover Institute Press).

Van Oudenaren, J. (1984), *The Soviet Union and Eastern Europe* (Santa Monica, Calif.: RAND).

Volten, P. M. E. (1982), *Brezhnev's Peace Program* (London: Westview).

Waller, D., Bruce, J. and Cook, D. (1986a), 'SDI: progress and challenges'. A Report submitted to Senator William Proxmire, Senator J. Bennett Johnston and Senator Lawton Chiles, 17 March.

Waller, D., Bruce, J. and Cook, D. (1986b), 'Star Wars: breakthrough or breakdown?' *Arms Control Today*, vol. 16, no. 4, pp. 8–12.

Wallin, L. B. (ed.) (1986), *Military Doctrine for Central Europe* (Stockholm: Swedish National Defence Research Institute).

Ward, P. D. (1979), *The Threat of Peace: James F. Byrnes and the Conference of Foreign Ministers 1945–1946* (Kent, Ohio: Kent State University Press).

Watt, D. C. (1984a), 'Britain, the United States and the opening of the Cold War', in R. Ovendale (ed.), *The Foreign Policy of the British Labour Governments 1945–1951* (Leicester: Leicester University Press), pp. 43–60.

Watt, D. C. (1984b), *Succeeding John Bull: America in Britain's Place* (Cambridge: Cambridge University Press).

Weickhardt, G. G. (1985a), 'Ustinov versus Ogarkov', *Problems of Communism*, vol. 34, pp. 77–82.

Weickhardt, G. G. (1985b), 'Ogarkov's latest fulminations on vigilance', *Radio Liberty Research Bulletin*, no. 41, (3350), 9 October, 325/85, pp. 1–8.

Werth, A. (1971), *Russia: the Postwar Years* (London: Hale).

Wesson, R. (1974), *The Russian Dilemma: A Political and Geopolitical View* (New Brunswick, NJ: Rutgers University Press).

White, B. P. (1981), 'The Concept of Détente', *Review of International Studies*, vol. 7, no. 3, pp. 165–71.

Williams, F. (1961), *A Prime Minister Remembers* (London: Heinemann).

Williams, M. (1980), *White among the Reds* (London: Shepheard-Walwyn).

Williams, P. (1986), 'Britain, Détente, and the Conference on Security and Cooperation in Europe', in K. Dyson (ed.), *European Détente* (London: Pinter), pp. 221–36.

Williams, P. M. (1979), *Hugh Gaitskell* (London: Cape).

Williams, P. M. (1983), *The Diary of Hugh Gaitskell 1945–1956* (London: Cape).

Wilson, G. (1986), '46 Senators seek to slow SDI research', *International Herald Tribune*, 24/25 May, p. 3.

Winterton, P. (1948), *Inquest on an Ally* (London: Cresset Press).

Wise, S. (1984), 'CPSU journal outlines Soviet stance on Warsaw Pact policy dispute', *Radio Liberty Review*, RL 173, 30 April.

Woodward, L. (1955), 'Some reflexions on British policy, 1939–45', *International Affairs* (London), vol. XXXI, pp. 273–90.

Wright, M. (1964), *Disarm and Verify* (New York: Praeger).

Yergin, D. (1978), *Shattered Peace: The Origins of the Cold War and the National Security State* (London: Deutsch).

Young, J. W. (1984), *Britain, France and the Unity of Europe 1945–51* (Leicester: Leicester University Press).

Zimmerman, P. (1986), 'Pork bellies and SDI', *Foreign Policy*, no. 63, pp. 76–87.

Zuckerman, Lord (1986), 'The wonders of Star Wars', *New York Review of Books*, 30 January, pp. 32–40.

Index